Embodied Meaning and Integration

Middle Way Philosophy

Series Editor: **Robert M. Ellis**, Middle Way Society

Middle Way Philosophy is a cross-disciplinary project developed by Robert M. Ellis over more than 20 years, to develop a consistently pragmatic approach to the justification of human judgement. It follows through the implications of the Buddha's Middle Way, rejecting absolute beliefs of a negative as well as a positive type, in the light of the developing modern understandings of uncertainty, scientific method, mindfulness, embodied meaning, neuroscience, cognitive and developmental psychology, systems theory, Jungian archetypes, and democratic political practice.

Diagnosing the central problem of absolutization that interferes with the justification of human judgement, it then seeks to identify the most effective responses to that problem. It does this through the rigorous application of pragmatic philosophy, drawing on a wide variety of evidence. Overall it thus offers a detailed normative ethical philosophy based in the conditions of psychology, and an overall framework to show the relationship of a variety of practices (from mindfulness to critical thinking) to the universal goal of improving each human judgement.

Published

Absolutization: The Source of Dogma, Repression, and Conflict
Robert M. Ellis
(Volume I)

The Five Principles of Middle Way Philosophy: Living Experientially in a World of Uncertainty
Robert M. Ellis
(Volume II)

A Systemic History of the Middle Way: Its Biological, Psycho-developmental, and Cultural Conditions
Robert M. Ellis
(Volume III)

Embodied Meaning and Integration

Overcoming the Abstracted Grip on Meaning in Theory and Practice

Robert M. Ellis

SHEFFIELD UK   BRISTOL CT

Published by Equinox Publishing Ltd.
UK: Office 415, The Workstation, 15 Paternoster Row, Sheffield,
        South Yorkshire S1 2BX
USA: ISD, 70 Enterprise Drive, Bristol, CT 06010

www.equinoxpub.com

First published 2025
© Robert M. Ellis 2025
All rights reserved. No part of this publication may be reproduced or transmitted in any form or by any means, electronic or mechanical, including photocopying, recording or any information storage or retrieval system, without prior permission in writing from the publishers.

British Library Cataloguing-in-Publication Data
A catalogue record for this book is available from the British Library.

ISBN-13 978 1 80050 556 8 (hardback)
         978 1 80050 557 5 (paperback)
         978 1 80050 558 2 (ePDF)
         978 1 80050 664 0 (ePub)

Library of Congress Cataloging-in-Publication Data

Names: Ellis, Robert M., author.
Title: Embodied meaning and integration : overcoming the abstracted grip on meaning in theory and practice / Robert M. Ellis.
Description: Sheffield, South Yorkshire ; Bristol, CT : Equinox Publishing Ltd, 2025. | Series: Middle way philosophy ; volume IV | Includes bibliographical references | Summary: "Embodied meaning is a new approach to understanding the significance of all symbols, including those of language, as association in human experience. Robert M. Ellis here develops a detailed multi-disciplinary account of the role of embodied meaning in the Middle Way as a practical path"-- Provided by publisher
Identifiers: LCCN 2025013306 (print) | LCCN 2025013307 (ebook) | ISBN 9781800505568 hardback | ISBN 9781800505575 paperback | ISBN 9781800505582 pdf | ISBN 9781800506640 epub
Subjects: LCSH: Middle Way (Buddhism) | Meaning (Philosophy)--Religious aspects--Buddhism
Classification: LCC BQ4280 .E434 2025 (print) | LCC BQ4280 (ebook)
LC record available at https://lccn.loc.gov/2025013306
LC ebook record available at https://lccn.loc.gov/2025013307

Typeset by S.J.I. Services, New Delhi, India

Contents

List of Diagrams	vii
Foreword to the Middle Way Philosophy Series *Iain McGilchrist*	viii
Acknowledgements	ix
Introduction	1
1. Embodied Meaning	**12**
a. Association in Living Systems	12
b. The Channelling of Desire	20
c. Differentiation and Integration	25
d. Symbols	31
e. Prototypes	36
f. Basic Level Categories	40
g. Embodied Schemas	44
h. Metaphorical Extension	49
i. Idealized Models	57
2. The Trouble with Representationalism	**62**
a. What is Representationalism?	62
b. Representationalism, the Left Hemisphere, and Propositional Sentences	69
c. Representation and Judgement	73
d. Representation and Communication	77
e. The Reduction of Meaning to 'Cognition'	84
f. Representation and Expression	88
g. Representationalism, Metaphysics, and Essentialism	92
h. Representation Blindness and the Subtilization Slope	97
3. Taking Embodied Meaning Seriously	**102**
a. The Lack of Need for 'Sense-making'	102
b. Archetypal Meaning, not Metaphysics	107

    c. The Tapering of Ineffability   112
    d. Non-linguistic Symbols and Beauty   117
    e. Representationalism and Religion   124
    f. Representationalism and Philosophy   134
    g. Representationalism and Politics   142

4. The Fragmentation of Meaning   **149**
    a. What are the Fragmentation and Integration of Meaning? 149
    b. Fragmentation of Meaning as a Condition for Conflict   155
    c. Babel: The Fragmentation of 'Cognitive' Understanding   160
    d. Planetary Indifference: The Fragmentation of 'Emotive' Understanding   165
    e. Linguistic and other Symbolic Fragmentation   170
    f. Cultural Fragmentation   174
    g. Archetypal Fragmentation   179
    h. Somatic Fragmentation   183

5. Integration of Meaning   **188**
    a. The Growth of Meaning Resources   188
    b. The Pruning and Clarification of Meaning   196
    c. Absorptive Methods of Meaning Integration   202
    d. Communicative Methods of Meaning Integration   210
    e. Expressive Methods of Meaning Integration   217
    f. Meditative Methods of Meaning Integration   222
    g. Ambiguity   227
    h. Synthesis   232
    i. Sublimity   237
    j. The Meaning of Absolutes   242

Conclusion   **246**

The Middle Way Philosophy Series   251

Bibliography   253

Index   258

List of Diagrams

Diagram 1.	Basic conditions of embodied meaning	13
Diagram 2.	The development of embodied meaning from its basic conditions to the most complex language	31
Diagram 3.	Representationalism: A mind map	63
Diagram 4.	Pyramidal embodied model of meaning as prior to belief or 'knowledge'	87
Diagram 5.	Fragmentation of meaning: A mind map	151
Diagram 6.	Integration of meaning: A mind map	189
Diagram 7.	The two mules	213

Foreword to the Middle Way Philosophy Series
Iain McGilchrist

The 'Middle Way' Ellis argues for so cogently is far from being a simple compromise between existing polarities, but a departure at right angles to typical thinking in the modern Western world, which looks to me like the path to ancient wisdom.

The perception that objectivity is neither an absolute, nor any the less real for that, is central. Ellis argues for an approach that is incremental and continuously responsive to what is given, rather than abstract and absolute. This is the difference, as he notes, between the pragmatic, provisional, nuanced, never fixed position of the right hemisphere in the face of the absolutism towards which the left hemisphere always tends.

The need for certainty must inevitably lead to illusion, whether in philosophy or in the business of living, and here too Ellis makes clear – as far as I am aware for the first time – the connections between the cognitive distortions known to psychology and the fallacies identified in the process of philosophy.

This is an important, original work, that should get the widest possible hearing.

Dr Iain McGilchrist is the author of The Master and his Emissary *and* The Matter with Things, *and a former psychiatrist.*
This foreword was originally written for the old Middle Way Philosophy series.

Acknowledgements

The biggest acknowledgements in this book must go to my wife, Viryanaya, who first got me interested in embodied meaning, as a product of her own studies, from around thirty years ago. Of course, her indirect contribution to my work through her personal support is also much bigger than this. I should also thank her for some comments on the manuscript of this book.

The ideas on which this book draws owe a great deal to the work of George Lakoff and Mark Johnson. Of these, I have had some direct contact with Mark Johnson, to whom I'm particularly grateful. I'd also like to thank Iain McGilchrist for his insights into the effects of brain lateralization on meaning, as well as more specifically for his general foreword to this series. I'd also like to thank Rodrigo Caceres Riquelme for some comments on the manuscript.

Introduction

Many of us, for a large proportion of the time, are disconnected from our bodies: 'in our heads'. We can, however, become aware of our interoception (our inner bodily experience): what it feels like to move our hands to pick up a book, tense and relax muscles in the shoulders, smile, or even notice the movements of breathing. Mindfulness, or any of a range of embodied and somatic practices, can help us directly with developing that awareness.

This book, whilst starting from basic experience of the body as the formative one for human beings, is not, however, about instruction in bodily practice. Instead, it tackles an underlying issue: the way our bodily disconnection has distorted our wider intellectual (and by implication, then, practical) understanding of what meaning is like. Meaning is the medium through which we shape our whole response to the world, and if we understand that medium as merely abstract (as has been our habit), it has a limiting and distorting effect on that response. Instead, meaning is embodied. That means that even the most abstract ideas are continually dependent on our bodily states and experience.

Most people have little understanding of how much we will need to rethink if we start to fully recognize that meaning is embodied. To begin to recognize its implications, unfortunately, doing yoga or mindfulness to raise bodily awareness is not enough by itself, because we are still subject to so many culturally entrenched disembodied assumptions. We need (perhaps counter-intuitively for some) to understand the disembodied web of assumptions we have been making, and the alternatives to it that are available – to start to *think* about meaning in a way that is compatible with embodiment. We will not be able to follow through the transformative possibilities of embodiment without addressing disembodied assumptions at their own relatively abstract level, to challenge them and replace them with approaches that allow us to proceed with active embodiment in a more consistent way. This process is not merely another reduction of embodiment to abstraction, as long as it remains practically motivated.

The good news is that we have many intellectual resources with which to do that, most of which have been developed in the last few decades. Many of them are still not familiar to the wider group of people for whom embodied practice is important, and are discussed only by a limited tribe of linguists and philosophers of language. At the same time, the theoreticians who do use them rarely seem to fully apply those new intellectual resources to practical ends, and, as I shall argue in this book, often still do so with restrictive assumptions that need to be challenged. A full discussion of meaning needs to bring together theory and practice as much as possible, as well as being interdisciplinary and synthetic. That is an approach that my Middle Way Philosophy series has in general tried to adopt, and this book offers an exploration of the important role of embodied meaning in the sustainable, practical, and interdisciplinary Middle Way approach.

Before I go further, I will attempt to introduce some of the prior intellectual resources that have influenced me in understanding embodied meaning, by saying a little about how I personally encountered them.

I first discovered the concept of embodied meaning in the early 1990s, when my wife, a philosophical linguist, got me interested in George Lakoff's rambling but mould-breaking volume *Women, Fire and Dangerous Things*.[1] Lakoff (and his associate Mark Johnson) threw down the gauntlet to representationalism, the traditional and still dominant understanding of meaning as dependent on the relationship between language and reality. His eye-catching title derived from an unusual categorization system from an indigenous Australian context, illustrating the ways that categorizations are dependent, not on a fixed relationship to 'reality', but on our culture and experience.

When, in the later 1990s, I began to develop Middle Way Philosophy, embodied meaning was absorbed into it as an integral part of its perspective. I began to realize then the relationship between what I had learned from Buddhist practice and embodied meaning. Our bodies provide a *context of experience* in which meaning is developed from infancy onwards, and where meaning can

---

1   Lakoff (1987).

be applied to our beliefs. Meaning involves constant association between experiences, and between experiences and symbols – association that also has the power to draw our attention and occupy our imagination.

One can experience that more fully and directly in mindfulness meditation, where we can gather and refine our imaginative associations through awareness of their bodily context. When we get caught up in a flow of distracting fantasy as we try to meditate, this is a narrow flow of meaning-association. For instance, we may find ourselves constantly repeating what we feel we should have said yesterday to get back at a disliked person who has slighted us. That narrow flow of obsessive fantasy is one we can broaden by extending the meaning of what we're experiencing in the context of our bodies – that feeling of hatred, for instance, is caught up in embodied states of restless energy that conflict with our desire to meditate. To put it in the context of bodily experience makes us see that it's only one of many things going on in the body, all of which are related in wider meaning. We can only broaden our hatred into love by seeing it as having a wider *meaning*.

It is that embodied *context* in our awareness (both within and beyond meditation) that also allows the Middle Way as an alternative option in each judgement we make, so that we are not simply dominated by absolutized binary alternatives – 'the truth' and its contradiction in 'falsehood'. If we can only recognize the embodiment of meaning (as I argued in *Absolutization*, the first volume of this series[2]), absolute claims become impossible, because they are dependent on the assumption that we can form sentences that *represent* truth or falsehood independently of the body and its associative process. If it is followed through fully in our understanding of everything we engage with, the body is thus our prime medium of flexibility in which rigid positions, and their attendant conflicts, can be dissolved.

We should not interpret the term 'body' itself too narrowly: it is the locus of our *experience* of sensing and imagining, in constant interplay with the judgements and actions that have steered that experience. The body constantly adjusts by *making connections*. It is not a set of beliefs, or the basis of any beliefs, about the 'physical

---

2   I.3.a. (See 'The Middle Way Philosophy Series' listed before the bibliography in this book.)

world' as an ultimate ground of beliefs, or of an unnecessary binary contrast with the 'mind'. Recognizing the body's formation of meaning, too, does not necessarily imply that direct awareness of the body is the only method of broadening our awareness of meaning: we can also extend imaginative awareness in the expansion of meaning through the arts, or help to motivate a search for new ideas through critical questioning. However, all of these require a wider embodied meaning framework of understanding to see most clearly how they help us.

More than a decade after my initial encounter with Lakoff and Johnson's work, I then read Iain McGilchrist's book *The Master and his Emissary*,[3] which provides another, neuroscientific, dimension to the recognition of embodiment. The locus of abstracted, proliferating absolute claims turns out to be the pre-frontal cortex of the left hemisphere of the brain, long thought to be the seat of language in general. It is the seat of language only in the sense that it brings together the symbols we use into grammatical propositions, that are assumed to potentially represent reality and provide the background conditions for the fulfilment of our goals. Meaning as understood through the body, however, is all processed through the right hemisphere. The account of embodied meaning in language offered by Lakoff and Johnson (which I will explore in this book) through basic categories, embodied schemas, and metaphors, all involves right-hemisphere processing. I thus began to recognize that the value of embodied meaning is also the value of remaining sufficiently in touch with new stimuli through the right hemisphere, rather than the all-encompassing beliefs of the dominating, proliferating, and confabulating left.

There are a whole set of *practices* that work on embodiment, directly in experience – not only meditation but, obviously, bodywork practices such as yoga, tai chi, or somatics. These connect us to the body as a wider context for our assumptions. They thus help to free us from the 'abstracted grip on meaning' that I mention in my subtitle to this book, particularly when combined with an intellectual understanding of embodied meaning. Other practices work even more directly with the uncovering of meaning as we encounter it in our awareness, such as *focusing* as developed by

---

[3] McGilchrist (2009).

Eugene Gendlin.[4] In focusing, either through a process of therapeutic dialogue or individual reflection, we use deliberate space and gently probing questioning to allow connected meaning to emerge in our experience. Although not a practice of exercising the whole body like, say, yoga, focusing (like mindfulness meditation) is nevertheless an embodied practice, precisely because it stimulates those right-hemisphere links for greater associative awareness. It often does this by focusing our attention inwardly on the sensations in the body and the meaning they have for us.

A final helpful element of the account of meaning that I have gradually assembled is indebted to the work of Carl Jung, whom I have written about (both appreciatively and critically) in my previous books *Red Book, Middle Way*[5] and *Archetypes in Religion and Beyond*.[6] Jung's concept of the 'image' foreshadows Lakoff and Johnson, and his understanding of *symbols* is that of ambiguous associations irreducible to fixed signs. That understanding of symbols and their role is one that I apply in this book. Even more importantly, Jung's concept of *integration* – bringing together conflicting elements in our experience over time (also discussed by Jung as 'individuation') can also be applied to meaning. The second half of this book is devoted to offering a full account both of the integration of meaning, and of the *fragmentation* that this integration can overcome.

The account of meaning in this book, then, is an independent one of synthetic origin. Whilst owing much to Lakoff and Johnson especially, it does not agree with them on every particular of the implications of their approach (for instance, it is not 'naturalist'). In academic discussion, Lakoff and Johnson's 'embodied meaning' has since developed into '4E cognition', which adds enactiveness, extension, and embeddedness to the initial 'E', embodiment. I have always taken these other three E's to be implicit in embodied meaning, so their addition contributes little to my thinking about it. However, I disagree with the framing that categorizes embodied meaning as a type of 'cognition', modelling our whole approach to meaning on the basis of 'knowledge' as a paradigm, and thus usually ignoring the vital distinction between meaning and belief. Categorizing embodied meaning as 'cognitive linguistics', when it is neither necessarily cognitive nor necessarily linguistic, seems

---

4   Gendlin (2003).
5   Ellis (2020).
6   Ellis (2022).

to me to be a massive academic assumption trap. Instead, I argue for thorough even-handed scepticism about 'knowledge' (which I explored in volume II of this series, *The Five Principles*[7]) and an account of both meaning and justification built on association and practical judgement.

One of the effects of bracketing meaning into a form of 'cognition' is also to perpetuate the false separation of 'cognitive' from 'emotive' meaning – of 'denotation' from 'connotation', or of 'semantics' from 'pragmatics'. That these different forms of meaning instead constantly interact within the same system, and need to be considered together, has major practical implications. This includes that the form of meaning that helps us to formulate our beliefs is *not separate* from the form of meaning that helps us to understand, value, and empathize. We find symbols meaningful because, in a specific situation, they have associations that have an impact on us – *both* a 'cognitive' *and* an 'emotive' impact.

That meaning is *prior* to belief (and thus also prior to 'knowledge' if we had it) is one of the major arguments of this book, and my protest against what has become the entrenched academic way of discussing embodied meaning. In our experience, we can clearly find things meaningful without believing in them – as in all the arts. For instance, I find the world of J.R.R. Tolkien's *Lord of the Rings* highly meaningful – all the more so because of the detail of its depiction – but I do not *believe* in this world, let alone have 'knowledge' of it. So why does the academic discussion continue to frame meaning as a sort of 'cognition', putting the cart of belief and/or knowledge in front of the horse of meaning? Entrenched cultural habit seems to be the only adequate explanation I can find for this. Even the most recent, detailed and nuanced academic account of embodied meaning, making strong use of a systems approach, *Linguistic Bodies*[8] (for which I have much respect) completely ignores the very possibility of meaning systems being understood separately from and prior to implicit belief systems. If we can free ourselves from the model conflating meaning and belief, it becomes a lot easier to think in a much more practically helpful way about the role of meaningful symbols in our lives: for instance that the value of religion is inspirational, not about 'beliefs'; that education is primarily about meaning, not

---

7   II.1.
8   Di Paolo, Cuffari, & De Jaegher (2018).

'knowledge'; that the arts are not primarily about ideology, and do not require 'suspension of disbelief', but are valuable because they enrich meaning.

The practical value of this way of approaching meaning also becomes clearer when we recognize its relationship to both internal and external conflict. Absolutized beliefs are ones that cannot be corrected in the light of experience, so they remain in intractable conflict with other absolutized beliefs[9] – as we see, for instance, in the opposed absolute views of groups that would rather kill each other than sympathetically examine each other's premises in relation to their own experience. However, these opposing beliefs each depend on meaning resources in the mind-bodies of those who employ them – meaning resources that are *prior* to those beliefs. We cannot frame our conflicting beliefs without meaningful language to express them in. These meaning resources can also be isolated from each other in ways that are *prior* to conflicts in belief: what I call *fragmentation of meaning*. Since most of what we call 'understanding' is about meaning, even though we wrongly frame it as belief or knowledge, it might be easiest to grasp this initially as *not understanding others* or *not understanding parts of ourselves*.

These gaps between experiences of meaning can be bridged through the practice of the *integration of meaning*. There are a variety of potential practices for integrating meaning, which I have already discussed in *The Five Principles*, including the arts, education, travel, humour, ritual, and political action to support meaning.[10] What they have in common is the making of new connections between symbols and experience, so that we are able to *understand* the world around us more fully and adequately. What we sometimes call 'learning', including of new vocabulary, as well as what we sometimes call 'sympathy' and 'imagination', are encompassed by the integration of meaning. Through the extraordinary power of ever-developing association, we are stimulated both to respond more fully to what we experience, and to associate it more widely with other ideas.

Meaning has a basic and central role in our practical lives: it is the medium between us and our assumed world, and the starting point from which increasingly adequate beliefs and actions can be developed. Nevertheless, it is easily confused, because for many people

---

9   I.5.a.
10 II.6.e & f.

it is too close to our immediate experience to conceptualize easily. To be used helpfully, it needs both conceptual clarification and the practical development of skills. What I will be mostly concerned with in this book is the former – but the latter, already outlined in the *Five Principles*, forms an important context for making sense of the conceptual approach.

There are a number of likely conceptual misunderstandings that it may be prudent to try to head off at the outset. One common confusion is between *embodiment* and *materialism* or *physicalism*. The account of meaning in this book is one based in the body *as we experience it*. In understanding that experience I also draw on the science that helps to illuminate that experience through the use of systematic observation and theorization. That does *not* mean that this is a reductive 'materialist' account of meaning, claiming that meaning is 'just' this or that. This book is part of the Middle Way Philosophy series, which overall systematically avoids metaphysical claims of any kind, including negative or reductive ones. It thus avoids idealist or Platonic views of meaning as well as materialist ones, navigating *between* the assumptions of freewill and determinism, theism and atheism, and so on. The Middle Way itself provides an alternative framework of assumptions that are provisional rather than metaphysical (a framework that I will go into in more depth philosophically in volume VI of this series). Here, though, I am avoiding the application of any metaphysical framework to our understanding of meaning.

Another whole set of misunderstandings will be discussed in section 3, and involve different ways that meaning has been co-opted by thinkers who do not clearly differentiate meaning from belief. These particularly include the treatment of meaning as an aspect of 'sense-making', where 'meaning' or 'sense' includes beliefs about the world as well as meaning proper. I am not concerned in this book with top-down ideas about 'the meaning of life', nor do I think we need to cultivate any such ideas to 'make sense' of our experience. Rather, a sufficient integration of meaning provides us with the resources to make all aspects of our experience meaningful. There are, of course, always conditions (such as depression) that make life as a whole seem less meaningful for individuals, but I don't accept the narrative that we are generally caught up in a 'meaning crisis'. Human beings constantly generate meaning through the body and right hemisphere of the brain, whether or not they acknowledge those sources of meaning. The over-dominance of the left hemisphere can lead us to *fragment* that meaning, but it is nevertheless still there. Such fragmentation is also not a uniquely modern phenomenon, but has been going on throughout human history, even though the causes of fragmentation have changed.

When people talk about a 'meaning crisis', what they often mean is a loss of inspiration. Inspiration is indeed a sort of meaning – the kind that motivates us through symbolic reminders of our motivation towards long-term or integrative judgements. As I argued in my previous book *Archetypes in Religion and Beyond*,[11] the archetypal functions of such figures as the hero, the anima/animus, and God are to operate in this way. Religious reminders of God, for instance, put people back in touch with their previous experiences of temporary integration (religious experience) through association. The entrenched projective usage of 'God' as a supernatural entity that either 'exists' or 'does not exist' is representationalist, and there is a completely different alternative way of seeing God as embodied *meaning* rather than belief. 'God' is a set of helpful associations *in our experience*, and only a quite unnecessary set of entrenched cultural habits leads us to assume that these associations are an object of absolute and metaphysical belief.

If the conditions of modern civilization have led us to lose our sources of inspiration in this way, then all we need to do is gather them together – integrate them. This requires a practice of the integration of meaning, whether pursued individually or socially or both. The main thing that stands in the way of integration of meaning is represented absolute belief, because absolute belief creates conflict by preventing any dialogical examination of opposing positions. If you believe that your way of interpreting the significance of the symbols you use is final and absolute, you are no longer in a position to understand those you have rejected. This is a particular problem for inspirational, archetypal symbols, because of the absolutizing conflicts created by those who constantly claim that they 'exist' or 'do not exist'. To integrate our inspirational symbols, we need a thoroughly embodied understanding of meaning, followed through to its conclusion – not further confusion of inspirational meaning with beliefs about the world.

11   Ellis (2022).

The final type of misunderstanding of an approach to embodied meaning that focuses on our *experience* of making associations is the assumption that it is intrinsically individualistic. This, however, imposes a false dichotomy: embodied meaning is *both* individual and social at the same time. Our experience of finding symbols meaningful involves a constant interplay with others, and is dependent on a complex system reaching far beyond the individual – one explored in detail in the aforementioned *Linguistic Bodies*.[12] However, we also have individual (*not* individualistic) experience of such meaning, of a kind that can be too quickly discounted if we assume that meaning is somehow intrinsically social, privileging the containing social system over the contained individual system. Neither of these aspects of meaning is prior to the other, and both of them are equally experienced in any instance of meaning. However, in treating both of them we need to prioritize experience over any theoretical preference for the social, and it is at the social level that merely abstract and implicitly representational claims about meaning can more easily supplant our view of it from experience.

Our need for affirmation from the group often overrides individual awareness, and imposes an absolute and dichotomous model (although this is not an inevitable feature of groups).[13] Far from the individual experience somehow demanding an inner/outer dichotomy that the social context does not, it is the individual perspective *referring to experience* that can more easily challenge socially assumed dichotomies (which are constantly reinforced by group biases), even when they involve individualistic beliefs. There is nothing that is necessarily 'inner' or individualistic about experience in a sense that excludes the 'outer' or the social, and nothing necessarily representationalist about a focus on embodied meaning in experience – but at the same time it is individual practical experience that can counteract socially imposed dogma (including individualistic dogma).

A helpful approach to embodied meaning thus needs to steer through a narrow passage between opposing dogmas at every stage. Not only does it need to avoid representationalism, but in the process also the opposing dogmas of idealism versus materialism, freewill versus determinism, religious 'belief' versus secularism,

---

12 Di Paolo, Cuffari, & De Jaegher (2018) p. 21.
13 I.5.e. Also see 2.d below.

intrinsic meaningfulness versus meaninglessness, and sociality versus individualism. A helpful understanding of meaning thus cannot be completely separated from the philosophical arguments for the Middle Way made throughout this series. However, this book focuses primarily on the development of a positive understanding of embodied meaning as a starting point for the Middle Way, aiming to show that an alternative model is possible even from the limitations of those approaches so far that have claimed to be 'embodied'.

1. Embodied Meaning

1.a. Association in Living Systems

> Embodied meaning is associative meaning, formed of links within the structure of an organism in response to electrical signals. Meaning without belief is association without potential action, and involves a shift throughout the internal system. The interdependent and *gestalt* nature of systemic meaning implies that it is only found in living organisms, not AI (which models only the left hemisphere). Only left-hemisphere overdominance makes computer models the norm, and interprets association deterministically.

The most basic starting point of embodied meaning is that it is *associative* rather than *representational*. That is, that meaning comes from a habitual relationship between symbol and experience (or, more basically, between two or more stimuli). If we perceive (or conceive) one thing, it reminds us of another thing. We can understand that habitual relationship physiologically, as neural links that have developed in an organism, or psychologically, as associations that we can recognize either through behaviour or directly through experience.

Association goes together with motive (see 1.b) and differentiation (see 1.c) to provide three basic conditions for embodied meaning **[diagram 1]** that are discussed respectively in the first three chapters of this section.

The beginnings of the recognition that meaning is associative go back to the work of the eighteenth-century empiricist philosopher David Hume, who identified three principles of association of ideas (resemblance, contiguity, and causality).[1] Its recognition in psychology goes back as early as the turn of the twentieth century, when Wernicke proposed that the repetition of similar experiences causes a pattern of activation that gradually strengthens a particular pattern of association.[2] Despite the constant presence of this understanding

---

1 Hume (1975) iii; (1978) i.iv.
2 Wernicke (1977).

in the background of scientific approaches to meaning, however, its implications seem to have never been fully followed through – probably because of the equally constant counter-influence of the more traditional view of meaning as dependent on representation.

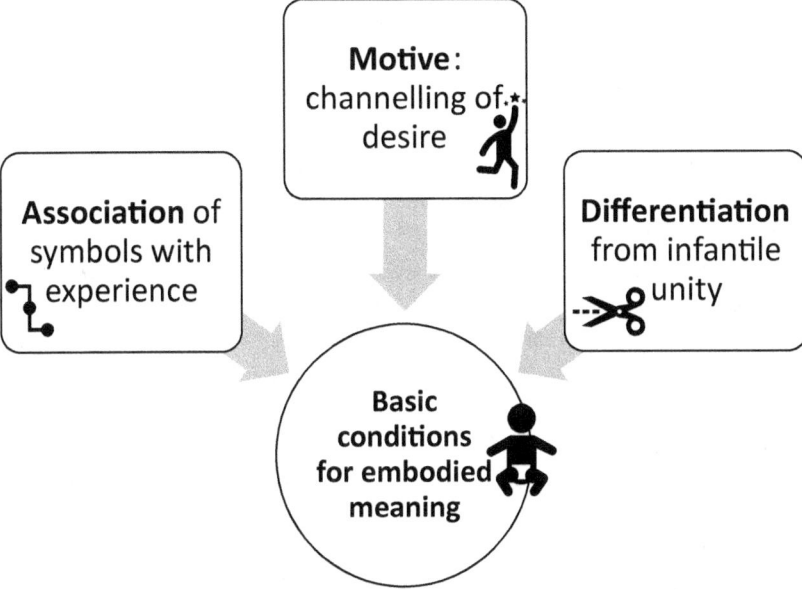

Diagram 1. Basic conditions of embodied meaning.

Humans and all kinds of organisms make such associations, so any account of embodied meaning in humans is continuous with our roots in pre-human life. In contrast, the idea of representation is much more specific, complex, and human-centred. However, I will return to the question of representation and why it is *not* meaning in the next section of this book. Through the whole of this first section, I will be focusing more on a positive account of how meaning is embodied.

Association is interaction of a kind that can be more readily repeated because of internal changes to make it so. It is part of a potential bank of adaptations to the surrounding environment. Living organisms are distinguished by their self-organization, so as to continue within particular boundaries that are semi-permeable, breached only to take in new information or food.[3] However, part

3   III.1.a. Maturana & Varela (1987) ch. 2.

of that self-organization is adaptable, and consists in potential ways of responding to the environment. If it encounters a particular food source, even a simple organism can 'remember' that food source: it becomes meaningful to the organism. One could say the same about a source of danger to be avoided. The meaningfulness of these stimuli to an organism is not necessarily the basis of a particular pre-determined action, although that is our only way, in practice, of detecting that meaning when we observe a simpler organism. All we can say is that the stimulus has re-organized the organism slightly in some way that may or may not affect its future responses.

Association is an interactive feature of living systems, both internally and externally. *Within* the system that is an organism, new electrical signals coming from outside interact with the prior organization of the organism, and have the effect of strengthening links.[4] *Beyond* the organism, the external stimulus is itself part of a wider system, such as an ecosystem, and the change in one organism responding to the stimulus may well modify its way of interacting with other parts of the system – for instance, it may advance on recognizing a food source or flee on recognizing a predator. *Meaning* for an organism is thus also equivalent to *memory*, as I will discuss further in 5.a. A particular kind of stimulus *means* food, just as the organism *remembers* that it is associated with food.

Here we have the basic distinction between meaning and belief: that is, that meaning alone merely changes the internal system, whilst belief changes the organism's way of interacting with its environment. This distinction is rarely a very clear one at the level of simple organisms, because it is very difficult, if not impossible, to tell how their internal states may have changed when these do not evidently change external relationships. However, when we get to more complex animals such as humans, it becomes much easier to differentiate meanings that do not directly affect beliefs: for instance, we may read *Pride and Prejudice,* and find Mr Darcy very meaningful, but still do not believe that he existed historically, or expect to visit his house. The ways that our reading is helpful to us are more indirect than this (see 5.c), though none the less important for all that.

This capacity for associative meaning is not merely a matter of making a systemic connection by itself, but comes from the capacity

---

4   III.1.b & f. Godfrey-Smith (2020) pp. 30–1.

to constantly adjust the associations forming that connection in relation to the whole of the rest of that internal system. This is a capacity that seems unique to living systems. In an age of constantly developing AI (artificial intelligence), it is worth reminding ourselves of this point at the outset. Because meaning is embodied, computers do not have meaning: instead, computers have consistent ways of interacting based on algorithms. In other words, computers have beliefs but no meaning. If you ask a complex computer algorithm such as ChatGPT a question, it will give you an answer based on its 'beliefs', which it has scraped from all the sources it is able to scan through on the internet. However, ChatGPT does not go through any kind of gestalt adjustment of the kind that all organisms, no matter how simple, go through on encountering new stimuli. It can 'learn' by adapting its responses in increasingly complex ways, but nevertheless ways that are still linear and programmed, not the result of the near-simultaneous activation of multiple links within a complex living system. Living meaning is *gestalt*, meaning that changes in the system pass a tipping point in which all the nodes in the system quickly adjust to each other. You can think of it as like the trillions of neuronal links in our brains all simultaneously playing the party game of musical chairs: when the music stops, they all have to find a new seat. Compared to their previous arrangement before the music started, they have all changed and adjusted to each other simultaneously, even though the overall arrangement is only marginally different from the previous one.

The distinction between a living system that is capable of meaning and a non-living system that is not was long ago identified by philosopher John Searle in his famous Chinese Room thought experiment.[5] Imagine that a non-Chinese speaker is locked in a room alone with a lot of instruction manuals for translating one set of Chinese symbols into another. A Chinese speaker then passes Chinese symbols to this person through a hatch, with no other interaction taking place, and the person in the room then looks up these meaningless symbols to find a programmed response. He then passes new symbols out to the Chinese speaker, to whom they are meaningful, so she believes that she is having a conversation in Chinese. However, at no point does the non-Chinese speaker understand (i.e. find

---

5   Searle (1989). See also discussion in VI.4.c of the place of this thought experiment in philosophy of mind.

meaningful) the symbols he is processing. Searle argues that the non-Chinese person locked in the room is equivalent to a computer, which can give complex responses that are meaningful to humans, but the computer itself merely processes, and does not appreciate the meaning of what it is processing.

To bring this point home, let's imagine that the Chinese speaker passes in a symbol that means 'tree', or something similar. The non-Chinese speaker, handling this symbol, does not recognize that it has anything to do with trees, even if he begins to develop any other associations. To the Chinese speaker, the associations of that symbol are ones that interact with many aspects of her experience: of climbing trees, appreciating the beauty of trees, perhaps even planting them or chopping them down. All of this is there in the background for a living organism – a simultaneous link with all the previous associations for that organism, insofar as they have been able to change that organism's structure in any way. The computer has no experience of acting in the world in this way, and thus no set of associations that give meaning to the symbol. The only mutual adjustments that it can make are those that it has been previously programmed to make.

So why do we wrongly interpret the non-living system, the computer, as having living experiences? I don't think we would be tempted by this kind of interpretation at all if we were not, ourselves, in some ways like the computer and in other ways not. We have only been able to design, build, and programme computers (or even complex AI systems based on networks of them) because of our own capacity for the kind of linear processing that computers can do. This capacity is found in the human left brain hemisphere – the part of us that, when over-dominant, thinks in solely representational ways.[6] Left-hemisphere representation depends on right-hemisphere meaning, but can constantly neglect or ignore this dependency and try to operate as though its representations were the whole story.

Where understanding of meaning is concerned, left-hemisphere over-dominance has resulted not just in representationalism and the modelling of organic meaning on computers, but also in a tendency to foreground belief and make it prior to meaning, even when our accounts of 'cognition' (as a whole process including both meaning

6   I.2.b, I.3.a, III.1.i.

Embodied Meaning 17

and belief) are 'embodied'. This can be seen in the accounts of 'meaning' that are actually accounts of beliefs, as I will discuss in section 3.

Association is often taken into account in theory, but in ways that fail to recognize its presence at the basis of the meaning of the very theory we have about it, because they rely on metaphysical belief that assumes representationalism. For instance, association can be interpreted as the basis of a deterministic account of how organisms act according to inevitable causal mechanisms, so that we are seen as *controlled* by association. Such deterministic theories may limit themselves behaviouristically to the kinds of beliefs (or so-called 'knowledge') we can get by *observing* other organisms. But this does not take into account the gestalt ways that living organisms associate, with complex systems operating simultaneously rather than through chains of detectable linear causes. We can never tell whether a living organism is 'free' or 'determined', and association does not leave us with one rather than the other. Rather the insistence on freewill and determinism as a structure of explanation is a product of absolutization of a particular set of 'factual' beliefs and interpretations, and of the representationalism that allows that absolutization. If we limit ourselves to the linear relationships between particular associations and their particular behavioural effects, we can do no justice at all to the immense systemic complexity of the meaning process in any organism, let alone in human beings where we also have copious experience of internal meaning.

Association *for a living system* is instead association *in the context of that living system*. There is a constantly adjusting, ever-humming mutual interaction going on, and a new associative experience makes its mark by creating new mutual adjustments in that system. These adjustments basically take the form of one stimulus reminding us of another. Of course, it can't remind us of everything: that would not usually fit our day-to-day practical purposes where we interact with objects and people that each have specific meaning. So another aspect of that association involves *differentiation*, where associations start to specialize and exclude, so as to more effectively associate particular experiences with each other. I will be discussing differentiation further in 1.c.

Overall, this process of association creates an ever more complex, ever shifting, ever adjusting relationship between what neuroscientists have called 'conceptual structure' and 'physical substrate' – a relationship that has been captured by Tononi et al. in what they call 'integrated information theory'. Direct observation of the brain tells us nothing very specific about the content of someone's experience: at best a probability that can be refined only by using large amounts of data.[7] However, there is clearer evidence that the *complexity* of the neural networks that are observed correspond to the *complexity* of attention, association, and meaning in phenomenological experience.[8] As long as we respect the complexity of the interactions within a whole that make this a living system (and do not confuse it with the linear movements even of large amounts of data), it is impossible to treat it reductively.

As we will see later in this section, those associative and differentiating adjustments may take one of a number of possible forms that build on each other. They may take a prototypical form, in which a particular kind of stimulus gains a wider resonance: for instance that we see a robin and begin to get an idea of what a bird is. They may take a basic categorical form, in which the similarities between particular stimuli allow us to recognize similar ones in future as in the same category. They may take a schematic form, in which a particular context of embodied experience allows us to both associate and differentiate within that context, for instance that the associated experience of 'container' allows us to ramify out to many different sorts of container. They may take a metaphorical form, in which association of one context with another allows us to transfer patterns of meaning between those contexts, like the association between running sands and passing time. Finally, they may also form *models* in which meaning interacts in mutual dependency with hypothetical belief: for instance, it could only be Wednesday if it was Tuesday yesterday. All of these forms of association will be discussed in more detail later in this section of the book (1.f–i).

It is only at the point of forming models (not before), that meaning becomes dependent on belief, and unable to function without it. Yet the traditional understanding of meaning seems to depend overwhelmingly on models, with the assumption that models *represent*, and a refusal to consider the building blocks and process of

---

7   Recent breakthroughs in 'semantic decoding', which appear to offer such specific information, are based on matching large data-sets of neural activity to data-sets of words (in a similar approach to Google Translate), not on any appreciation of the meaning of neural input by AI. See Tang et al. (2023).

8   Tononi et al. (2016).

development of models in our experience as offering a prior understanding of meaning.

It is by considering all the forms of associative meaning, prior to and including models, that I should be able to offer an account, by the end of this section, of how living association makes not just all aspects of our language meaningful, but also all other symbols (such as visual images or musical patterns). Such a positive understanding is necessary for the arguments that then follow about the implications of embodied meaning and its use in practice.

1.b. The Channelling of Desire

> Desire and meaning are highly interdependent, with meaning channelling the energy of desire through specific forms. Our motives for engagement with meaningful objects are not just a matter of 'emotive' meaning, but are a condition for all aspects of meaning as we experience it. Our desires can be engaged in meaning even when there are no beliefs or goals involved, as we particularly see in the experience of beauty.

Although most of this book will be concerned with the relationship between meaning and belief in various forms, before we go any further we must also consider the equally important relationship between meaning and *desire*. Desire is the energy that motivates organisms to fulfil their goals: goals which can only take specific form because of meaning. Those desires may be associated with positive goals, but may also be concerned with avoidance, making fear a sort of desire. Meaning can thus be described as the channelling of desire. Without meaning, desire would be inchoate. Without desire, on the other hand, meaning would be powerless. Although the distinction between meaning and desire is analytically helpful, in practice the two are interdependent to the extent that we could not have one without the other.

However, the relationship will probably not become fully clear unless we also consider it in relation to belief. Belief is the basis of activity, the assumed representation that forms the background to our goals – whether these are immediate goals like reaching the object on the other side of the room, or long-term ambitions like winning a Nobel prize. We are motivated to pursue these goals by desire, but we are only able to shape our view of them through meaning. Suppose my goal is to fetch a book from the other side of the room: to fulfil that goal I will need to believe that there is a book of a particular description, that it is in a particular location relative to other things, and that I am capable of moving to it, picking it up, and making use of it. The meaning that gives me the potential to have these beliefs will include associations between the general and specific description of the book and my understanding of how it might help me, as well as my past bodily experience of movement and action that gives me the raw materials for my belief that I can cross the room and pick up the book. However, that meaning and that belief will not become actuated, and may not become fully relevant, without my also having the *desire* to fetch the book, driving my experience of those meaning-associations into the more solid form of belief, and then enabling me to act according to those beliefs.

I could also channel my desires towards something that I did not believe. For instance, I could be immersed in a novel and desire to pick up the novel again and re-immerse myself in it. There are then practical beliefs surrounding the reading process, but not about the meaning that I get from that process. My desire to read is not a desire for the act of reading – rather it is a desire for the meaning I get from that reading. The meaning I get from the novel does not directly modify my beliefs about the world in any immediate way, though of course it could have various long-term effects on my attitudes (such as by offering archetypal inspiration).

However, I could not find something meaningful without my desires being engaged in that meaning. Without that desire, I will not pay any attention to a symbol, and it will cease to be meaningful. This is another way of discussing 'cognitive' and 'emotive' meaning (meaning as equivalent language versus meaning as feeling), often turned into a false dichotomy by linguists and philosophers (that will be discussed in more detail in 2.e). What is often thought of as 'cognitive' and 'emotive' meaning is an increment[1] – a spectrum of responses to a symbol dependent on how much our desires are invested in its meaning. Without both cognitive *and* emotive meaning to some degree, a symbol is not meaningful at all. We all have the experience of alienation from language that is supposed to be cognitively meaningful, produced in an abstracted bureaucratic context that neglects emotive meaning, but when used in a specific context where people's desires are not engaged, it becomes 'meaningless'. Take, for instance, routine safety announcements on aircraft or for fire evacuation from buildings, which is often repeated regardless of how many people present have heard the same announcement many times before. The language of functionaries that are merely stating the official view of an organization for legal purposes can be similar, as is the language of someone performing an inherited ritual that no longer has a purpose that its participants identify with. Such language is assumed to be 'meaningful' regardless of who utters or listens to it, but actually has very little meaning, unless we make

1   II.3.

the effort to listen to it. That is because our 'cognitive' response is entirely interdependent, in practice, with our 'emotive' one.

We engage in the meaning of a symbol by giving attention to it. However, the motivator of our attention does not have to be beliefs about its direct usefulness in the fulfilment of goals. Our motives can be much broader than that, which is why meaning can engage our desires without belief. Our motives can instead be part of an interaction with some sort of context in which we find a symbol meaningful in relation to our total experience, so that we become *interested* in it only as a way of exploring our wider experience, with only a vague potential for future application in the pursuit of goals.

The engagement of our attention through meaning is not just a matter of opening our senses, but is also often an active process, part of all the ways we interact with the world. Thus another helpful way of understanding meaning, apart from belief, is that of *play*. Play is characterized by an open 'flow' state of association in which we temporarily free up our expectations of the world around us, shaking it up so as to allow us to try out new creative relationships with it. We might do this, for instance, through imaginative construction, story-telling, or role-playing. When we play, it may well have some value for our future beliefs and actions, but this value remains indirect. As soon as our constructions need to be tested or our stories verified, we have left the playful world of mere meaning and passed on to the more serious world of belief, even though the beliefs may remain provisional. To engage with meaning without belief, it may well help us to recall the play states of childhood, and perhaps to actively cultivate the openness of that play state in adulthood.

The contexts that grab our attention and direct it at new symbols may be aesthetic, symbolic, archetypal, or conceptual. An aesthetic context is one where our motives interact with the senses, and where we thus get drawn into increasing appreciation of sensual form, proportion, and detail – for instance, the context of an artist working on a picture, gradually intensifying her engagement as she is drawn into an imaginative vision of the result. A symbolic context is one where our motives interact with imaginative links between a symbol we are experiencing and other symbols that we already find meaningful – for instance, a Christian hearing an unfamiliar Old Testament passage in church, engaged by connecting the meaning of that passage with the more central Christian meaning

Embodied Meaning 23

as he understands it from the gospels and Church teaching. An archetypal context is also symbolic, but is one where symbolic links are also ones that offer us long-term inspiration – so that the same Christian, for instance, may recall the Old Testament passage later, and find a new connection to the inspiration of God through it. That inspiration may also be of an emotionally negative kind, priming us to look out for threats. A conceptual context is one where we examine a concept in appreciation of its relationship to other concepts within a cognitive model, and are motivated by exploring and perfecting that web of conceptual relationships – for instance, a mathematics student learning a new proof, her attention grabbed by the meaningful relationships between the elements of the mathematical model.

If our desires are engaged deeply enough to channel our attention in any of these ways on a particular occasion, we may encounter beauty. I will discuss beauty further both later in this book (3.d), and in much greater depth in volume VII of this series.[2] Overall, though, our experience of beauty provides a further reason for recognizing the distinction between meaning and belief. Beauty seizes our attention because of the *meaning* of what we experience, not because of our beliefs about it. Although of course there are a few cases where we can associate attention to beauty being connected to predictable goals (a man entranced by the loveliness of a woman, say), there are many, many more where we have no particular goals in mind for appreciating beauty other than our enjoyment of it: why else do we enjoy sunsets, or even the contemplation of clouds in the sky or the swaying leaves of trees? Our desires are quite capable of being engaged by meaning alone, resulting on some occasions even in the intense integrative phenomena of *sublimity* (which I will return to in 5.i).

In understanding meaning as motivated by desire, then, we need to avoid reductive interpretations of our relationships to meaning that treat it solely in terms of beliefs about goals. Our left hemisphere forms goals and beliefs in relation to those goals, but the right is capable of appreciating meaning without any direct reference to goals, because it is open and alert and willing to explore new experiences and make new links between those experiences. When our desires are motivated only by meaning and not by more specific belief, they are much more exploratory desires. One could,

[2] VII.1.

of course, give an overall explanation for why we have such exploratory desires, based on how they help us in the longer term: for instance, we may be looking out for possible new threats or opportunities. However, these possible threats and opportunities are not the motives for paying attention to experiences that have meaning for us. We are not yet acquainted with what any of these threats or opportunities may be yet, so we are merely open – at play rather than narrowly focused on purposes. We are not *looking out for* particular kinds of threats or opportunities (which would require the belief that they are imminent), but merely looking out (or listening, feeling, smelling, tasting, imagining). Our desires are not channelled into one particular represented goal, but spread out widely into a variety of possible channels, moulded only by our wider embodied situation rather than by our specific goals.

Our wider embodied situation does have an effect on the meaning we experience, in a wide variety of ways, and thus on the directions in which our desires engage. As I will discuss in the next chapter, early infancy offers a specific type of embodied situation in which meaning (and thus also desire) are largely undifferentiated. This creates a very different experience from that of an over-stimulated adult with highly differentiated objects of meaning, and many different demands on that adult's attention, all of which are meaningful. In contrast to the adult's, the infant's expressions of desire are thus inchoate and somewhat unpredictable, until it has at least got more into the habit of paying more attention to some aspects of its experience rather than others. With no developed channels of meaning for desire to flow down, it could burst out almost anywhere.

Our embodied situation also moulds desire through meaning in specific ways later in life, whether through deeply entrenched biological processes or through more contingent cultural ones. For instance, sex and sexuality obviously also mould some of our desires in particular ways, in the process making certain symbols highly meaningful (for instance, making it hard to see breasts only as fatty tissue). At the other end of the spectrum, language and culture also offer us ready symbols that shape our sense of what is meaningful much more contingently, for instance, in Inuit languages differentiating between different categories of snow. Regardless of their causes, all such particularities of meaning shape our attention through the intensification of desire in some directions rather than others.

1.c. Differentiation and Integration

> The specific associations of embodied meaning only become possible through initial differentiation of our associative experience in infancy. However, at some stage the learning process passes from one of differentiation to one of integration – that is, of remaking lost (fragmented) connections between the meanings of symbols in different contexts. Differentiation does not necessarily cause fragmentation, because the latter involves loss of awareness of the underlying connections between differentiated symbols.

In early infancy, as well as in states of deep sleep, our meaning is undifferentiated. Our whole experience may be one of association, but we do not associate distinct experiences as symbolic of other distinct experiences. Rather, all our experiences are associated with each other. An infant whose only experience is being held and nursed by the mother has only that as a basis of association. Any other experiences the baby has, such as the maternal heartbeat or other rhythms sensed before birth, become associated with that undifferentiated state and its emotional reassurance. It is only when the mother is no longer the sole object of attention that differentiation begins: the baby experiences not-mother in contrast to mother.

The subsequent *differentiation* of meaning is shaped by the development of the senses, the neural connections that help us to learn from them, and then by the motor skills that enable us to interact with our world.[1] The elements into which meaning is differentiated by these processes will be discussed in more detail later in this section, but they begin with basic level categories and embodied schemas. We have particular kinds of experiences that may be associated with regular features of objects or other organisms we interact with: 'Mum', 'cat', 'tree', 'book'. We may begin to find these meaningful before we associate them with words, but those words will make a big contribution to differentiating them, as we share these words with others and thus come to learn the categories that others use. We may also link meanings with particular kinds of activity that become schematic, so that linked words or other symbols become meaningful in the context of that activity: a 'path' becomes something we walk along, a 'box' something that is hollow and contains other things that we may put in or take out.

1   III.1.b. Johnson (2007) ch. 2.

As we differentiate, we learn language, and stimulate the linguistic centres of the left pre-frontal cortex. But the meaning we learn is not only linguistic. We also learn to associate objects or people with each other: an aunt is associated with her child, the park with its pond. We also learn to associate pictures of objects with the objects they depict, based on the resemblance, and to recognize onomatopoeic representations of noises such as grrr. The differentiation is not merely 'cognitive', but just as much 'emotional', and may be idiosyncratically individual in some cases, rather than only following cultural and linguistic norms. The child who begins to interact directly with the world is learning not only to name the things in it, but also to relate directly to them, rather than only to the undifferentiated womb. People and objects become sources of identification just as they become sources of association: their meaning is always emotionally loaded.

As we learn through connection, we also unlearn through disconnection. We may forget words or people that we don't care about sufficiently (see 5.b on the 'pruning' of neural connections), and avoid those that have negative associations. We will learn symbols from those we associate with, and as we do so, gradually identify more with the group that shares those symbols, rather than with other groups. Our conflicts with others are partly a matter of beliefs about them, but we are also separated from them by a lack of shared meaning: even if we do share some symbols with them, these may not be sufficient for mutual understanding, so the conditions for conflict may remain unaddressed. Differentiated meaning can thus also become *fragmented* (see section 4 below). It is not fragmented only because it is differentiated, but because differentiated symbols are no longer associated with each other sufficiently for us to find them meaningful, when we have lost our awareness of an underlying connection.

Meaning that is fragmented, however, may also become integrated. Whilst integration in general (introduced in *The Five Principles*[2]) overcomes conflict between opposing desires and beliefs, integration of meaning does not directly resolve conflict – rather it defragments by creating understanding where it was previously lacking. Where there is understanding, we have a crucial and

---

2   II.5.

necessary but not sufficient condition for the integration of belief. For more about integration of meaning, see section 5 of this book.

What we often call 'learning' and 'understanding' (and may wrongly identify with 'knowledge') is meaning in the process of integration. Such learning and understanding spans a spectrum from the predominantly cognitive to the predominantly emotive: for instance, learning a new word in a language is predominantly (but not solely) cognitive, whilst recognizing your teenage son's motives where there was previously a barrier is predominantly emotive. Education is primarily a matter of integrating meaning: its main achievement is to get us interested in new symbols that are synthesized with our existing experience. New links get added to an existing web of links. This is not 'knowledge' – no facts have necessarily been learnt (or if they have this is incidental) nor propositions affirmed. Nor is it necessarily a matter of belief: I do not need to form propositions of belief out of the new words I learn in German, nor do I need to believe or disbelieve what my teenage son may say when I start listening to him. The integrative process consists in the way that new meaning is incorporated into the resources available to me.

The boundary between differentiation and integration is a vague one, as both can be forms of learning, and superficially they appear opposed. To understand the relationship between them, we need to start by recognizing that the undifferentiated state of an infant superficially looks like an integrated state. However, to treat the undifferentiated state as an integrated state is to fall into what Ken Wilber calls the *pre-trans fallacy*, confusing a state before integration is possible with one after it has been achieved to some degree. There can be no integration without prior differentiation, or there is nothing to integrate. However, the prior memory of an undifferentiated state, as I have previously argued elsewhere,[3] may provide us with a symbolic reminder of what integration is like, and also a notional idea of its completion (see 5.j). To provide us with that reminder, that prior undifferentiated experience does not have to actually be an experience of integration, only to resemble it in certain respects.

Differentiation may to some degree also create fragmentation, dependent on how far we remain in touch with that underlying awareness of the possibility of integration. It is a background sense

---

3   III.1.j; Wilber (1982).

of the possibility of integration that allows the infant to develop meaning in all sorts of other ways whilst remaining confident of his or her basic security and the meaningfulness of his/her world. However, to the extent that that security is broken, fragmentation starts to result. This is very much a matter of degree: people with traumatic childhoods and highly insecure maternal attachment do not thereby become completely incapable of learning. However, there may be a lot of fragmentation of meaning created by that early experience that will need stitching back together in the process of learning, and may create considerable difficulties for them. Someone with secure attachments is also not entirely devoid of fragmentation, because there can be a variety of possible causes for us losing track of the connection between different meanings (not just insecure maternal attachment). We all suffer from some degree of fragmentation interfering with our capacity to learn by preventing us engaging as much as we might with the new meaning around us.

The point in our development where integration learning takes over from differentiation learning is probably one where basic adaptation to our environment has already taken place to an extent that enables us to become increasingly independent. The young child does not have to stretch himself to encounter a spoon or a door, and to start to associate words with these objects, because they are regular parts of his environment that he is obliged to interact with: they interpose themselves readily before him. However, the adult who finds a new plant in his garden and makes the effort to look up what it is called, or who meets a new person and makes the effort to find something out about their background, is not so much obliged to find these new symbols meaningful in order to operate in his environment. He could 'get by' without doing so. If he has no previous experience of engaging with botany at all, there is a fragmentation between the web of symbols associated with the details of plant life and his existing web of symbols, just as there might be between his existing social links and the stranger. To talk about 'making an effort' in such cases is probably to miss the crucial element in the process: namely the creation of a new link where one was not present before. It matters little to what extent the absence of that link is due to unfamiliarity, and to what extent to emotional resistance, because we have an emotional resistance to the unfamiliar, and what we are unfamiliar with becomes an object of emotional resistance. Such resistance is not because we lack 'knowledge' of the unfamiliar, but because of fragmentation of meaning.

Another way of thinking of this distinction is in terms of reinforcing and balancing feedback loops. Differentiation is primarily the continuing way in which an organism perpetuates itself, reproducing patterns that already exist. It may depend on initial observation (for instance, of a new object, or of a word associated with that object), but that observation is incorporated into and serves a pre-existing pattern of life. Integration, on the other hand, is mainly concerned with *adjusting* that pattern of life in the light of new information. Differentiation is thus primarily a matter for the left hemisphere, which constantly creates new categories to further its goals, whilst integration is primarily a matter for the right hemisphere. That the early differentiation of the young child is also accompanied by many right-hemisphere qualities (such as intense curiosity) is a reminder of how effectively the hemispheres can work together, and of the ways that categorization still depends on new meaning. Nevertheless, the *separation* of the symbols is the most important process that is going on in that early learning. Often we start off with very vague associations, but have to clarify them when it becomes relevant to our needs. For instance, as a young child with two older sisters, I recall assuming that sisters were always older siblings and brothers younger ones. It was only by having to interact with other families where there were older brothers and younger sisters that I was forced to separate the concepts of sex and relative age in my use of the terms.[4]

There can also be no precise boundary, but again only a general description, of how differentiation can turn into fragmentation. We can only fail to engage with something unfamiliar because we have separated it out from the rest of our experience in some way, to make it an object of ignorance. Socio-cultural groupings are the most obvious example of differentiation that can rapidly form the basis of fragmentation, as we separate out the other from our own group, and then cease to try to understand what is other. Both the language and the motives of the other then cease to be an object of curiosity. Of course, this process can also be accompanied by absolutized beliefs that rationalize that non-engagement (the effect of

---

[4] See 5.b below for further discussion of the implications of this same example.

group biases): however, even in the absence of such beliefs, fragmentation can provide an initial resistance to engaging with the other.

Integration of meaning is thus an interdependent element in the pyramid of integration that begins with integration of desire and culminates with integration of belief.[5] We can only engage with new meaning because we desire to do so, which in turn requires our background beliefs to be adjusted towards doing so. However, openness to learning is only the starting point for an integration of belief that overcomes the longer-term sources of conflict. Sources of conflicting desire and belief, and/or of fragmented meaning, may be a legacy of infancy, or may also be affected by our ongoing practice. What judgements do we make at every point? Do we choose to step forward towards new understanding, or away from it? For us to do this effectively requires clarity about the embodiment of the whole process, so that we can address the conditions for it in our experience, and avoid the false shortcuts offered by any supposed God's eye view.

Sections 4 and 5 of this book will engage with the fragmentation and integration of meaning as aspects of Middle Way practice in much more detail. However, for the moment we need to note the place that both differentiation and integration of meaning have in the way that embodied meaning is shaped in our experience. In particular, it needs to be a prompt to keep synthesizing psychological awareness of our wider states, and moral understanding of the direction we can steer them in, with our understanding of meaning. Meaning is a much bigger and more important matter than should be left solely to linguists and to the relatively narrow framing they often give to its discussion.

---

5   II.5.d.

1.d. Symbols

> Symbols are any experiences that are associated with other experiences – including any object, person, image, or word. Our focusing of attention makes them meaningful along with association. Symbols are multivalent, unlike the univalent signs relied on by representationalism, which mistakes a practical need for shared fixity of meaning in particular circumstances for a general condition. Such symbols *can* be 'private' even if that limits their use.

Having identified three basic conditions for embodied meaning, we now need to show how these basic conditions can account for every type of meaning, including the most complex linguistic meaning (the kind that non-embodied accounts tend to over-privilege). My account of how embodied meaning can be built up from the basic conditions to any level of abstraction owes a great deal to the work of Lakoff and Johnson (though also with some modifications), and can be visualized as a hierarchical pyramid structure **[diagram 2]**.

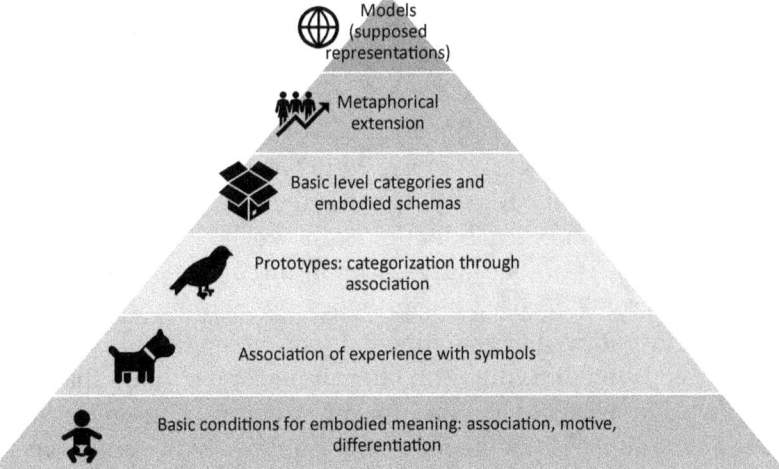

Diagram 2. The development of embodied meaning from its basic conditions to the most complex language.

The idea of a *symbol* is a crucial aspect of embodied meaning that should be clarified before we go too much further. Embodied meaning is *not* just a theory of language, but more widely a theory of symbolic meaning encompassing language – which is why we do not just have 'linguistic bodies', but rather, 'symbolic bodies'.

So far, I have mentioned symbols as associations with experiences: so most basically, symbols are experiences that we associate with other experiences. This places no other requirements on what can or cannot serve as a symbol. Anything at all in our experience can serve as a symbol if we associate it with something else: not just a word or a visual icon but also a sound, an object, or a person *as we experience them*. An aspect of the way we experience them is that they are already overlaid with interpretation as we encounter them. We cannot encounter them on the basis of a blank slate, but always do so on the basis of previous experience and of all the neural links we have already made with them or with similar things.

That *anything* can be a symbol does not of course require that *everything* is a symbol – or at least not in practice. Some things are far more meaningful to us than other things. For instance, as I look out of my window, some things that I see are far more symbolically loaded and thus meaningful to me than other things. A red kite that flies into view is meaningful because it is relatively unusual, living, active, and distinctive. The trees, flowers, and grass that I can see are only moderately meaningful, more in general than in particular, unless I have some reason for focusing on a particular detail. The clouds are again only moderately and generally meaningful, unless I happen to see a cloud that visually resembles something else – in which case it starts to become symbolic. A cloud might also start to become more meaningful if I focused my attention on appreciating its shape aesthetically, regardless of symbolic associations.

The attention and the fascination with which I examine my experience is the basis of its beauty, as I will discuss in detail in a later book of this series focused on aesthetics.[1] Sometimes that beauty is symbolic in nature, but sometimes it may be entirely aesthetic, or possibly conceptual. Symbolism, then, is one of the things that grabs our attention and provides beauty, prompting increasingly mindful examination, but not the only thing. Although the conditions for meaning are created by all the associations we have built up consciously or unconsciously over our whole lives, it is attention that modifies that meaning for us in the present. It is our ability to contextualize symbolic meaning in wider aesthetic experience that can give us some freedom to modify meaning by varying the intensity of our experience of it. A symbol accompanied by aesthetically-based

1   VII.

attention becomes stronger, as many artists, dramatists, and film-makers are aware, and one that lacks such attention often weakens. For example, we have a stronger response to a powerful figure on a stage highlighted by spotlights, than one in the shadows that we can only just see: the light level changes the aesthetic context of the symbolic figure, but not its symbolic meaning.

The embodied and associative basis of symbols makes their meaning multivalent: that is, any given symbol has a variety of meanings. We may even be aware of the ambiguity and vagueness of a symbol as we contemplate it, but even when we are not, symbols change their meaning over time, just as the human bodies that find them meaningful change. It also should be exceedingly obvious (though often neglected in practice) that 'the same' symbol (i.e. one with a largely unchanging form in key relevant respects, such as a written word) means different things to different people. How could it be otherwise, when they have different bodies, giving different experiences of the meaning of the symbol?

I thus follow Jung in making a distinction between *symbols* and *signs*, whereby symbols are multivalent (having many meanings) but signs are univalent (having one meaning). I'm aware that the usage of these two terms varies in different contexts of discussion, so all one can do is stipulate what one believes to be the most helpful usage. Signs, *in theory*, have only one meaning: for instance, a red traffic light means 'stop'. That would mean that the sign could be 'translated' into an equivalent definition without loss of meaning. If a word has multiple meanings, when it is treated as a sign, it needs to be analysed so as to separate out those different meanings (as they are listed in a dictionary), each of which is a separate sign that (again, in theory) can then be exchanged between people whilst maintaining the same meaning. Where words are treated as signs, there is assumed to be denotation as opposed to connotation, so that a word *represents* an object rather than merely being associated with it. These theoretical properties of signs are all assumptions of representationalism – which will be criticized in more detail in section 2.

If meaning is embodied, however, this implies that there can only be symbols, not signs. There is not pure denotation. Every word (or icon, or significant object) is multivalent, because its meaning is entirely dependent on its embodied context and the associations that context gives it. The idea of denotation has a *practical* usage within a shared model in which people are collaborating, as the fulfilment of shared goals can only be adequately planned with an assumption of shared language. However, such practical usage constantly has to adapt to the differences in interpretation of the same language used by participants, even after shared definition of terms and shared instruction in the same model. We are not using signs that we poetically expand into symbols on special occasions. Instead we are using symbols that we constantly have to keep trimming to try to make them into signs, even though they constantly spread their meaning like vigorous weeds.

If there is no pure denotation, there can also be no essentialism: there is no essential or 'proper' meaning for a symbol, only an approximately shared meaning in communication that can serve (or fail to serve) particular purposes. Essentialism takes a limited discourse for granted and ignores the wider context of meaning: 'that's not what it really means'. The appeal to a dictionary tells us only the prejudices of society about ways that the meaning of a word should be limited, as documented by the lexicographer. The constraint of language to 'essential' purposes through limiting assumptions about its meaning also constrains the resources we can use to consider and examine our beliefs, thus serving ideological purposes. For instance, if a view is dismissed as not 'true Marxism' in a group of Marxists, it will not be further explored, nor its possible value understood.

If the key requirement for a symbol is association, that association may or may not necessarily be shared. We do learn much of our interpretation of symbols through shared culture, especially the symbols of language, which depend for their form on cultural transmission. However, before we reduce even linguistic symbols to their communicative function (in the fashion of Wittgenstein), it's important to recall the constant dependence of communication on shared meaning, and shared meaning on individual experiences. There can be no cultural transmission of the meaning of symbols without individual experience of their meaningfulness: you can instruct children all day on the socially-agreed meaning of symbols in a classroom (what a lot of education traditionally amounts to!) and yet it will create no meaning at all if the children are not interested (that is, if they don't have an individual experience of the meaningfulness of those symbols).

It may well be that our capacity for finding symbols meaningful depends in some respects on social stimulus of that capacity in general. However, the developmental activation of a capacity should not be used as a basis for constraining our understanding of its subsequent use. Once we have activated our symbolic and linguistic capacities, there is no reason why we cannot use them independently to create new symbols that are entirely private to us. These can be 'private' in the sense that we are aware of no overlap between the meaning of a symbol to us and its meaning to others, as in Wittgenstein's example of a secret mark in a diary recording an individual sensation.[2] We may be unable to use such symbols as *signs*, which will need to be shared with others for a purpose, but that is an entirely different issue to their *meaning* as symbols. In a wider sense, all symbols are private, because only I have the exact experience connoted by the symbol. Even the meaning of a sentence in a paper about physics has a meaning for me that is different from its meaning for others, even if the social emphasis is on the practically shared relationship between that sentence and reproducible universal phenomena.

Overall, then, the emphasis in our understanding of symbols in embodied meaning needs to be on the continuity of the phenomenon of meaning across types of symbol. 'Meaning' in the sense of the meaning of the tree to me on my regular walk, or the meaning of a smile I detect on a friend's face, is continuous with 'meaning' in the sense of the meaning of the most abstracted collections of supposedly representative signs – say, the working of a mathematical problem, or an engineering plan. In all such uses of symbols, connotation is prior to denotation, because denotation is specific only to a practical shared context, whilst connotation shapes our whole experience. For the same reason, meaning (which is connotative) is prior to supposedly denotative belief. This does not entail that we give up using signs for particular purposes in particular contexts: for instance, I hope that the linguistic symbols that I am using now in writing this book will fulfil some of the functions of signs, in enabling practical goals that we may share, as well as the wider functions of symbols. However, whenever we narrow our sense of meaning in this way, we need to remain aware of the limitations and costs of doing so.

---

2   II.1.f. Wittgenstein (1967) § 258. Also see 2.d below.

1.e. Prototypes

> Prototype theory lies at the roots of embodied meaning, as it shows how our categorizations are based on association rather than absolute definition. This also shows how meaning is incremental, even if we define categories absolutely for practical purposes. Prototype theory looks most at nouns, but it can also be applied to other words and to non-linguistic symbols. Prototypes should not be confused with archetypes, although the empirical evidence for each may have a similar structure.

The theory of prototypes provides one of the basic types of evidence that initially aided Lakoff and Johnson in developing embodied meaning theory.[1] It also helps to illuminate the ways in which association can provide the basis of the categories we use in language (such as 'thing', 'elephant', 'graduate') – categories that we might initially assume to be given meaning by formal abstract definitions telling us what does or does not belong in that category. Initially developed by Eleanor Rosch, prototype theory identifies the ways in which categories can become more meaningful, not from definition, but through their association with examples: for example, 'robin' as a prototype of the category 'bird'. When we first learn the term 'bird' as a young child, we have little idea of the zoological definition of the term. Rather, we encounter an example (which may be a live bird or a picture) and associate the word with the example. We then learn to extend that association to other examples.

Of course those associations may vary a good deal, but they also follow cultural patterns. For instance, the category of 'bird' may well be represented for a British person by a robin: a bird that is both distinctive and familiar in Britain. When settlers brought British culture to America, they missed the robin (which only occurs in the Old World), so their cultural association led them to name an unrelated but superficially similar bird (the American robin) 'robin', showing something of the power of that association. Whether the associations begin in culture or in personal experience, though, the crucial point is that we learn to understand categories in this associative way, and as a result, this is *how* we understand categories.

The vital element introduced by prototypes as an approach to meaning is their *incrementality*. Instead of a given object in experience

---

1   Lakoff (1987) pp. 39 ff.

either being a bird or not a bird, it is more or less birdy. As I have argued previously,[2] incrementality is a basic feature of organic systems that our conceptual understanding needs to attempt to track. Meaning for an organism involves a change in structure in response to a stimulus, but each change in structure depends on autocatalysis[3] – a gradual, not instantaneous, process. It would be the height of arrogance to assume that our categorizations are somehow immune from this general feature of organic meaning, and it is prototype theory that first showed how we could understand our categorizations of meaning in more helpful incremental terms.

Prototype theory thus challenges the abstract representationalist assumption that language is fundamentally different from other types of meaning, because the meanings of the categories it uses have to be determined in top-down conceptual ways. On the contrary, the ways in which we understand categories are very much bottom-up. We adopt a category that is used in our social context, but it becomes meaningful to us as individuals because of the *associations* we have with that category.

Many of the criticisms that have been made of prototype theory, since its inception in the 1970s, have failed to understand this point, because they assume a representationalist framework in which concepts have to be definable in terms of other concepts. Whilst accepting the empirical evidence drawn on by prototype theory of how people learn and use categories, then, critics have objected that the mere typicality of an example does not enable us to distinguish its boundaries: for instance if a prototypical apple is a green apple, this doesn't enable us to recognize that apples can also be red, yellow, or brown.[4] This misses the point that it is socially-accepted linguistic conventions, not *meaning*, that help us to determine the boundaries of categories. To work out what counts as an apple we might need to consult socially-agreed models (which I will discuss further in 1.i). However, to understand the *meaning* of 'apple' we need to recognize its associations in experience – vague and indeterminate as these will undoubtedly be.

The prototype phenomenon most obviously applies to nouns, but it also has implications for other types of words. There are prototypical ways of acting in the meaning of a verb to us, and prototypical

2   II.3.a, III.1.b.
3   III.1.a.
4   Hampton (2006).

adjectival or adverbial descriptions. For instance, 'to kill' is more likely to be associated with a murder than a suicide,[5] and 'red' is universally prototypically centred around a particular point on the spectrum (even though it doesn't precisely define it).[6] Empirical evidence for such effects can obviously only detect cultural (or cross-cultural) elements in prototyping, but there may also be personal variations and personal effects. Prototypical colours are likely to be affected both by your colour vision and by the predominant colours in your early environment, whilst prototypical birds may depend both on your environment and the direction of your interest in it. There will also be a lot of personal variation in the emotional associations with particular words, particularly for those with some degree of trauma or phobia.

Although it's not discussed in the academic literature, I see no reason why prototype effects shouldn't also apply to non-linguistic symbols. For instance, the meaning of the Christian cross may vary a great deal depending on whether or not one has a Christian background (and if so, which church and what sort of environment): there may be theological differences in how far it primarily means the crucifixion or the resurrection (the 'empty cross'), variations of whether it means love and peace or war and aggression, and associations with boredom on the one hand or excitement on the other. With non-linguistic symbols (not only icons but also pictures, sounds, smells, objects, etc.) it becomes increasingly obvious that there is no single 'definition' of the meaning of the symbol, so the question then becomes why we should treat linguistic symbols any differently from this.

Prototype theory makes it clear that the general form by which we should understand *meaning* (as opposed to communicative conventions) is to start with prototypical meaning and work outwards from there. Prototypical meaning will offer the most deeply-rooted associations for any symbol, but each symbol can also be seen as a subsystem of the overall web of associative links that is meaning, with many connections to other symbols with which it is interdependent. That subsystem develops in practice through growth in relation to embodied activity. We develop basic level categories and schemas in early infancy in relation to embodied experience, these

5   Stamenkovic (2011).
6   Berlin & Kay (1969) p. 13.

offering prototypical patterns. These categories and schemas then extend metaphorically and metonymically, again in relation to our activity as we develop organically. This process will be charted in more detail in the next three chapters.

Prototypes should not be confused with archetypes, as they often are. A prototype offers a starting point for the growth of meaning in a symbolic subsystem. Archetypes, on the other hand, are prompts for integrative growth in the human system of meaning as a whole. On a helpful understanding compatible with embodied meaning, neither offer any kind of essentiality, which is the shortcut way of thinking about them that may make them appear superficially similar. The idea of essentiality comes from a definitional approach to identifying the boundaries of how we use symbols, whether linguistic or non-linguistic. These boundaries are often worth clarifying in practice, but only on the basis of a pragmatic argument about usage, not on the basis of any belief about the 'essence' of any phenomenon, which we can have no access to in experience. Prototypes are not the essence of words, but the way in which we find them meaningful, just as archetypes are not the essence ('unconscious' or otherwise) of inspirational symbols, but a way of talking about commonalities of function between them.

However, I have previously suggested that supportive evidence about archetypes could be gathered by a similar approach to that taken in prototype research.[7] This assumes that, rather than the relationship between symbols and essences of meaning for those symbols, the relationship between either prototypes or archetypes and symbols is like that between a schema and the metaphorical or metonymic extensions of that schema. How this might work should become clearer when I discuss schemas below. Tracing back our various extensions of a web of meaning to their schematic root can help us both to vivify the meaning of those extensions (very helpful for learning), and to understand how they have developed, whether we are dealing simply with the meaning of category words like 'bird' or with the inspirational meaning of, say, 'God'. In both cases we should equally avoid the Platonic approach that leads us straight into abstraction and thence absolutization through essences, but this does not exclude a process of digging and discovery.

---

7   Ellis (2022) pp. 59–60.

1.f. Basic Level Categories

> Basic level categories are the initial associations of terms that we make in relation to objects and similar types of objects, making these terms meaningful at the level we interact with them. Objects are most basically meaningful somewhere in the middle of the range between generality and specificity. We need to combine basic level categories with embodied schemas and metaphors to understand contexts, but we often rely instead on abstract extension of absolutized categories.

Basic level categories are one of the early staging posts in the differentiation of meaning, and were early identified by Lakoff and a number of his forerunners in the development of embodied meaning theories.[1] They provide us with our first associative relationship with phenomenal[2] objects in the world. This association is primarily that between certain key nouns and objects or types of objects, but can also be seen in the association between pictures (including simplified pictorial icons) and objects, or between objects and the noise they make (or are conventionally thought of as making, such as 'woof' with a dog), or between any two differing experiences of an object.

Our assumptions of sameness start here. How do I 'know' that the noise of a dog barking comes from the 'same' dog that I see the next moment, or indeed that this 'dog', a spaniel, belongs to the same category as the wolfhound I saw yesterday? Applying the principles of scepticism discussed in *The Five Principles*, I do not 'know' anything of the kind: it is not a question of 'knowledge' but of meaning. I *associate* the word 'dog' with my different experiences both of one given animal and with other similar animals. There can thus be no right or wrong association with a categorizing symbol, only associations that are shared with others to a greater or lesser extent.

Association does not distinguish between individual objects and types of objects – 'mama' from 'cat' – until we come across more similar examples of a type. So we could at first think of basic level categories as applying either to individual objects, or to types of object with obvious similarities. Later, we can start to distinguish

1   Lakoff (1987) pp. 31-55.
2   'Phenomenal' means 'as we experience', and thus should be distinguished from any metaphysical beliefs about objects, which extend beyond experience.

wider categories from unique objects – 'women' from 'mamas'. We can also refine our understanding of a category: for instance, to identify the relevant criteria so that we can separate cats from dogs. To start with, though, it is enough that we make links between identifiable words and identifiable aspects of experience. Even if we assume that all women are mamas and all furry animals are cats, we have made a start in our differentiation of the world.

Such early categorization is called 'basic level' because it is the starting point for further differentiation. Such later differentiation may come in the form of higher categories with larger semantic fields (hypernyms) or of lower categories with smaller semantic fields (hyponyms): for instance, if our basic level category is a 'tree', we may then learn the meaning of a more specific type of tree ('oak'), or of a wider category of which tree is a part ('plant'). This associative pattern follows the same prototypical pattern through which we started to find basic categories meaningful, so that, for instance, we might find trees more 'planty' than rushes because we have learned to understand the meaning of plants through the meaning of trees. Such categorization can also apply to adjectives and verbs: if 'red' is a basic level category, then 'crimson' may be a hyponym and 'colour' a hypernym subsequently learned in relation to that initial category. Similarly, 'go' may be a basic level category with 'walk' as a more detailed application, and 'move' as a more general one.

Because basic level categories are embodied and depend on the initial level at which we engage with the world, they may vary according to our culture and environment. If you live in a culture where a particular animal or plant is important, you may begin with a particular species as a basic level category, whilst those for whom it is less important will differentiate less. For a country-dweller with an oak tree right in front of their house, 'oak' is much more likely to be a basic level category than it is for a city-dweller who encounters vaguely differentiated trees only on occasional visits to the park.

Although we may come to understand basic level categories and their extension in relation to the common and/or scientific classification of objects in higher or lower categories, it is important to note that such classification is a later development in our grasp of meaning, dependent on our acquisition of representational models (see 1.i below). The level of classification that we find most *meaningful* is contingent on our embodied engagement with it, not on whatever may be the more general or more specific level of the classification system when considered abstractly. It is also prototypical, as discussed in the previous chapter. This point becomes even more obvious if we try to trace hypernyms or hyponyms up or down the tree beyond a point of familiarity: at the most general level, we get lost in theoretical physics, and at the most specific, in the endless distinctions of hyper-specialization, such as species and sub-species and minor variants. We not only do not, but could not, start at one end of the spectrum of classification or the other: rather, we have to start in the middle.

Basic level categories tell us something about the object-related level of meaning as we first encounter it. However, they don't tell us anything about the context of those objects. That context is crucial in its influence on meaning, because without taking it into account we can treat objects as separated from their surrounding conditions, thus forming beliefs that underestimate the interdependence that has crucial practical effects. The operation of basic level categories is thus constantly interdependent with that of embodied schemas, which I will discuss in the next chapter. Of course, we do need to be able to treat objects that often operate separately as though they were separate: a pile of bricks, for example, is something we can make a great variety of constructions with because of the separateness of each brick. Organisms also have separateness that is dependent on their self-perpetuating boundaries. However, we also need to be able to look beyond those boundaries to appreciate how organisms are also part of ecosystems, and bricks are also parts of constructions – indeed of cities. To label an 'object' using a basic level category is to start to get ourselves into the habit of putting labels on objects, and thus giving them assumed boundaries. However, these boundaries are maladaptive when they distract us from systemic relationships.

The consideration of basic level categories in relation to schemas and metaphors is the way to give a bigger context to the category, but this is often not the route we take. Instead, when our basic level categories prove inadequate, we start to use higher or lower level categories instead: we ascend into generalized abstraction, or lose our perspective in analytic precision about specific detail (which also includes its share of generalized abstractions). In other words, we continue to treat meaning as though it was based on objects with clear boundaries, but make the objects bigger or smaller so that the boundaries are less clear. We construct objects that we then treat as metaphysical by putting them into absolute beliefs – God, or nature, or freewill, or reason – and assume that these objects have the same kinds of boundaries that ordinary basic-level objects have, but also have a universal application far beyond concrete objects: for example, that we can make claims about God that are simultaneously universal and specifically human.

Basic level categorization lays down neural channels that then enable us to find increasingly complex language or other symbology meaningful. It is then easy to lose all recognition of their role in our apparently direct interaction with more complex symbols. For instance, a trained zoologist with a complex understanding of the relationships between all the different levels of scientific classification of animals, based on different defining features, is no longer directly conscious of the process by which she formed initial understanding even of the general term 'animal', let alone of all these details. Nevertheless that process continues to give a general shape to the meaning of animal terms to her, in a sense that unites 'cognitive' and 'emotive' elements: for instance, the initial enthusiasm of relating to cats, dogs, or other familiar animals in early childhood is still part of the *meaning* of all the animal terms that depends on them through basic level categorization. In an important sense, then, meaning is individual associative history. Like a plant growing towards the light, we cannot completely undo the kinks that direct our neural stems in particular directions in particular conditions, and these remain part of the structure underlying our responses to the world even many decades later.

1.g. Embodied Schemas

> Embodied schemas (or 'image schemas') are associative patterns of interaction with our environment which provide clusters of meaning for symbols. They combine different sense experiences, interaction, and cultural embeddedness to provide meaning context both through our bodily experience and our relation to objects. They are both 'cognitive' and 'emotive'. They link basic level categories, and can be extended to new spheres by metaphor.

Embodied schemas, like basic level categories, are associations. However, they are wider contextualizing associations between kinds of experience and fields of associated symbols. Meaning cannot simply be associated with objects or types of objects, because its whole function is to link experiences together: those objects have a context in which we encounter them. It is our embodiment that creates the areas of associated experience in which the schemas operate. Let's take an initial example: the source-path-goal schema. This offers a sphere of meanings associated with the embodied experience of *moving along a path from a starting point* (source) *to an anticipated end point* (goal). This schema gives meaning to a whole range of concepts, such as 'journey', 'road', 'origin', or 'end'. I will return to it below. However, first we need a little more on the idea of an embodied schema in general.

I am using the term 'embodied schemas' here to initially try to avoid any confusion with other uses of the term 'schema': particularly the Kantian use, which is purely conceptual and concerned with the models or frameworks used in belief (see 1.i below). However, generally I will subsequently refer to 'embodied schemas' as just 'schemas', on the assumption that this is understood. The original term used for them, in the work of Lakoff and Johnson, was 'image schemas': however, they are not only formed from visual images, but from every aspect of our senses and of the interaction of our senses with bodily activity. As Johnson defines an image schema, it is 'a dynamic, recurring pattern of organism-environment interactions'.[1] In Lakoff and Johnson's account, 'image schemas' are preconceptual, gestalt, continuous, and internally structured.[2] We use them to form concepts rather than them being dependent on

1 Johnson (2007) p. 136.
2 Hampe (2005).

concepts; we experience them as instantaneous wholes; they have no clear boundaries from our embodied experience or conceptual application; and they are not dependent on structures elsewhere in our mind-body (such as representations).

Embodiment creates the forms of schemas along with the other E's beloved of cognitive scientists discussing this area: enaction, extension, and embeddedness. In early childhood we develop associations in the course of *acting* and *interacting* in the world. We do so in a context of space and time where our bodies and other objects have *extension* – they take up space and continue over time, rather than being limited to a particular point in either: this moulds the whole way we interact with things. Our experience is also *embedded* in a whole set of other systems: ecological, biological, and cultural. We would not come to make many of our associations without being in some way directed towards them by our interactions with others, all within a wider socio-cultural framework.

To apply these E's to the source-path-goal schema, we need to recall that we get our understanding of what it is to follow a path from the experience of moving through space, with bodily effort and represented goals. A young child may crawl forwards to grasp a toy. I may get up to cross the room to fetch a book. In both cases we are interacting with objects in space in a way that depends on the kinds of goals we have as humans, and on the bodily equipment (nerves, muscles, legs, opposable thumbs, etc.) for fulfilling those goals at different points in space. The ways that our bodies move through space may vary (crawling, walking, taking a bus, etc.), but they all involve the movement of bodies that are themselves extended in space. Our movement is also environmentally embedded, because the form taken by my path is constantly interdependent with the opportunities and formats offered by that environment.

It would not be enough, in understanding the meaning of 'path' to us, to merely try to apply basic level categories. A 'path' may sometimes take the form of a concrete object (such as a line of bare earth worn through grass), but it may not be visible or otherwise noticeable at all without its relationship to our source and goal (a 'path through the air', for instance). It is not a complete abstraction, because we *experience* what it is like to follow a path, but only in a given type of embodied situation. It is only in such an embodied situation that we understand words for sources, paths, or goals, not in isolation.

A given schema is thus not just the source of meaning for one symbol, but for many associated ones. As previously, we may be primarily thinking in linguistic terms, but schemas can also contribute to non-linguistic meaning. For instance, a circular target made up of concentric circles (as traditionally used by archers) is an easily recognizable iconic visual representation of a goal. However, this is meaningful to us only in relation to our schematic understanding of the relationship between sources, paths, and goals. The arrow can only have a target because its source is some distance from the target, and it needs to follow a line in space from the source to the target. Our active experience of the schema can also help us to understand it in relation to the activity of other people, animals, machines, or even inanimate objects such as hailstones or planets. Whether or not we are correct in any sense to attribute a 'goal' to a planet (the philosophical problem of teleology), our understanding of the orbital *path* of a planet depends on anticipation of the point it will reach in future – even if that anticipation only happens in our own minds and nowhere else.

There is no complete list of embodied schemas, but below is a partial list of some of the ones that have been proposed.[3] Many of these are dependent on previous ones, with those underlined in bold evidently being the most basic. The relationship of derivation of the dependent schemas from the more basic ones can be seen as applications of a prototype (as discussed in 1.e), or metaphorical developments (as discussed in the next chapter).

- **<u>Source-path-goal</u>** (already discussed above)
- *Process:* the experience of connected linear causal events, giving meaning to terms like cause, beginning, end
- *Cycle:* the experience of a circular process
- *Iteration:* the experience of repeated similar processes
- **<u>Container</u>**: the experience of some things being inside or outside other things, thus giving meaning to terms like box, field, in, out, into, etc.
- *Full-empty:* the experience of degrees of filling of a container
- **<u>Link</u>**: the experience of connection, giving meaning to terms like attachment, connect, web

---

3   Adapted and re-ordered from Hampe (2005), drawing in turn on Lakoff and Johnson.

Embodied Meaning

- *Contact:* the experience of close physical proximity creating touch sensations, giving meaning to terms like feel, touch, embrace
- **Part-whole**: the experience of some things being part of other things, giving meaning to terms like bit, ingredient, total
- **Centre-periphery**: the experience of some things being closer to the centre of an area than others, giving meaning to terms like middle, edge, extension
- *Surface:* the experience of contrast between the outside of an object and its hidden inside
- **Body orientation schemas**: up-down, front-back and left-right
- **Balance**: the experience of maintaining an upright pose (or not), giving meaning to terms like fall, poise, wobble
- **Object schema**: the experience of interacting with a discrete object, which can be seen as the basis of basic level categories
- *Schemas for relationships between objects: merging, matching, splitting, collection*
- *Scale:* the experience of comparative object size, giving meaning to terms like big and little, and to comparative and superlative adjectives
- *Near-far:* the experience of sensing objects as closer or further off
- **Force schemas**: *enablement, blockage, counterforce, attraction, compulsion, restraint, removal, diversion*

These schemas are all primarily focused on linguistic forms. However, when it comes to non-linguistic meaning (see 3.d below), I would suggest that some more need to be added:

- Perspective: the experience of having a specific visual vantage point that structures and connects our experience of the spatial relationship between objects and their relative scale
- Rhythm: the experience of iterated marked events over time, given particular meaning by its relationship to our bodily rhythms of heartbeat and pulse
- Melody: the experience of tone patterns, given particular meaning by its link to emotional expression in the human voice

It will be seen here that all of these schemas relate to bodily activity in the world. Although they include schemas for objects themselves, these are objects as we experience and interact with them. In some cases the basic experience providing meaning for us will be that of experiencing our bodies themselves (for example, one basic way of relating to the container schema is of what is inside or outside our bodies). In other cases, we relate to the sensual experience of objects beyond our bodies, but with our experience continually affected by the way that our body interacts with those objects. For example, it is often we who merge, match, split, or collect objects, often also by exerting force on them. We may also experience other people doing the same things, which helps to create a meaningful link between our direct experience of activity and our observation.

This list of embodied schemas can only create a general impression of the range of sources of meaning they offer. It needs to be constantly borne in mind that the meaning in these schematic forms is *both* 'cognitive' and 'emotive' (although the academic sources tend to concentrate rather one-sidedly on the 'cognitive'). To recall the emotive side, we just need to recall the strength of *identification* we are likely to have with a goal (for instance), and thus the motivation it will give us for following a path. If this motivation is then *blocked* (one of the force schemas), we will feel frustration. For another example, we identify more with the centre than with the periphery of our bodies, or of an object that we identify with. This schema thus helps us to calibrate the scale of our response to any perceived attack or interference on ourselves or such an object, so that we respond more strongly to a stabbing than to someone treading on our toe, and more to a break-in than to a scuff on our front door. We also identify more with wholes than parts, more with what is near than with what is far, and so on. Schemas that may be most strongly associated with our own bodies or with aspects of our immediate environment may also be extended so that they help us identify with the corresponding aspects of others' bodies or of more remote objects.

As we will see in the next chapter, these embodied schemas can be applied to a vast range of linguistic and symbolic meaning, beyond the immediate concerns of infancy, through metaphorical and metonymic extension. In doing this they also constantly interact with basic level categories.

1.h. Metaphorical Extension

> Metaphor extends meaning by associating one context (the 'source domain') to another (the 'target domain'), in both linguistic and non-linguistic symbols. It follows the same pattern of meaning extension as prototypes. It is supplemented by metonymy, which associates a part with a whole – although this can also be used dissociatively. By this means, basic level categories and embodied schemas can be extended to provide embodied meaning even to the most abstracted 'cognitive' propositions.

Despite the range of the embodied experience that can be related to symbols through basic level categories and embodied schemas, it may still be unclear to anyone unfamiliar with embodied meaning how the rich complexity and flexibility of human language can be understood in embodied terms. If you take, say, a historical proposition: 'William of Normandy conquered England at the Battle of Hastings in 1066', or a scientific one, 'Lithium reacts with water to release hydrogen, generate heat, and create lithium hydroxide': how, we may ask, can the meaning of such statements depend on our bodies? We are accustomed to the widespread cultural assumption that the meaning of such statements depends on a relationship between the words used and the states of affairs in the world that they refer to (representationalism). In this way of thinking, the meaning of such statements is purely cognitive, and the emotive elements are contingent and incidental. It doesn't matter how I feel about the Norman Invasion or about lithium – the sentences are supposed to be meaningful because of the 'facts' they refer to. To see that this is not the case requires us to relate such complex linguistic constructions to their source of meaning in basic level categories and embodied schemas.

The way in which they are related is primarily through *metaphor*, along with metonymy and modelling. If we can understand these processes adequately, then there should be no 'representational' piece of language that we could not (at least in principle) be able to relate to its embodied meaning. This way of understanding the operation of metaphor is very much indebted to Lakoff and Johnson's book *Metaphors We Live By* (1980), one of the seminal texts of embodied meaning.[1] As we will also see, the ability to 'defuse'

1 Lakoff & Johnson (1980).

representational claims by understanding them in embodied terms is also a valuable practical tool for our avoidance of absolutization.

Metaphor is not mere literary embellishment, but the process we constantly use to associate one context of experience with another. We use it, particularly, to associate prototypical meanings with further, non-prototypical ones, and thus to extend our use of symbols within a developing web. We may, for instance, start off with a prototypical sense of a bird as being like a robin, but then recognize the ways that a penguin is like a robin. It's through a metaphorical process, then, that we recognize that a penguin *is* a bird like a robin, associating one context of experience with another. We may then go on to consider an aeroplane, or a fragile old woman, or a jazz musician, to be 'metaphorically' a bird: but if we do that, we are just further extending a metaphorical process that began with our extension of the basic concept beyond its initial prototype.

As we have seen, our basic experience of meaning depends on our early embodied interactions with the world. However, as we grow up, we become aware of more and more meaningful contexts, some of them remote for us, or entirely abstracted. Rather than only using words associated with our immediate activities and relationships, we start to discuss plans for next year, new events in distant countries, generalized relationships between types of objects or organisms in the world, or even what we take to be the most general 'truths' foundational to all human existence. We manage this, broadly, by associating the more remote contexts with the more immediate ones, mapping the less familiar in the terms of the more familiar. We cannot start from scratch in 'representing' the world, but rather build up a capacity to symbolize remote things in terms of nearer ones. The way in which we build up that capacity then forms the underlying processes of association that shape the way we understand the world for the rest of our lives.

Metaphor is seen as relating a *source domain* to a *target domain*, so that the meaning of the target domain is at least partially structured by the meaning of the source domain. The source domain may be a basic level category, an embodied schema, or another metaphor. A diagram of ancestral relationships (target domain) is seen in terms of the basic level category of a tree (source domain), to create the notion of a 'family tree'. Individual experience of living a life (target domain) is seen in terms of a container (embodied schema as a source domain), in the phrase 'my life is very full'. In a further extension, a series of relationships between spiritual teachers and disciples (target domain) can then be seen in terms of a family tree (source domain), creating a metaphor of a metaphor – the idea of spiritual lineage.

The direction of metaphorical development is said to be overwhelmingly *unidirectional*, in that it consists of more concrete source domains being used to provide meaning to more abstract target domains.[2] It is of course possible, but unusual, to have an abstract source domain and a concrete target domain – so unusual that we are likely to find it comic: like describing a baby's grimaces on passing wind as Aristophenian, or a log as mindfully undistracted. The process of concrete meaning being refined into abstract target domains, however, is not only developed in individual creative uses of metaphor, but unconsciously entrenched in much of the historical development of our language in all its idiomatic forms. In his guide to the forms taken by metaphor, Kövesces lists thirteen common concrete source domains: the human body, health and illness, animals, plants, buildings and construction, machines and tools, games and sport, money and economic transactions, cooking and food, heat and cold, light and darkness, forces, and movement and direction. Thirteen common target domains are then emotion, desire, morality, thought, society or nation, politics, economy, human relationships, communication, time, life and death, religion, and events and actions.[3] For instance, the term 'heart of the problem' uses the human body as a source domain, and thought as a target domain. The idea of 'enlightenment' uses the source domain of light and dark and the target domain of morality, thought, or religion.

Lakoff and Johnson also make a distinction between *structural metaphors* and *orientational metaphors*. In a structural metaphor, it is the structure of meaning in the source domain that is extended to the structure in a target domain. All the examples already given are structural – for instance, 'my life is very full' maps the physical structure of a container onto the temporal structure of a life. An orientational metaphor, instead, 'organizes a whole system of concepts with respect to one another',[4] usually using a spatial basis of organization. One of their examples is 'happy is up', with the converse 'sad

2 Kövesces (2002) p. 25.
3 Ibid. pp. 16–25.
4 Lakoff & Johnson (1980) p. 14.

is down', as applied to phrases like 'my spirits rose' and 'I fell into a depression'. In a similar way, up-down spatial orientation tends to be correlated to consciousness, health, control, status, morality, and any kind of arithmetical increase. There are direct correlations in our embodied experience that help to reinforce these orientational metaphors: for instance, the way that an upright spine enables us to feel more energy in our bodies compared to a slouched position, the energy and muscular preparation required to jump into the air against gravity, and the ways that a lack of energy or effort lead us to assume lower positions where less muscular activity is required (lying down or slumping in an armchair). Such metaphors thus seem 'natural', but they are the product of our environment, reinforced by cultural habit. In a world without gravity, we would presumably not have heaven in the sky and hell beneath the earth. Sometimes we may be constrained by the metaphorical habits of our culture, which make it counter-intuitive, for instance, to think that we might be happier with less money, or able to be more moral with a 'low' social status.

One way in which I disagree with Lakoff and Johnson is in their identification of what they call 'ontological metaphors'. These are said to be 'ways of viewing events, activities, emotions, ideas etc as entities and substances',[5] and are taken to be metaphorical because the idea of a discrete object is the source domain and an abstract idea is the target domain. For instance, they suggest 'inflation' as in 'inflation is lowering our standard of living' as such an 'ontological metaphor', because it involves the reification of a process of prices and wages rising into an abstract thing. However, I see nothing metaphorical about this process, given that metaphors of any other type all involve a right-hemisphere based association between experience and symbol through imagination. Reification is not such a process, but rather a left-hemisphere based attempt to pin a fluid phenomenon into a clear representation. Metaphors like 'my life is full' or 'I fell into a depression' provide us with symbols to relate to our experience, but reification is not a new symbolization of experience, rather a limitation and regimentation of existing symbols so as to serve a propositional function. At the initial level of the object schema, there is thus a process of association, but not after that. Unfortunately the whole idea of an 'ontological metaphor' is

5   Ibid. p. 25.

another of many examples of the misuse of the term 'ontology' in a way that confuses absolutizing claims with experiential ones, often thus leading us into absolutizing claims through equivocation.[6]

In Lakoff and Johnson's otherwise excellent account, metaphor needs to be supplemented by metonymy: which is not strictly metaphor, but serves a similar role in some cases for extending meaning. Metonymy is the use of 'part for whole', that is, the association of the meaning of the whole with a symbol associated with a part or an aspect of that whole: for instance 'Washington' for 'The government of the United States' or 'the ham sandwich' for 'the customer who ordered a ham sandwich'. Quite often such metonyms are just linguistic shortcuts that we have adopted by convention, such as the use of an author for his or her writings ('You'll find some bizarre arguments in Ellis'), but at others they may have the reductive or devitalizing effect of focusing our attention on a limited functional part of something at the expense of the rest of it ('We need more hands at the mill'; 'We have 100 head of stock'). Metonymy is nowhere near as significant as metaphor as an aspect of the extension of meaning, but its capacity for aiding reductive appropriation is worth noting. It takes a right-hemisphere act of the imagination to *associate* a part with a whole, but a further act of the left hemisphere to then decontextualize the resulting metonymic expression so that we *disassociate* the part from the whole whilst appropriating some of the functions of the whole. Hands by themselves cannot do work in a factory, for instance (they need whole people attached to them), but the decontextualization of the over-dominant left hemisphere allows us to take this for granted whilst focusing narrowly on the operation of the hands alone. Iain McGilchrist extensively discusses the ways this is particularly done by schizophrenics.[7]

We generally *extend* meaning through metaphor or metonymy to enable us to apply the meaning-associations we have initially developed in relation to basic level categories and embodied schemas to new, more abstracted or more generalized, contexts. Let me return to the example propositions with which I began this chapter: 'William of Normandy conquered England at the Battle of Hastings in 1066': how has our understanding of this sentence been developed from our more immediate embodied associations? Well, all the proper

---

6   This is an example of the inflation of metaphysics, discussed in I.4.f. Also see V.2.i on the dangers of equivocation between absolute and non-absolute senses.
7   McGilchrist (2021) ch. 9.

nouns in this sentence (William of Normandy, England, Battle of Hastings) refer to specific examples of people, places, or events that we can come to understand in relation to basic level categories with their extension into further categories. William of Normandy is an example of a man (whom we might have first recognized in relation to Daddy), which we then differentiated into specific types of man such as a duke or king, perhaps using an implicit metaphor of upness for his high social status as such. Our understanding of 'England' depends on our ability to understand areas of land, which uses the container schema: England is a container within its borders, but one that is, of course, coloured by many other associations. The 'Battle of Hastings' depends on our reification (using the object schema) of a process of fighting as an event – something we might initially understand from our own experience of physical fighting in ourselves or others. The association with that event of fighting in a particular place, Hastings, depends on our schematic ability to relate the part to the whole (Hastings as a place in England). To understand the idea of 'conquering' we also need to employ the force schema of compulsion, metaphorically extended from a physical compulsion in individual experience to a political compulsion as Norman rule was imposed on the Anglo-Saxons. This compulsion schema is combined with the container schema as we imagine the application of compulsion to a delimited area, England. Finally, the date of the battle, 1066, depends on cognitive modelling of time – something I will return to in the next chapter.

To turn to my other example, 'Lithium reacts with water to release hydrogen, generate heat, and create lithium hydroxide': here we are talking about kinds of substances that we are likely to understand as a development of basic level categories. 'Water' and 'heat' might well be basic level categories, directly encountered in infancy, but most infants will not meet lithium until they are older (unless they are weaned in a laboratory!), so may come to understand it by first developing a hypernym from objects they encounter (substance, or more specifically metal or malleable substance), then descending from this to a new hyponym (lithium). We would also use the schemas for merging and splitting to understand how a reaction between chemical elements combining may then result in separated substances (hydrogen and lithium hydroxide), even though the lithium hydroxide also involves merging. We may also use the process schema to understand how the merging and splitting fit together in a causal process. It is debatable whether any of our thinking in relation to this sentence is metaphorical: does the lithium react, generate, and create in metaphorical extension of the way humans do these things, or is it part of our basic understanding of these things that they are also done by inanimate substances? We do not have to resolve such questions to see that a process of extension from concrete to abstract, from simple to complex, and from early experiences to more mature ones, is constantly at work, developing our capacity for meaning in new forms.

The result of such extension, of course, is that most of the time it embeds itself into our culture and language, so that we rely on metaphorical extension for meaning. To recognize many metaphors, we have to dig back into the etymology of words, or at least pay new attention to the cliches we habitually employ. An act of awareness is needed to consider that a 'noble' gesture, associating certain kinds of virtue with high social status, might just as well be applied to those with low status. An act of awareness may also be needed to recognize that William of Normandy's 'conquest' of England was not as simple as the use of sufficient force to compel a stuck door to open, but rather consisted of the complex decision-making of many thousands of people, accepting him as their king because of their awareness of the negative consequences of not doing so. If we form *beliefs* on the basis of these metaphorical constructions, and then absolutize those beliefs, the limitations of the metaphor then limit the conditions addressed by the beliefs.

It is also worth pointing out that even though metaphor has these complex functions in language, it is a general means for the development of meaning and is thus not limited to language. The extension of meaning from a source domain to a target domain can use other kinds of structure than linguistic ones. The Christian cross, for instance, is an iconic image that extends the meaning of a physical cross (the actual pieces of wood used to crucify Jesus) to a reminder of suffering (the instrument of suffering is suffering itself) and then to an abstract idea of redemption through suffering. A piece of music, through embodied schemas of rhythmic movement and voice tone, can extend the meaning of particular rhythms, tones, and instrumental qualities metaphorically so that they become associated with, say, war (Tchaikovsky's 1812 Overture) or bucolic pleasure (Beethoven's Pastoral Symphony). Of course, one could hear Beethoven's Pastoral Symphony and then go through a linguistic process of associating it with the countryside: but the meaning of the music for us can have far more immediate associations than that, not necessitating any linguistic process, but nevertheless going through the associative development that metaphor offers.

The metaphorical extension of meaning thus enables us to create symbols that engage with an ever wider set of conditions in a complex world, but in the process also creates new scope for damaging absolutization as the left hemisphere takes over from the right. As we habitually employ metaphors, but forget that we are doing so, through cultural embedding or personal habituation, we create new hostages to fortune and tools for dogma. At the heart of this limitation is the point that the source domain of a metaphor can never be exactly the same as the target domain: the metaphor thus helps us to engage with the conditions as we did in the source domain only to the extent that they are the same in the target domain. If we consider argument or medicine to be combat, for instance, we are likely to neglect the ways that argument also requires sensitivity, and medicine also requires tolerant nurture. This creates the fallacy of weak analogy, to be discussed further in the next volume.[8]

---

8 V.2.j.

1.i. Idealized Models

> Models (known widely as 'cognitive' models) are our supposed representations, dependent on basic categories, schemas, and metaphors. They offer coherent possible beliefs within a framework, but are structures of meaning, not belief or 'knowledge'. Idealizing a model involves implicit absolutization of the meaning conditions to produce representationalism. This is especially common in relation to mathematics and to essentialized definitional frameworks of language – the basis of rationalistic errors in philosophy.

It is only when we have followed the tree of meaning up from its roots in embodied experience and neural association, up the trunk of undifferentiated meaning and the branches of basic level categories and embodied schemas, then through the twigs of metaphor to the leaves of meaningful symbols, that we finally reach the occasional fruit of representation as an aspect of meaning. The use of representation, though, does not have to mean representational-*ism*. Representations are subsidiary to and dependent on basic and extended categories, schemas, and metaphors for their meaning, just as fruit can only develop on a tree that has already grown branches and twigs, and has had some leaves and flowers. These representations do not give us the source of meaning from their relationship with 'reality' as representationalism insists (to be discussed in the next section). Rather, they rely on particular metaphors and cultural assumptions to create a coherent structure of relationships between linguistic terms (and we are now only dealing with language).

Examples of such coherent structures would be the relationship between the meanings of numbers (and indeed all other symbols in mathematics), and the relationship between terms for points or periods in time – such as the division of the day into hours, minutes, and seconds, the days of the week, and the months of the year. There is also at least implicitly such a structure whenever a word is used in relation to a definitional framework, so that it is no longer just our associations that determine its meaning, but our expectations of how well it conforms to certain rules or norms that check its relationship to a model. I will say more below about how these example structures are developed from schema and metaphor.

Developing these structures is not an easy or instantaneous process: think of a young child laboriously learning to tell the time.

However, once we have developed them, all the intermediary links of learning are facilitated through a rapid and unconscious process, and this process starts to seem independent of the effort we put in to acquire it. Focusing only on the explicit representation of the results in our left hemispheres, and remaining unaware of the continuing work in the right hemisphere that makes them meaningful, we tend to forget that there was ever a learning process for them, and assume that the structures themselves are immediately derived from a world that they correspond with. This confuses the final stage or top layer of association with the totality of conditions for it, like assuming that the eucalyptus pastilles that relieved your cold symptoms cured the cold. It is this focus on surface structures that creates representationalism as the apparently intuitive or 'natural' explanatory framework when most people consider meaning.

These structures are called 'idealized cognitive models' by Lakoff.[1] They are used throughout language, particularly when we try to make the meanings of words explicit: definitions of words, for instance, give us a model for how a word should be used that is embedded within a particular set of (mainly cultural) conditions. We *idealize* this when we start to believe that the model is 'natural' or 'essential', rather than recognizing all the contingent conditions that have created it. We might, for instance, assume that we must always think in terms of weeks made up of seven days (despite counter-examples from other cultures, such as a Balinese one discussed by Lakoff[2]). Or we might assume that mothers must always essentially give birth to their children, so that the marginal examples of foster mothers or surrogate mothers are 'not real mothers'.

So I am following Lakoff in continuing to use the terms 'idealized' and 'model' to label these structures, but dropping the 'cognitive' in between. These models or structures are not merely cognitive, but also emotive: for instance, the meaning of the term 'Saturday' is not only dependent on its place in the modelled structure of the days of the week (for many people it is also strongly associated with a sense of freedom from the onerous work responsibilities of weekdays). I also avoid the term 'cognition' as much as possible in any case (as already discussed in the introduction), because it tends to associate processes of meaning with 'knowledge'. Idealized models are not

---

1 Lakoff (1987) pp. 68 ff.
2 Ibid. p. 69.

structures of knowledge, they are structures of meaning. Not only do they not have to be true, but we do not even have to believe in them. Wednesday does not come after Tuesday because it is 'true' that it does, beyond our linguistic conventions, nor even because I believe that it does: it comes after Tuesday as an aspect of the modelled structure of symbols employed, just as B follows A according to the conventions of the alphabet.

Lakoff evidently believes that the 'cognitive' element is necessary to show that an idealized model can be tested against a range of conditions and be judged as fitting or not fitting them to varying degrees (which a 'non-cognitive' theory would not).[3] However, a 'non-cognitive' theory is just another kind of (less appropriate) cognitive theory (still assuming a topsy-turvy paradigm in which 'knowledge' precedes everything else, but non-incrementally). The whole contested label of 'cognitive linguistics' seems to be very much the accidental product of the academic environment in which it originated, but this label unnecessarily perpetuates some of the assumptions of the ontological obsession in academic tradition that it potentially does so much to challenge.

The process of idealizing a model is parallel to that of absolutizing a belief, and indeed it implicitly includes absolutized beliefs (ones about meaning), even if it is not then used to help create further absolutized beliefs. An idealized model, like an absolutization (as described in *Absolutization*) is often characterized by mental proliferation, the exclusion of options, reinforcing feedback loops, assumed system independence, fragility, various kinds of denial of embodiment, discontinuity, formalization in metaphysical theory, foundationalism, circularity, infinite rationalization, claimed inevitability, inflated significance, repression, conflict, projection, confirmation bias, substitution, and group binding.[4] When the idealized model is implicitly challenged by experienced meaning that does not fit it, we exclude these alternatives from consideration, maintain self-perpetuating dogmatic mechanisms of exclusion, and endlessly rationalize it. Because the basic mechanism is the same as that of absolutization, disputes about the meanings of words can be just as heated as those about the 'truth' of propositions (think of debates about who is really a Christian, or on the definition of

3 Ibid. p. 71.
4 I.1–5.

art). Restrictive meaning then becomes an important part of every absolutizing belief: for propositions to match reality, the words that comprise them also need to have determinate relations with it, and thus to have an 'essential' meaning.

The arguments for maintaining idealized models involve ignoring the meaning processes by which those models are built up and sustained, in a way that parallels the discontinuity and assumed system independence of absolutizing beliefs. Awareness of these processes can thus be a helpful antidote to the idealization of models. As mathematics provides the most commonly idealized model ('So isn't it essentially true that 2+2=4?'), it may be of particular value to reflect on schemas and metaphors that give it meaning. I can only give a brief idea of that here, but for full details I highly recommend Lakoff and Nuñez's *Where Mathematics Comes From*.[5]

Our understanding of numbers depends on the object schema and the collection sub-schema, which help us to separate the meaning of one object from that of another. This schema seems to be present in young babies and many animals, who can intuitively notice the differences between groups with differing numbers of up to four objects.[6] Mother ducks whose nests have been parasitized with extra eggs by another duck also seem to recognize the change in the number of eggs and reduce their own laying.[7] Lakoff and Nuñez also discuss the role of other schemas: the source-path goal schema giving us the idea of progression as we count, the part-whole schema giving us a sense of larger numbers containing smaller ones, and a schema of measurement coming from the physical activity of marking points along a stick. All of these schemas are interdependent, and are extended by interaction with further schemas.[8]

To understand numbers as abstract symbols, we apply a metaphorical extension whereby objects and their collections are the source domain, and arithmetical numbers are the target domain. I understand the concept of, say, '37' through the use of a model, using that metaphorical extension, that implies a coherent and consistent relationship between all the numbers. For example. one feature of concrete object collections is that whenever you put together two collections, you get a larger combined collection. We

5 Lakoff & Nuñez (2000).
6 Lakoff & Nuñez (2000) pp. 15–23.
7 Ehrlich, Dobkin, & Wheye (1988).
8 Lakoff & Nuñez (2000) pp. 60–74.

metaphorically extend this to the stability of results in numbers, expecting that whenever we add two numbers together, we get the same result (or that if we do not, we have done so incorrectly). Similarly, concrete 'addition' with collections of objects is commutative (we can add two numbers together either way round and get the same result: 2+1 or 1+2 = 3) and transitive (if 3 is greater than 2 and 2 is greater than 1, 3 is greater than 1). So we transfer these qualities to the target domain of abstract arithmetic. Similarly with the source-path-goal, part-whole, and other schemas drawn on, our ability to associate experience of these symbols at a concrete level is applied metaphorically to numbers.

This only deals with basic arithmetic, but Lakoff and Nuñez go much further, offering embodied explanations of all other common mathematical operations. It is thus not necessary to idealize the model to explain the meaning of mathematics. The recognition that we do not have to idealize even such a commonly idealized model has far-reaching implications in challenging rationalist styles of philosophy that take these absolutized meanings as a basis of certainty and thus of 'knowledge'. Mathematics, like any other model, is not a source of Platonic truth, but a structure of *meaning* that we may or may not apply in our understanding of experience, however far-reaching and apparently universal the application of that model may be.

The idealization of models clearly forms the key condition for the next section of this book. Having surveyed embodied meaning as an overall explanation of meaning, I now need to discuss representationalism: why it has arisen, why it is wrong, its effects and its implications.

2. The Trouble with Representationalism

2.a. What is Representationalism?

> 'Representationalism' is not defined here as narrowly as in most philosophy and cognitive science. It refers to any view according to which meaning is dependent on a metaphysical state via an idealized model. It does not depend on any particular metaphysical distinction (e.g. realism or idealism). Representationalism is generally marked by abstraction (e.g. in computationalism) and by assumed isomorphic relationships between language and reality (for which our experience of meaning gives no grounds).

Section 1 of this book should have provided enough of an understanding of embodied meaning to provide a starting point for understanding our relationship with meaning, symbols, and language. However, to begin to dismantle the entrenched *non-embodied* approaches in practice, we need not only a positive idea of an alternative, but also an adequate understanding of all their drawbacks. I am thus attempting a critical survey of representationalism in section 2. This critical survey is summarized in an accompanying mind map **[diagram 3]**.

I am also concerned that following the initial impetus provided by Lakoff and Johnson, the theorization of embodied meaning has gone badly wrong – effectively being re-appropriated by the entrenched approaches that it challenged – and that is my topic for section 3 of this book. Before we try to understand the misunderstandings of embodied meaning, though, we need a deeper exploration of representationalism itself: what it is, its disastrous consequences, and why there is such strong pressure for its cultural entrenchment. These issues cannot be understood entirely separately from those of absolutization and the Middle Way, of which they form a key element.

To be clear about what exactly representationalism is, I will need to engage in some philosophical stipulation in this chapter. This will be followed up in the succeeding chapters by an identification of representationalism in neuroscientific terms (2.b), in the psychology

The Trouble with Representationalism 63

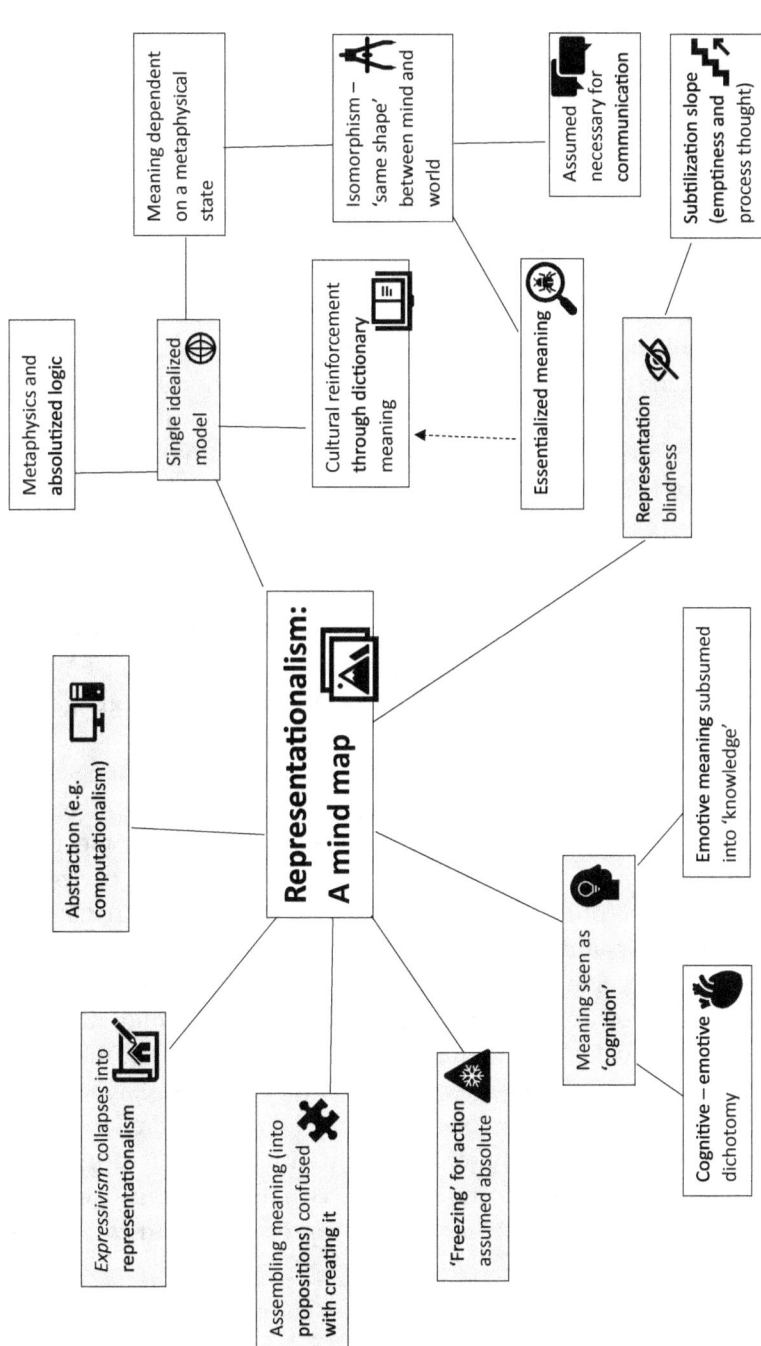

Diagram 3. Representationalism: A mind map.

of judgement (2.c), and in the linguistics of communication (2.d). All of these approaches will help us both to distinguish representationalism, and to understand why it is entrenched and problematic. The remainder of this section of the book will then be concerned with the ways that representationalism is or has been applied – with disastrous effect – to distinguish 'cognition' from 'emotion', to isolate creative expression from representation, and to justify metaphysics and absolutized logic in all areas of discussion – especially religion, philosophy, and politics.

I am going to engage in stipulation to define 'representationalism' more closely, because, astoundingly, there appears to currently be no established word with the scope of what I call representationalism. One could talk about 'non-embodied' views of meaning, but for those who either don't understand why meaning should be embodied in the first place, or don't understand why their 'embodied' view of it is not, this conveys little. The most obvious reason why there is no word for the entrenched view of meaning is that people don't recognize its assumptions as present: fish don't have a word for 'sea', they just swim in it and take it for granted. As always, then, if we don't have a word for it, or if that word is confused or appropriated, people don't recognize a problem. This is also more generally the case with the inflation of metaphysical language, as discussed in *Absolutization*.[1]

The term 'representationalism' *is* currently used (interchangeably with 'representionism') in philosophy, linguistics, and cognitive science, but in these contexts it usually has a much narrower meaning than the one I am employing. It seems to have two different narrower meanings. In the philosophy of perception, 'representationalism' is another term for 'indirect realism' – the belief that our perceptions allow us to perceive what is 'real', but only via a 'representation' that changes their form. In cognitive science, 'representationalism' seems to be the belief that we have internal representations that substitute or 'stand in' for an external state, and that these have causal power to change our behaviour.[2] The way I am using the term here is broader than either of these. Representationalism may often take a metaphysically realist form, but this is not a definitive feature, and it makes no difference whether representationalists believe

1 I.4.f.
2 Haselager, De Groot, & Van Rappard (2003).

that we perceive the 'real world' directly or indirectly. Nor does the representation necessarily have to substitute for an external state or have a causal role in behaviour to count.

Instead, representationalism is treated here as any view according to which *meaning* is dependent on a relationship with a metaphysical state, using an idealized model of that state (as discussed in 1.i). This does not involve any specification of the precise theorized nature of the metaphysical state: the debates between different metaphysical positions being proliferating and irrelevant. Nor does it involve any requirement for beliefs or 'knowledge' that may be formed on the basis of those representations. Typically, the debates in philosophy, cognitive science, and linguistics that form these narrower views of 'representationalism' are not concerned with *meaning* at all, except insofar as meaning is swept up into 'cognition', and 'cognition' is dependent on trying to explain, in one way or another, how we have 'knowledge', despite the uncertainty of our embodied state. Any account of how representationalism typifies an unhelpful view of *meaning*, however, must begin with meaning as a set of associations made by organisms, distinct from belief because they do not necessarily form the basis of judgement or behaviour. Representationalism is thus any view that insists that our associative experience of meaning must be understood in terms of its representational value in relation to a metaphysical state.

In previous discussions of this topic, I have categorized representationalism within a wider notional approach of 'linguistic idealism'.[3] The 'idealist' aspect of this, as I conceived it, was the set of signs in our minds that determinately referred to objects-out-there and falsely limited what we could refer to. This terminology was derived from Thomas Nagel, whose challenge to the false limitation of what we are supposed to be able to meaningfully refer to (in much philosophy of language) seemed a helpful one.[4] I then distinguished two types of linguistic idealism – representationalism and expressivism, according to whether the limited signs in our minds were supposed to get their meaning from an external state in the world (representationalism) or an internal one in our minds (expressivism). Since 2013, when I wrote in those terms, my understanding of this area has moved on, and I now

3   iii.3.a.
4   Nagel (1986) pp. 95 ff.

consider the formulations of both 'linguistic idealism' and 'expressivism' unnecessary. They were unnecessarily engaging in some of the current concerns of the analytic philosophy of language, when most of these concerns are irrelevant to embodied meaning. If our understanding of meaning is embodied, then there is, indeed, no determinate zone as to what our language can refer to or not refer to (for more on this see 3.c). However, talk of 'idealism' of any kind is liable to cause confusion with metaphysical idealism, and the distinction between representationalism and expressivism involves unnecessary engagement in the polarizing metaphysical games of philosophers. Applying the principle of agnosticism to metaphysical claims of all kinds, we should recognize that there is no relevance in distinguishing different supposed ultimate sources of meaning beyond experience (whether 'internal' or 'external'), just as there is no relevance in distinguishing between realist and idealist accounts of 'the world', when our experience evidently involves a complex mixture of our own preconceptions and the world-out-there.

'Representationalism', then, covers all forms of theory or assumption that take meaning to lie anywhere other than in our embodied experience. It covers the classic linguistic 'truth-conditional theory of meaning', but it also covers many other assumptions about meaning that are not explicitly theorized in the same way. It also covers what I used to call 'expressivism', but in fact failed to find in a pure form anywhere: that is, a belief that our symbols gain their meanings solely from being expressions of an 'inner' state (see 2.f below). The term also covers Wittgensteinian reductions of meaning to social communication, and 'truth-conditional pragmatics', as I will discuss in 2.d.

As suggested in the sub-title of this book, representationalism is distinguished for its *abstraction* of meaning from experience. Academic discussion of non-embodied meaning has also identified this abstraction with computational models, with the manipulation of arbitrary symbols, and with amodality (that is, lack of relationship to any particular type of sense-experience). Not all representationalism is necessarily computational, but the assumption that meaning has the merely formal qualities that can be manipulated by a machine without bodily experience is a common one in representationalism. John Searle's famous Chinese Room thought experiment (as already discussed in 1.a) readily captures why computational models have nothing to do with *meaning*. The commands and responses of computers are compared to those of a non-Chinese person who is passed messages in Chinese, and looks up convincing responses to them in a manual, without any understanding of the meaning of those messages to Chinese speakers. Searle's point is one of the earliest and clearest distillations of the insight that *meaning requires a body*, not just the manipulation of symbols that may seem to us entirely arbitrary. Symbols, of course, do not have any *intrinsic* meaning (so we should avoid essentialist, etymological, or onomatopoeic fallacies when identifying the meaning of words): they have only the meaning that we give to them, but that meaning cannot be given by a machine. That meaning is also cross-modal rather than amodal, resulting from a concatenation of associated sense experiences rather than an isolation from all sense experience.

Another feature of representationalism is that of the parallel between the representation in an idealized model and the 'reality' (actual or hypothetical) with which it is correlated. As Alfred Korzybski pointed out, 'the map is not the territory':[5] our representation cannot possibly have all the features of what is being represented, even in theory. You can walk around the territory, but you cannot walk around the map. So what is the relationship supposed to be? The most common answer to this is some type of *isomorphism*: that is, that the map resembles the territory and its form in certain key respects that can be abstracted. On a scale map, for instance, the ratios between the distances between different objects will be the same as the ratios in the territory, so that if the scale is, say, 1 cm to 2 km, two represented buildings 1 cm apart on the map will be reliably 2 km apart on the territory. However, we cannot readily apply even this limited account of representation on a map to linguistic symbolism in general, and it becomes increasingly difficult to do so as we deal with more abstract pieces of language. 'Inflation is rising', for instance, is only remotely comprehensible through the metaphor that links numerical increases with up. There is no 'territory' in which the marked prices in the shops are 'literally' floating up towards the sky. But even the numerical increases themselves are a generalization based on a range of data. We can't understand 'inflation is rising' by relating it to anything 'rising' in the world, but only through a habitual process of metaphorical extension and

5   Korzybski (1933) p. 498.

abstraction. There is no isomorphism here, and we can insist on it only by ignoring the process by which we understand the language.

Through its abstraction of meaning from experience, representationalism sets up all the conditions that we need for absolutization. As I have previously argued, representationalism is a general aspect of absolutization that underlies all forms of metaphysics.[6] As such it needs to be treated more as a facet of absolutization in general rather than a specific metaphysical belief (as I did previously). It is a way of describing the absolutization of idealized models in general, not a description of a specific model or definition of a specific theory. Its relationship to metaphysics in general will be explored further in 2.g. below.

6   I.3.a.

2.b. Representationalism, the Left Hemisphere, and Propositional Sentences

> Neuroscience gives additional, non-reductive, evidence against representationalism. It shows meaning not to be merely processed in Broca's Region of the left hemisphere, but instead more widely in the right, dependent on perceptual, emotional, and motor systems. Broca's Region assembles prior meaning into propositions that can represent possible states of affairs, rather than creating meaning in the first place.

One fruitful way of understanding representationalism and its limitations is neuroscientific. That does not mean that an explanation of the distinction between representationalism and embodied meaning can be reduced to neuroscience, nor that a neuroscientific explanation is essential to understanding that distinction. However, in my view it offers a very helpful perspective. That perspective is not one in which the external, scientific perspective of neuroscience in any way overrules our experience of meaning and the experiential basis that is needed for our rejection of the abstracted grip on meaning of representationalism. Instead, it is an additional, complementary perspective. One of the great achievements of the work of Iain McGilchrist is the recognition that neuroscience can be used in this way: that far from being a dogmatically-wielded reductive tool, it can be an integrative tool.

One level at which neuroscience can be used might be described as pre-hemispheric: that is, it gives further evidence for the embodiment of meaning through evidence of the relationship between meaning on the one hand, and perceptual and motor systems in the brain on the other. If representationalism was correct, and meaning was entirely a matter of representational models, we would expect it to be processed entirely in the region of the brain that deals with propositional relationships within idealized models. However, the findings of brain scanning for some time have been of a far wider distribution of activity than that. Meaning is integrated with the parts of our brains that deal with perceptual, motor, and emotional activity, regardless of the hemispheric distribution of that activity.[1]

However, a very rich further dimension is added to our understanding of the neuroscience of embodied meaning by the perspective

---

1 Just (2008).

of brain lateralization. The contrast between the two hemispheres of the brain is described by McGilchrist as that between two different ways of paying attention. The left hemisphere pays attention in a predatory, goal-driven way, focused on the objects of desire. Meanwhile the right hemisphere is much more widely alert for new possibilities. These ways of paying attention thus have correlative contrasting approaches to meaning attached to them: the left hemisphere's approach to meaning being in terms of idealized models that can form the basis of goals, whilst the right hemisphere's is that of sensitivity to a range of wider experience.

In short, then, the left hemisphere is our inner representationalist, and as long as the left hemisphere is over-dominant in its repression of the right, we are likely to continue to think in representationalist ways. However, the relationship between these two types of meaning is asymmetrical, with idealized models being constantly dependent for their meaningfulness on the right-hemisphere based process by which embodied meaning is built up (as described in section 1): basic categories and schemas creating associations through prototypical experience, which are then extended through metaphor. The senses and the imagination, which form the basis of embodied meaning, are right hemisphere functions.

I have already discussed the relationship between brain lateralization and representationalism both in *Absolutization* (as an aspect of absolutization) and in the *Systemic History* (in relation to its evolution from earlier animals). In *Absolutization* I discussed the evidence that Broca's Region in the left pre-frontal cortex is the main seat, not of meaning in general, but specifically of syntactic processing and semantic understanding.[2] This can be particularly clinched by observations that patients with lesions in this area do not lack a sense of meaning, but are unable to put together propositional sentences to represent a state of affairs.[3] McGilchrist also points out the proximity and close relationship between the centres for linguistic representation and the centres for manipulation in this area of the left hemisphere, suggesting that their dominance is due to an inhibition of the parallel areas of the right hemisphere.[4] In the *Systemic History*, I also considered the substantial evidence that bilateral asymmetry

2   I.3.a. Key references on Broca's Region are Friederici (2002) and Scott et al. (2000).
3   Kolk & Heeschen (2007).
4   McGilchrist (2009) p. 100.

of the brain and nervous system was already well-developed in animals through the evolutionary tree from early fishes onwards, only to be further emphasized in human brains because of their relatively greater complexity.[5] The *representational* features of the human left hemisphere have developed organically from the *predatory* function of the left hemisphere in our evolutionary ancestors.

The previously dominant neurolinguistic view that Broca's Region is the seat of linguistic meaning itself, then, came from a traditional bias towards representationalism that neglected all the complex conditions of meaning that are needed to make the final development of meaning into idealized models possible. Idealized models are propositional because, like propositional sentences, they assemble assumed objects into relationships within a framework (this framework itself rapidly becoming a new object). If we take a simple example of a propositional sentence, 'John loves Clelia', this introduces us to a hypothetical or possible world in which John, Clelia, and a one-way transitive action of loving are assumed to 'exist'. Linked to this model are many other assumptions, such as that John and Clelia are people (not pencil-sharpeners), and probably that the 'love' here is heterosexual desire of a male for a female (not, for instance, an archetypal longing with Clelia being a symbolic saint, or a gastronomic 'love' with John as a gourmand and Clelia a dish).

The prior materials, in the example sentence, are 'John', 'love', and 'Clelia', all of which have independent meaning as symbols, regardless of their place in the idealized representational model of relationships marked by the sentence. 'John' and 'Clelia' represent individuals, so you may associate them primarily with individuals you have encountered with those names (it is the framing provided by their use in an example that probably makes you interpret them as *example* names). 'Love', whether as a noun or as a verb, has substantial associative meaning for us that is probably connected to feelings in our bodies. It is only when we put it in a sentence (with the third-person singular verb ending 's') that its meaning then becomes constrained by grammar to a particular role in the sentence. The meaning of these *elements* of the sentence is provided by the right hemisphere, based on weak associative links between sense experiences, internal experiences, and symbols.

5   III.1.h & i.

The framework of interpretation provided by the left hemisphere then 'brings forth a world' (to use the expression of Maturana and Varela), whether or not we believe that world to 'exist'. In that world, there is a parallel relationship between linguistic symbols on the one hand and a hypothesized world on the other, such that the former 'represents' the latter. It is the left hemisphere that does this 'representing' by bringing together the materials provided by the right. As I will discuss in the next chapter, this representing is clearly related to practical judgement.

In the classic version of formalized linguistic representationalism, the truth-dependent theory of meaning, this 'representing' of a model is only said to work for *propositional* sentences, that is, ones making a statement of some kind: a question ('Does John love Clelia?') or an exclamation ('John loves Clelia!') are not supposed to be propositional, because they have different linguistic functions. Embodied humans use language in all sorts of ways, including to elicit new information and to express emotion, but this cannot be taken into account in this form of representationalism, which uses only one linguistic form as the basis of meaning. There are other forms of representationalism in which other human communicative functions are taken into account, because the representational relationship is shifted from one between sentence and reality to one between language in a wider sense and human functions in a *social* version of reality. I will return to this in 2.d.

Overall, then, we need to see the role of the brain hemispheres as asymmetrical contributors to meaning. It is the right hemisphere that provides us with the raw materials of meaning, but Broca's Region in the left hemisphere that assembles these raw materials of meaning into propositions. It is that role of assembling prior elements that representationalists have long mistaken for the generation of meaning itself. Meaning for representationalists is thus like 'Yorkshire Tea' or 'Dundee Marmalade' – it is given its supposed identity based on its final phase of manufacture and packaging, regardless of the origin of tea in India and oranges in Spain. Without oranges, there is no marmalade; and without sensitivity to the body and its processes, there is no meaning.

2.c. Representation and Judgement

> The 'freezing' of models is a necessary prerequisite for action, as it provides an assumed context to act in. However, this 'freezing' is a provisional representation and does not have to be interpreted absolutely: rather an integration of meaning allows our beliefs to be reassessed at any point. Representationalism, on the other hand, requires implicitly absolute representations appealing to 'reality', with accompanying essentialism and denial of the possibility of provisionality.

Idealized models clearly have an essential practical role in our lives, as they provide the basis of judgement. This is where many thinkers have failed to distinguish provisional from absolute judgement, because they have assumed that this practical need requires absolute representation. Representationalism for many may thus seem like practical common sense, because our assumptions about the world around us also seem to be the ones that make it meaningful (hence the confused term 'sense-making' which I will tackle below in 3.c). If we can clearly separate out what we find meaningful from what we believe as a basis of action, though, it becomes possible to understand this whole area quite differently. It then becomes possible to understand how provisionality and action are compatible, with our sense of what is meaningful being embodied and thus entirely prior.

The basic link between representation and judgement is the 'freezing' of a model at the moment we make a judgement based on it. That freezing is necessary for the effectiveness of our actions, but nevertheless its rigidity in the longer term may negatively impact that effectiveness. For example, if I am picking slugs off a vulnerable plant in the twilight, I can't actually see the slugs very well: rather I'm reliant on a model of what sorts of objects are slugs, that becomes 'frozen' as the basis of my belief and my action. What slug *means* for me then, according to the model I have adopted, is a squishy, slimy, roughly oval object a few centimetres long, moving very slowly over a plant or the adjacent ground. This model is the basis of my belief that these slugs are engaged in destruction of plants with long-term negative consequences for me, motivating my action of interfering with their activities. The word 'slug' would have a similar meaning regardless of whether or not I also believed that they were in conflict with my goals, though of course I would have less motive for taking any interest in them. Nevertheless, my beliefs and actions are dependent on taking the meaning of 'slug' for granted. That might make a difference in some circumstances: for instance, there are larger slugs, such as leopard slugs (*Limax maximus*) that prey on smaller slugs and do little damage to plants, so the effectiveness of my action in removing 'slugs' to protect plants might be more effective if I discriminate in the meaning of 'slug' between larger and smaller varieties. If I slightly adjust my understanding of the meaning of the 'slugs' I am hunting, next time round my dependent beliefs and actions will be slightly adapted.

It needs to be noted that the freezing is entirely contextual. I do need to make a judgement *at that time* and *in that situation*, based on my best evidence as to the best way to respond to the situation. However, this involves no requirement that I should necessarily maintain the same freezing of meaning later in a different situation. Sometimes, indeed, it is beneficial to maintain both meanings and beliefs in a stable pattern, until the reasons to change them become overwhelming – this is both for reasons of communication and for reasons of consistency in action. Consistency of assumed meaning is what makes communication possible, as I will explore in the next chapter. Consistency of meaning applied to our actions is also a key condition for moral practice and the use of principles of any kind: for instance, if I decide to give up alcohol for clear practical reasons, I need a consistent definition of what counts as 'alcohol'. Consistency has value, but we *give* things consistency as a matter of practice – they are not a 'given' from outside, and adaptivity demands inconsistency with the assumptions we followed before. Language is constantly changing in its meaning, because people and conditions keep changing, but whenever we can identify a clear practical justification for doing so (taking all the effects into account), we should be prepared to change the meanings we apply to words (I will return to this point in 3.g).

Perhaps it can be seen from examples like that of the slugs how much provisionality of belief[1] depends on the adjustment of meaning. When we make judgements, we tend to take the meanings we are relying on for granted, and focus only on our beliefs about the world around us. However, these beliefs have been pre-formatted by the associations of meaning that we have built up throughout

1 II.2.a.

our lives, and by the models we have created out of that associative meaning. It is thus unlikely that we will adjust our beliefs without adjusting our meanings to some extent too. If someone were to give me a new argument for tolerating slugs in the garden, for instance, that might lead me to shift my beliefs about how I should act, but at the same time I would be changing the meaning of 'slugs' (and also perhaps of 'garden') to broaden my associations with them.

It is more likely, on the other hand, that I could extend my meaning associations with a symbol without changing my beliefs about it: this is very much the sphere of the arts and religion. For instance, I could learn all about the Hindu elephant-headed god Ganesha without changing any of my beliefs about elephants, such as their likely behaviour or how they should be treated. This is, indeed, how I will approach the topic of the integration of meaning in section 5 of this book. There would be no point in differentiating the integration of meaning from the integration of belief if they referred to the same process, but the integration of meaning extends my associations and links them together, in a way that can provide future resources for the integration of belief (overcoming conflicts), directing my attention and my depth of engagement. I can be *inspired* by a symbol without changing my view of what I think it represents.

If we can develop a coherent view of the way flexibility of meaning can enable provisionality, and of the way representation can be used for judgement in an entirely contingent way in a context of individual experience, we can free ourselves from the unnecessary but entrenched assumptions of representationalism. These are, as I take it:

- That there can be no such thing as provisional representation: all representation is assumed to be absolute because of its dependent relationship with 'reality'
- That essential meanings for linguistic symbols provide absolute stability for this relationship to endure
- That changes of meaning are reducible to changes of belief within this meaning-system

Spelled out thus, it becomes much more obvious why representationalism is completely inadequate in its account of judgement. That this is not obvious to most people is probably due to widespread implicit use of absolute assumptions in contexts that are thought of as not absolute. For instance, the absoluteness of the dependent relationship of representationalism with 'reality' is made reasonably explicit in the truth-dependent theory of meaning (unless one fails to recognize the absoluteness of 'truth'!), but may be less obvious to Wittgensteinians who use communication conventions in the same way as the source of 'truth', just displacing this external reality to the social realm. The test of this is determinacy: both truth-dependence theorists and Wittgensteinians assume that there are some symbols that are 'meaningless' or 'ineffable' because they *fail* to match representation to assumed reality. The same assumptions are adopted more popularly by those who dismiss such-and-such an utterance as 'meaningless' (in general terms, not just lacking in meaning for them). If there is any criterion for meaninglessness, there must also be an implicit essentiality – that is, a range of meanings within which representation continues to occur in relation to a specific symbol, and beyond which it does not. A panda, they may say, is not a worm. A Christian is not a Hindu. These are implicitly essential boundaries for the meanings of these linguistic symbols.

Our judgement can only be set free to make representation *provisional* if we are prepared to let go of these representationalist assumptions and recognize the fluidity of meaning as association. Letting go of them does not imply letting go of communication, effective belief, or timely action: rather it gives us a more adequate standpoint from which to understand these things. Our recognition of the *contingency* of all the symbols we use, including those of language, needs to be thorough-going, not just an empiricist sticking-plaster on a creaking rationalist superstructure.

2.d. Representation and Communication

> Communication is necessary for learning meaning, but is not sufficient for it, and meaning should not be reduced to communication. The 'privacy' of individual meaning does not completely prevent checking of boundaries, and boundaries need to be adequately (not absolutely) shared in communication for practical purposes. Dictionary definitions tell us about idealized shared models, not meaning, and essentializing meaning to them is an absolutizing shortcut.

Communication is obviously central to human life, but it is a social bias that leads us to *reduce* linguistic symbols to communication: an approach that confuses initial necessity with sufficiency. Empirically, all the evidence suggests that we learn our capacity for language from others: there are some famous cases of isolated children failing to acquire normal language skills,[1] and even language-producing machines fail to stimulate children's language learning.[2] Of course, the forms used by language (that is, the precise sounds and grammatical conventions of a particular language) are also socially acquired: if you put a Chinese baby in France, it will learn French. These points suggest that communication is *necessary* for language, but not that it is *sufficient*. Psychological conditions of active association are also required for language to be meaningful to us. Even the necessity of social stimulus in language appears to be restricted to an initial learning period in which communication is acquired, there being no evidence that social isolation after the acquisition of meaningful linguistic symbols and grammar leads people to forget them. Once we have those neural links, those symbols are meaningful to us, and will remain so as long as we use them and as long as our brains and bodies maintain the underlying capabilities (though see 5.b for more discussion of synaptic pruning and of the loss of meaning). We can maintain those linguistic capabilities by other means than social communication, such as through talking to ourselves, sub-vocalizing, keeping a private diary, or just thinking in a verbal form.

Communication is a form of action, requiring the 'freezing' of models and assumptions (as mentioned in the previous chapter), as well as the maintenance of beliefs that are consistent with the

1   McNeil, Polloway, & Smith (1984).
2   Lytle & Kuhl (2017).

act of communication. That does not mean, of course, that when we communicate we necessarily have to articulate our beliefs – but even if we are describing a fantasy or telling a deliberate lie, there will be an implicit set of beliefs underlying that communicative act, such as that it is good or justifiable to communicate these things to others, or that they convey our experience. Communication requires beliefs of some kind, whereas private reflections may consist only of meaning. The distinction between meaning and belief, that as we have seen makes provisionality possible and representationalism unnecessary, can appear in our experience only because we can become aware of meaning without communicating it. This is a sort of 'privacy', within which meaning can be clearly separated from belief, though we need to be careful about exactly what we mean by 'privacy'.

It is the idea of 'privacy' that seems to have shaped Wittgenstein's influential 'private language argument' (actually an anti-private language argument).[3] Wittgenstein considered some form of defeasibility to be a necessary condition of meaning: that is, we needed to know under what circumstances a symbol would or would not have certain meaning. In the absence of methods of checking that meaning, he thought, there could be no meaning. Thus, he argued, if we recorded a symbol in a private diary that was intended to record a particular sensation, and did so on a number of occasions, we would have no way of knowing that the symbols referred to the same sensation. In the absence of external checks, he thought, the symbol would be 'meaningless' because of its indeterminacy. This situation of the absence of external checks is that of 'privacy', and this concept of 'privacy' shaped his view that meaning depended on the social conventions used in communication.

This unfortunately influential argument makes at least two unjustified assumptions: firstly, that meaning depends on determinate checking of boundaries; secondly, that 'private' experience lacks standpoints for checking or consistency of a kind that are necessarily available to public communication.

Why should meaning need determinate boundaries? Where there is an association, there is meaning, whether it is vague or precise. The attempt to give *absolutely* clear boundaries to meaning is moreover doomed to fail, as we are reminded whenever we misunderstand

---

3   Wittgenstein (1967) § 258. Also see 1.d above.

or are confused by others' (or even our own) language. Boundaries are a function of communication, not of meaning. We can agree on *practical* boundaries in the terms of an idealized model, the terms of which need to coincide sufficiently for the practical purposes of communication to take place. For instance, if we are both sorting large stones from small ones, we can agree that a stone counts as 'large' if its longest dimension is more than 2 cm, but there will still be boundary cases where measurement is insufficiently precise to ensure agreement, and where we might make different judgements.

Some method of checking is thus necessary to ensure consistency in the way we use terms within models, but Wittgenstein is mistaken in assuming that we are unable to ensure some degree of consistency within our own 'private' meanings. The method is, of course, memory. If I have a certain type of headache today that I call a 'gwuh', I can recognize that I also had a 'gwuh' yesterday, because I recall, imprecisely and fallibly, having the same experiences. From the standpoint of memory, indeed, there is a type of 'publicity' between my own experiences at different times, in which I can make comparisons, because the associations at different times are similar, and these associations can be compared with my immediate impressions. The fallibility of this process is not a fallibility that is somehow missing from 'public' comparisons, which also depend on memory, and where, moreover, an additional element of fallibility due to differing associations in different people is introduced.

Wittgensteinian attacks on 'private' meaning seem to be motivated particularly by concern to avoid 'solipsism'. Solipsism is, itself, a confusing term, as it strictly means the belief that one is alone in the universe: however, almost nobody seriously believes this apart from some people with mental illnesses such as schizophrenia. The term is often used far more loosely than this as a scare-word against any perspective that is not socially reductive, somehow associating the recognition of the importance of 'private' experience with schizophrenic-like states. It tends to assume that 'private' experience confines us to a single perspective – that is, our identifications and beliefs at the present moment – neglecting the integrative perspective that is added by awareness of our changing states over time. If meaning is indeed in a sense 'private', inaccessible to others in any direct way because it is associated with awareness of our own bodily states, then that does not at all imply that it is 'solipsistic'. On the contrary, awareness of different sources of meaning within our experience over time is the fount of provisionality. In particular, we may benefit from periods of solitude in which we become more aware of those different sources of meaning and of different beliefs formed from that meaning in our own experience, without the constant pressure of communication drawing our attention only to the idealized models we share with others.[4]

There is thus no reason to think that meaning is in any way diminished in 'private' contexts, let alone that it 'solipsistic', or that it is in any way dependent on communication, except in initial learning. Nevertheless, of course, communication is extremely important to human beings, and can particularly have a crucial role in processes of integration. It is thus helpful here to offer more of a positive account of the implications of embodied meaning for communication.

Rather than thinking of communication as a matching exercise in which isomorphic representations (see 2.a) in one person are transferred to another, we need to start here by recognizing that the unavoidable position for people with different bodies is different meanings. I cannot give my meaning to you, nor vice-versa. All I can do is stimulate a state in which you will experience similar meanings to me. What gives us some hope of having similar meaning experiences is the similarity in form of our bodies. Our brains have broadly the same structure and capacities, our senses similar wavelength limits and sensitivities, our limbs normally give us similar capacities for moving around and interacting with the world, and our similar needs for air, water, food, etc. give us similar motives. At the same time divergent meaning experiences can be created by widely differing culture, language, gender, age, and disability, but these divergences can still be held within a wider biological similarity.

Without that basic similarity, communication would be much harder and more limited. As Wittgenstein famously wrote: 'If a lion could talk, we would not understand him.'[5] Wittgenstein was here recognizing the ways that context provides meaning, although he understood that context as merely social – instead, though, it is biological. There are some limited ways that a lion and a human can communicate with each other (ask a lion-tamer), but there are also

---

4 See also VI.3.d.
5 Wittgenstein (1967) p. 223.

a lot of basic-level categories and schemas dependent on human bodies and experience that the lion does not share. If we imagine that the lion had a complex enough neural system to develop its own categories and schemas, it would still also have difficulty understanding our categories and schemas.

Obviously, the use of language or other symbols is the way we tend to stimulate experiences that are probably similar, but not identical, in others. If, for instance, I say (or write) the word 'dog', the meaning of that word for you is irreducibly different for you from its meaning for me. For instance, you may have been brought up with an Irish wolfhound and I with a Scotch terrier; our prototypes are thus quite different. At the same time, we probably share an idealized model of the definition of 'dog', based roughly on its scientific classification. For most practical purposes, that idealized model serves its purpose of providing sufficient consistency between our understandings of the term. We are all able to readily understand that idealized model because of the degree of similarity in our basic-level categories, schemas, and metaphorical extensions.

The practical test of whether communication has taken place is not one of isomorphism, but of adequacy. We don't need to have exactly the same idea in our minds, and indeed it is impossible that we should. Instead, though, the idea needs to be similar enough to result in compatible actions, including those of further communication. If you ask me to feed the dog and I feed the cat instead, sufficient communication has obviously not taken place. In most cases though, which are not subject to 'misunderstanding' (that is, inadequate similarity of meaning), our practical responses are based on similar enough meaning-experiences to *work*.

There is, of course, a common use of the word 'meaning' that refers only to consistent use of the idealized model. This is the 'meaning' of a word as we can look it up in a dictionary. Dictionaries are obviously very useful sources of information – but this is information about the shared cultural conventions in the use of the idealized model, not information of any kind about our *experience* as associated with the symbol. Our experience, as I will discuss further in the next chapter, covers *both* of the domains that have been often falsely separated into 'cognition' and 'emotion', both of which are interdependent aspects of meaning as a whole.

The dictionary definition not only tells you nothing about the 'emotional' meaning of 'dog' (such as how you feel about Fido), but it also does not tell you anything about how you understand the connection between the symbol and the experience – it tells you nothing about the specific process by which that symbol has expanded in its meaning from a prototype, or about the embodied schemas in which it was encountered. It may not even tell you anything about the way we have understood categorial[6] relationships, because although dictionaries may categorize, they always do so from the top down, not from the middle where we begin experientially. A dictionary or encyclopedia will tell you that 'dog' is the species *Canis familiaris*, from the genus *Canis*, the family *Canidae*, the order *Carnivora*, the class *Mammalia*, the phylum *Chordata*, and the kingdom *Animalia*. It may also give hyponyms: subspecies, breeds, or other subdivisions of dog. This will also not tell you that an aspect of your very understanding of what a 'mammal' is may depend on your prior acquaintance with dogs, though in some other cases dictionaries may also help reveal some aspects of metaphorical structures through information about etymology.

Information about the idealized model of a word or phrase, then, is geared towards aiding communication, not towards understanding meaning, even though dictionary information about a specific idealized model may aid us in relatively peripheral ways in forming such an understanding. We typically use a dictionary either to understand what someone else is saying (e.g. looking up an unknown word), or to make sure others can understand what we are trying to communicate (e.g. checking our spelling and/or usage as we write). Dictionaries can also be used more combatively to try to police usage ('that's not the meaning of "Christian" in the Oxford Dictionary'). In that case the idealized model becomes absolutized as the basis of *essentialism*, and the dictionary becomes an authority to appeal to. I will return in 2.g to further discussion of the ways that essentialism is an obvious product of representationalism, and its damaging effects in repressing stipulation and the creative use of language. Not all representationalists are formally essentialists, but in practice essentialism is often the product of entrenched representationalist thinking. We encounter it whenever someone thinks they know what a word 'really' means.

---

6   'Categorial' here means 'of categories', and is used in distinction from 'categorical', because the latter can also mean 'definite'.

Many of our unhelpful attitudes to meaning, then, seem to come from a confusion of meaning with communication, and the attempt to enforce norms that are needed for practical communication onto meaning as a wider phenomenon. It is not surprising that we do this, because it is easier. It is a kind of shortcut or substitution, because communicative conventions are easier to understand and communicate than is meaning itself. In some cases, the shortcut does not create any immediate practical difficulties, because the idealized model that we have absolutized is adequate to a particular set of limited conditions where it is used. As generally with absolutization, though, the wider we range through changing conditions, the more likely that shortcut is to create inadequacy in response to them. We need to be able to question idealized models to be able to think provisionally and change our beliefs when necessary, and this implies that we also need to be able to consider the symbols used in developing those beliefs apart from their entrenched social use in a particular context. 'Private' meaning thus proves to be crucial to provisionality, giving us the leverage to use imagination to range beyond the idealized models, and then to bring the products of that process back to 'public' discourse in the form of new meaning that we then try to communicate.

2.e. The Reduction of Meaning to 'Cognition'

> Meaning should not be reduced to 'cognition', as academics almost universally do, reinforcing representationalism. This either reinforces the absolutizing cognitive-emotive dichotomy, or subsumes emotive meaning into 'knowledge' – an absolute term – in a way that obscures our lack of it and conflates meaning with belief. Instead we need a pyramidal conceptual model with meaning at the bottom and 'knowledge' (if there is any) only at the tip.

The common academic assumption that meaning can be understood as a form of 'cognition' seems to me most unhelpful, and to effectively rest on representationalist assumptions. On the one hand, 'cognition' can either be sharply divided from 'emotion' because cognitive meaning is supposedly representable in ways emotive meaning is not. On the other hand, emotive meaning can be swept into and appropriated into an expanded notion of 'cognition', which ends up being no better, because it reduces emotive meaning to 'cognitive' and thus still implicitly representational terms. The first of these approaches creates an explicit false dichotomy,[1] absolutizing the cognition-emotion distinction that has at best only highly contextual and contingent uses. The second is also dualistic by implication, since it reduces one supposed form of meaning (emotive) to the terms of the other (cognitive), rather than integrating them in a way that questions the basis of the division.

'Cognition', according to the Oxford Dictionary, is 'the action or faculty of knowing'. Some definitions include awareness as well as knowing in the definition, but in a way that fails to separate awareness from the dominant idea of knowing. The most widely accepted philosophical definition of knowledge is 'justified true belief' (with some objections to this, such as Gettier's, offering only minor modifications). To treat meaning as 'cognition' then, is to reduce it from the beginning to a form of belief, ignoring all the cases where we find symbols meaningful without turning them into beliefs, such as in the arts. It is also to yoke meaning to the idea of 'truth', which is even more explicitly representationalist. The idea of a 'justified true belief' cannot avoid representationalist assumptions, because the language forming the belief has to represent the world out there in

1   V.2.d.

order to be 'true'. This entrenched association undermines the process of justification rather than aiding it, since effective justification demands that we avoid absolutizations.[2] To avoid absolutization we also need to avoid representationalism and to separate meaning from belief, so the whole idea of a 'justified true belief' can be seen as conflicted or self-contradictory.

This representationalist approach to meaning then needs some way of trying to account for the meaning we experience that is not 'cognitive' in this sense, so a separate type of meaning, the 'emotive', is devised. This 'meaning' is, for instance, the negative feelings we get when someone calls us 'pig-headed', even though we don't believe that we have the head of a pig. It's also the meaning we get from poetry or music. According to this approach, we then have two classes of meaning, despite the way in which association creates them together interdependently. 'Emotive' meanings have all the same embodied origins, as discussed in section 1, as 'cognitive' ones: for instance the impact of 'pig-headed' as an insult depends on two metaphorical extensions: not only our head being like that of a pig, but also our minds being our heads. 'Pig' is probably a basic-level category for most people, but one which has associations with eating things in dirt (and thus often of disgust) which for many people may even be more basic than appreciation of any of the basic zoological features of a pig. 'Emotive' meaning is a response to a stimulus in accordance with association, but then so also is 'cognitive' meaning.

A more recent, and generally more thoughtful, approach is to treat emotion as an aspect of cognition, but in terms that are framed by cognition. Here the meaning of 'cognition' may be expanded to include ideas of adaptivity or adequacy, as it is in the work of Maturana and Varela.[3] Emotional responses in humans are adaptations to the environment, just as cognitive ones are, even though they may vary in their adequacy. Grief, for example, helps one adapt to loss in the same way as information about what one has lost. Some emotional responses, such as anger, may be less well-adapted, but they are attempts to remove an obstacle to our goals which are adaptive in a similar way to our representations of what we do or do not want. Maturana and Varela treat the adaptation of

2   II.2.g.
3   Maturana & Varela (1980, 1987).

all life in a way that is continuous with human life, and thus implies the inseparability of cognition and emotion.

Nevertheless, the terms in which they choose to do this are the terms of cognition, as the title of their very useful introductory book, *The Tree of Knowledge*, makes clear. The whole book, they say, 'is a sort of invitation to refrain from the habit of falling into the temptation of certainty'.[4] Yet how could we do this whilst framing our understanding of that adaptation in the representationalist terms of 'knowledge'? They define 'knowing' as 'effective action', explaining it in terms of 'structural coupling' (that is, the genetic and individual modifications made to an organism in response to its environment) and action in accordance with the modifications thus made that test them in relation to that environment.[5] But 'knowledge' is an absolute, not an incremental, term (you either 'know' or you don't). Not only is this usage a potentially highly confusing complete change in the meaning of 'knowledge' that threatens to obscure our *lack* of it in the normal representationalist sense (thus encouraging absolutization), but it also continues to conflate meaning with belief, even though Maturana and Varela elsewhere give us an embryonic distinction between the two.[6] *Meaning* can be adaptive in long-term and indirect ways, but only by providing a wider possible fund of resources from which *belief* can be formed. Some meaning in human experience is completely 'useless' and possibly damaging, though we cannot tell in advance which, just as we could not predict the evolutionary blind alleys created by modifications in other organisms. Beliefs, on the other hand, can be applied and tested in feedback loops at any point.

The movement beyond representationalism thus remains incomplete where its academic exponents insist on framing the alternative in the implicitly representationalist terms of 'knowing' or 'cognition'. Instead we need ways of understanding meaning that are independent of belief, and that allow equally for emotive responses (whether these are adaptive or non-adaptive). The structure of our concepts on the subject needs to work upwards from an embodied base in which each new step of the pyramid is contingently dependent on the previous one **[diagram 4]**, whereas the topsy-turvy approach dependent on 'cognition' mistakes the tip of the pyramid

---

4   Maturana & Varela (1987) p. 18.
5   Ibid. p. 29.
6   III.1.b, which quotes op. cit. p. 175.

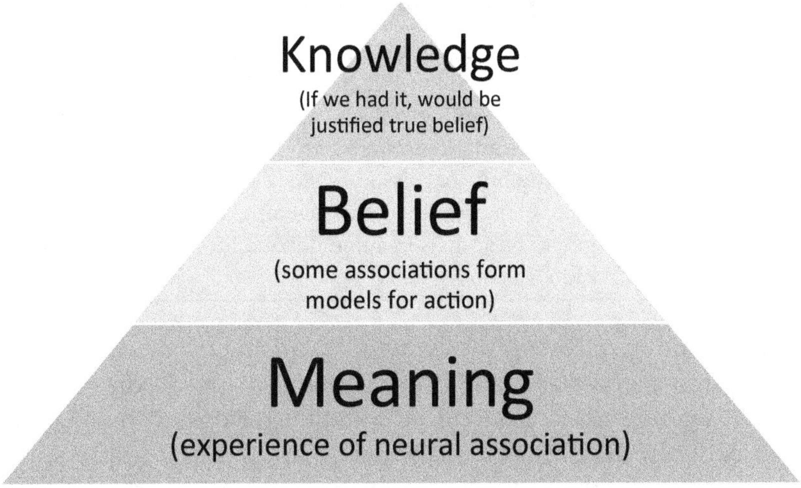

Knowledge
(If we had it, would be justified true belief)

Belief
(some associations form models for action)

Meaning
(experience of neural association)

Diagram 4. Pyramidal embodied model of meaning as prior to belief or 'knowledge'.

('knowing') for its base. This understanding of the pyramid implies the integration of emotive with cognitive meaning at every level, and also incorporates the recognition of right-hemisphere processes as underlying the representation of left-hemisphere ones.

2.f. Representation and Expression

> Expressivism is a dummy counterpart in supposed opposition to representationalism, seeing meaning only as expression of inner feeling, that collapses into representationalism when examined. It relies on an inward-outward dichotomy that assumes far more than is necessary from the individuality of our experience of meaning. Both representation and expression need to be seen as incremental qualities of meaning, not as total accounts of it.

Another perspective sees meaning as arising from our *expression* of inner experience, which symbols then put in an outward form. Meaning, then, it might be thought, resides in the relationship between the symbols and what we are trying to express. For instance, when an artist creates a sculpture, is the work of art not then given its meaning by what the artist is expressing? Even when another person then views that sculpture, is the meaning of it not found in the relationship with that person's inner states? The problem with this is that it offers a partial picture, reifying 'inner states', and assumes that this idea of an inner state offers a complete picture of meaning – which it does not: even for these examples, let alone for instances where 'expression' is less obvious, as in scientific language.

As already briefly mentioned in 2.a, representationalism has a kind of dummy or empty counterpart in expressivism Both representation and expression clearly take place in our experience of meaning – that is, we try to represent things that we believe to be 'out there' in the world, and we also try to express things that we believe to be 'in there' in ourselves. However, representation, as I have been arguing, is not the source of meaning; and for the same reasons, nor is expression. When we examine the idea of expression, it turns out to be another version of representation, and the belief that it is the source of meaning is just as reliant on the cognitive-emotive dichotomy as is representationalism. Moreover, expressivism seems to be a dummy or empty category, because nobody appears to put it forward seriously as a theory of meaning (at least, I have yet to find a theorist who does).

The distinction between representation and expression depends on an inward-outward dichotomy. In representation, we may imagine an outward state of affairs being 'represented' inwardly, whilst in expression, we may imagine the opposite: an inward state of affairs being 'expressed' outwardly. The difference then seems to lie in where the symbols are: do we think of the symbols as something 'outward', a cultural artefact, or something 'inward', a mental state of recognition? If they lie 'outward', the 'meaning' apparently has to be 'inward', whereas if they are 'inward', the meaning apparently has to be 'outward'.

However, the distinction between inward and outward is not so clear and unambiguous: particularly, talk of our 'inward' states at other times than the current one may seem 'outward', as when we talk dispassionately about our past feelings in childhood. There is a constant interdependence that makes the two impossible to separate in practice, both parts of a system best understood in terms of mutual rather than linear causality (a constant and unpredictable interplay). Moreover, expression can easily be re-described as representation ('this poem tells you how I felt…') and representation as expression ('this theory is biased…').

Very often, too, the 'inward' v 'outward' dichotomy maps onto the 'cognitive' v 'emotive' dichotomy, as emotions are seen as 'subjective' states being expressed outwardly from an inner origin, and cognition as an engagement with the 'objective' because it is supposed to be mapping what is really there. As we have already seen in the previous chapter, this dichotomy is inadequate for understanding meaning, in which cognitive and emotive elements are always inextricably interlocked, just as are the 'inward' and 'outward' elements.

Both representationalism and expressivism, even if they were genuinely distinct from each other, make the mistake of assuming that meaning lies somewhere other than in our actual experience of finding symbols meaningful. As already discussed in 2.d, there is a sense in which our experience of symbols is indeed 'private', or 'inward' – but this is solely a matter of the nervous systems of different individuals being not directly connected, even though there are many forms of communication and sympathetic resonances between them. However, there is a widespread tendency to over-interpret this 'privacy' and build absolute beliefs on it. It does not imply 'subjectivity' as opposed to 'objectivity' in the absolute senses of those terms. Facing up to the individual basis of meaning experience does not imply that meaning is solely 'expressive', or that we should rigidify our use of the container schema in any other metaphorical applications. Expression and representation are incremental features of the meaning we experience, usually experienced to different extents simultaneously.

This incrementality is perhaps most obvious in the arts, where attempts to represent the 'content' (in a summary, say) or to pinpoint what has been expressed through interpretation, do not have exactly the same meaning as a work of art itself – though nor are they entirely separate from it. A piece of music has a meaningful impact on our pulse, our muscles, and our feelings that a musicological representation on the programme notes does not: but the musicological discussion is still interdependent with experience of the music, on which it depends for its meaning. The same can be said for the feelings that the composer was expressing when she wrote the work. Even an academic paper read at a conference has a different meaning for us from either an outline of its argument or a discussion of the 'expressive' intentions of its author.

One common tendency is to substitute an idea of what is expressed for a work of art itself, creating a supposed representation that also often tries to appropriate an expression. This can perhaps be seen in our over-concern with the biographies of artists, musicians, and writers. Sometimes such exploration of the background of an artist can *add* to the meaning we already have from their works, but at other times it can provide a shortcut or substitution, because the meaning of the artist's life is easier to engage with than the work itself. That shortcut can then provide a theoretical expressivist reduction of the meaning of the work ('Oh, that poem is just an expression of his emotional crisis when he broke up with his lover'). However, the poem might be just as powerful for us without any awareness at all of the poet's life-history, because we relate to it through our own experience. That experience as a whole, however, also cannot be reduced to an expressivist account of our own lives. If we have just had a break-up ourselves, this may add a special punch to a poem that expresses the pain of that break-up for us, but that is not the entirety of the meaning of the poem, which is 'recollected in tranquillity' as Wordsworth put it – that is, it adds a context of greater awareness to its account of experience. 'Expression', like 'representation' is a frozen snapshot for particular purposes – albeit a snapshot of an inner rather than an outer state. It does not take into account the wider context of its total meaning in our experience over time.

Expression thus plays a part in meaning, just as representation does, but it is a mistake to use it as the basis of an account of meaning. More broadly, it is a mistake to take the predominantly right-hemisphere-led features of expression, like those of emotion, and over-compensate for left-hemisphere representational repression by using a conceptual reduction of them in the same framework of assumptions as that created by representational repression. In this sense, there is a Middle Way to be found between representationalism and expressivism – but as often, the weight and influence of the views on either side of the way are far from equal.

2.g. Representationalism, Metaphysics, and Essentialism

> Representationalism and metaphysics are both dimensions of absolutization arising from the rigid idealization of models. Metaphysics depends not just on the exact words used in a claim, but on the essentialism in their interpretation, with alternative interpretations excluded. It is perpetuated by absolutized logic and *ad hoc* defensive argument. Essentialism both restricts the options and maintains culturally entrenched narrowness of interpretation.

The most practically significant drawback with representationalism comes from its close relationship with metaphysics. As I previously argued in *Absolutization*, representationalism is one of the key dimensions of absolutization, and makes possible metaphysics – that is, claims about 'reality' beyond experience.[1] As I also argued in *Absolutization*, metaphysics cannot avoid absolutization.[2] Metaphysical beliefs are often mutually reinforcing, connected together with absolutized logic.[3] All such metaphysical belief requires is the absolute idealization of models in place of embodied meaning. Metaphysics and absolutized logic occur when an idealized representational model can no longer be adapted in the light of new meaningful information arriving via the right hemisphere (our senses and imagination). We start to believe that some things *must* be the case when we begin to repress alternative possibilities.

Representationalism and metaphysics are different dimensions of absolutization, related in a sense that is not deductively equivalent *a priori*, but rather systemic. Differing conditions bring differing aspects of these systemic features to light and reveal their interdependence.[4] Metaphysics comes to the fore when absolutized beliefs are formally stated in any way, whilst representationalism comes to the fore when we consider what assumptions about meaning have to be made to allow absolutization.

Metaphysics consists of generalizations over time, space or categorization, when those generalizations are not provisional, but rather *essentialized*: so that we consider them true not because that's how it seems so far, but because that's just how things are, following

1 I.3.a.
2 I.4.a.
3 I.4.b.
4 I.6.b.

a necessity or building on a supposed foundation. For instance: 'You can't trust Republicans' could be a provisional or an absolute metaphysical claim, depending on whether or not openness to the possibility of a trustworthy Republican is present. 'I can never do mathematical calculations in my head without getting confused' is a generalization over time, even though it only applies to one person. It could either be an absolutized metaphysical claim or a provisional so-far observation, depending primarily on the emotional state of the speaker, and whether or not they have enough confidence to be able to potentially improve their practice of mental arithmetic.

That essentialization also gives metaphysical claims infinite scope in at least one respect: 'You can't trust lawyers' applies to a potentially infinite number of lawyers – however many you may encounter, they will all be untrustworthy regardless. 'I can *never* do mathematical calculations in my head...' makes clear the infinite scope in its use of *never*. As discussed in *Absolutization*, this infinite scope has a crucial role in the entrenchment of metaphysical beliefs, making them impossible to disprove, because there will always be further possible exceptions to any possible counter-evidence.[5] *Ad hoc* reasoning can then be used to dispose of any contrary experience. One example of a trustworthy lawyer is dismissed as not a 'real' lawyer ('He did some *pro bono* work last year; he's not as selfish as the rest of his profession'). A mental calculation I managed to make without confusion is dismissed ('It doesn't really count because that was too easy'). When we think we have an essential meaning to a term like *lawyer* or *mathematical calculation*, then claims about them become impregnable to any supposed counter-example.

Essentialization is a feature of representationalism, because both assume a link between 'reality' and an idealized model. That idealized model specifies certain 'real' features of objects in a given category (nouns, whether concrete or abstract). It may also extend to features of those objects marked by adjectives ('Pink is an intrinsically sickly colour'), or actions marked by verb gerunds ('To garden is to participate in the ultimate sacredness of the living world'). We can (evidently – so far) only do this when our assumptions about meaning are implicitly representationalist: that is, we have an absolute belief about something 'ultimate', 'real', 'essential', 'necessary', etc. to justify those assumptions. Our belief in the idealized model

---

5   I.4.d.

limits the options to that model, so it thus seems unavoidable that meaning will be dependent on it alone. The model is treated as 'reality' both as a matter of belief about the grounds of meaning and as the source of meaning itself, increasing the likelihood that meaning and belief will be confused.

The links between different propositions in an idealized model also create the absolutization of logic. Again, if a given model is treated as the ultimate reality, the 'true' model, and this model consists of an interdependent web of relationships between 'true' propositions, then the logical relationships between all the elements in the propositional web will become 'necessary' or 'a priori'. This is what links representationalism, essentialism, and rationalist certainty. It becomes 'true', not just a feature of a very useful and widespread model, that 2+2=4, and that a bachelor is an unmarried man. The idea that logical relationships can be deductively 'valid' and 'invalid' follows. A 'valid' proposition contains apparently 'essential' assumptions: a bachelor is an unmarried man, so it becomes essential that a bachelor is a man (a woman can't be a bachelor) and essential that a bachelor is unmarried (a married man can't be a bachelor). There is nothing false about such validity, but it applies *only within a model dependent on embodied meaning*. This, again, is explored in more detail in *Absolutization*.[6]

The effects of essentialism can be readily seen if we consider discussions in which it is used as a shortcut to limit the new meaning we can develop in relation to a concept (and thus to limit options and defend absolutized beliefs). For instance, discussions about religious traditions are often a classic case of entrenched essentialism. If one suggests that Christian tradition can be interpreted so as to treat God and Jesus as meaningful archetypal symbols, whilst avoiding absolute beliefs about them,[7] a common response in my experience is that 'that is not Christianity'. So what is Christianity? Often it is defined as a set of *beliefs* about God – that he is an infinite, perfect, supernatural creator – and about Christ – that he offers salvation for human beings through his atoning sacrifice. If you examine Christianity as a *tradition* (that is, as a system evolving over time), however, it appears much more than that: as a set of inspired responses that cluster around certain *symbols*, and include a great

---

6   I.4.b.
7   As I did in Ellis (2018).

variety of beliefs. Such traditions are constantly taking new forms that are nevertheless inspired by and linked to the previous ones. They do not have any such determinate boundaries based on essential characteristics derived from fixed relationships between theological concepts in a single model. They are responses to human embodiment, expressed in a particular cultural stream.

Here, then, essentialism is a crucial element in the bundle of interdependent factors that maintain metaphysical beliefs. It is not only used defensively to keep restricting the options, but also in the way that people typically learn about new concepts. Although we learn language during early life in a much more embodied way (as discussed in section 1), in adulthood we are more likely to learn a new abstract concept by seeking a definition of it – giving us an understanding of its supposed 'essential' features. However, the more abstract the concept, generally speaking, the more that approach is likely to lead to absolutizing beliefs using that concept. It can be practically quite beneficial if we are precise in our essentialization of features in, say, identifying a plant or diagnosing a disease (even though we may need flexibility there, too, in the longer-term). However, such 'precision' about very general abstract terms like 'nature', 'art', 'religion', etc. merely impoverishes our view of them, making us over-dependent on a particular model to give meaning to that term, and greatly limiting our capacity to associate it with a range of embodied sources of meaning connected with different experiences. The meaning of 'Christianity' may have been learned in one particular context in a church or school, for instance. Is that all it means? Can we imagine other, probably contrasting, contexts of use, perhaps just reconstructing them from more sketchy experiences of its meaning elsewhere? Can we bring a wider range of sense-experiences, metaphors, and interactions to bear, in contrast to an over-dominant abstract definition?

Language is constantly changing and evolving, but it is the effects of that development that we need to be able to assess. Sometimes language changes in creative ways, to help us break out of meanings based on idealized models which greatly restricted the options. Sometimes, on the other hand, language change can entrench an absolutization by substituting a narrower meaning for a wider one. One example of the latter is the phenomenon of 'political correctness gone mad' in the use of language, in which social disapproval and even sometimes legal definitions may be used to reinforce a limited interpretation that may be offensive to some people some of the time. The White Cliffs of Dover, for instance, are not (generally) racist because they have that name, nor is a 'brainstorm' offensive to people with epilepsy, even if these may occasionally be part of the meanings of these terms to some people. The problem with such interpretations of language is not that they violate essential or 'common sense' beliefs about the meanings of terms, but that they unnecessarily entrench conflict through a narrowly negative interpretation of their meaning (one that becomes just as essentialized as the more traditional essentialization they may be objecting to). Openness to language change is often a sign of provisionality, unless it is promoted in the interests of narrowing interpretation.

2.h. Representation Blindness and the Subtilization Slope

> A further feature of representationalism is blindness of itself and its assumptions, even extending to unawareness of representation as a chosen basis for meaning. The relationship between meaning and represented object is assumed to be transparent. This also leads to the subtilization slope in which process or emptiness type philosophies seek increasingly refined metaphysical beliefs, rather than realizing that we lack the meaning basis to justify any view of such beliefs.

Why is it that we often do not become aware of the fact that we are representing – and thus of the limitations of our representation? One of the traits of representationalism seems to be more or less complete blindness to itself – both to the process of creating representations, and to the assumed belief that representations are the source of meaning. This is not blindness to the contents of the assumed representation itself, but to the process. It is thus more akin to the 'blind spot' in our optical perception generally, or of a driver reversing a vehicle. When we have a blind spot, we don't realize that we have a blind spot. We explain away any possible inconsistencies in our view through confabulation. We assume that our view is complete, after the general fashion of the left hemisphere.

Another way of putting this would be in terms of assumed transparency. Representationalists may from time to time recognize isolated features of representation and the ways it interferes with their experience, but the default assumption is one of transparency – that there are no distorting elements between our experience and a represented object. Note that I am not talking here about sceptical arguments or biases that affect the justification of our *beliefs* about the world, but about the transparency of relationships between language and the meaning that is a prior condition for us being able to use it for forming beliefs. As I noted in my discussion of sceptical arguments in *The Five Principles*, one form of sceptical argument is linguistic, because the lack of representational meaning is one thing that makes it impossible for us to have 'knowledge'.[1] However, not all sceptical arguments are linguistic, and the remainder depend on the lack of justification for belief, not on prior meaning. Nevertheless, the assumption of 'knowledge' can also be easily

1   II.1.a.

projected back into supposed transparency of meaning. The linguistic type of sceptical argument just points out the lack of any such transparency, assumed when we claim to have knowledge. So if we choose to ignore sceptical argument of all kinds and its implications, we will also simultaneously maintain representation blindness.

It's this lack of awareness of representationalism itself amongst representationalists that probably leads, as already mentioned, to the fact that there is no widely used term with the scope of 'representationalism' as I use it (see 2.a), and to the tendency to use that term more narrowly instead. The same can be said of the term 'representation'. Although there is substantial discussion of the term 'representation' in philosophy, the questions that philosophers are inclined to ask about it are merely clarificatory ones about how representation works, not the more basic practical question of whether it's helpful to assume that we have representation at all. They ask, for instance, whether representation is related to reality through structural features (isomorphism), or whether we should adopt instead a 'deflationary' or 'pragmatic' view of it.[2] The supposedly deflationary and pragmatic views, however, turn out not to actually question the central role of representation itself, but merely to offer different possible accounts of how it does its (still) supposed central task in creating (or not creating) a 'substantive' relationship between representation and target when used in our statements of beliefs. In spite of all the accounts of embodied meaning that have been developed, there is still not even any conversation going on, it seems, about the psychological implications and negative effects of adopting an implicitly representational view, or of the value of framing our view of meaning differently. It is just assumed to be obvious that representation is what meaning is about.

A further effect of representation blindness can be found in thinkers who may in theory have no commitment to representationalism, but who nevertheless end up reinforcing it by continuing within the framework it creates, even when they are sincerely struggling to get beyond some of the conditioning effects of representationalism. The reason for this is that they think in terms of making representation more accurate, in more and more subtle and abstract ways, rather than recasting their understanding in non-representational terms. I will call this the *subtilization slope*. This is what I see as the major

---

2   E.g. Suarez (2015).

problem with process philosophies, such as that of Whitehead, and with much Mahayana Buddhist philosophy, including, for instance, the Middle Way philosophy of Nagarjuna. Although there is an understanding of some aspects of the Middle Way in such approaches, advocates of such philosophies have generally yet to grasp the implications of embodied meaning.

Advocates of such process or emptiness type philosophies continue to assume that the answer to absolutization is to merely improve our representation of 'reality' and make it more 'accurate'. Rather than making an ultimate metaphysical description of the universe as substantive objects of any kind, then, they will make a new, better, metaphysical description in terms of process. Alternatively, they may describe the universe as 'empty', i.e. lacking either the presence or absence of ultimate objects. What this fails to do is to reconsider the very metaphysical approach that is at stake. The metaphysical approach is also the representationalist approach, failing to adapt to the kind of meaning available to us as embodied beings.

As embodied, we can only justify provisional, contextual, and conditional statements about the world, accepting that these statements gain meaning for us from a process of association, and are adopted for practical purposes. The statements we make can include provisional generalizations, because our practical purposes do carry us further beyond our immediate context into our expectations of other contexts,[3] but it is nevertheless vital to distinguish those generalizations from absolutes. As I argued in *Absolutization*, it is not possible to make *ultimate* (i.e. metaphysical) statements that are explicitly intended as such, and that are provisional in this way.[4] One of the key reasons for this is that by making statements that can only gain their meaning from representation, we constantly reinforce our denial of their embodied meaning, and thus also of their embodied limitations as a basis of belief. It makes no difference, then, if the *content* of metaphysical claims is processual: it is the fact of making a metaphysical claim itself that is far more significant.

The subtilization slope involves a continuing focus on the content of the metaphysical claim, with the assumption that introducing more and more explicit corrections into the metaphysical framework

3   I.8.
4   I.4.a.

will help us to avoid using that framework. Instead, however, the more subtle the distinctions within the metaphysical framework, the more our attention is drawn to it, rather than to wider aspects of experience, and the more the idealized model of metaphysics itself is reinforced. This typically also leads to paradox, as more and more metaphysical statements are made that fruitlessly try to get beyond the metaphysical framework, but fail to do so – resulting in contradictions that are wrongly believed to have an increasingly profound meaning or to be practically valuable in some way.

For example, in Mahayana Buddhist *Prajñaparamita* teachings, nirvana is said to be ultimately no different from samsara: both are 'empty' (*shunya*). This obviously results in paradox, and this paradox helps us to maintain the assumptions of the idealized model containing both samsara and nirvana, by continuing the separation between them in essentialized meaning. We are asked to believe that samsara and nirvana are distinct and also identical at the same time – the 'two truths'. What is excluded by this is any incrementality in our sense of the meanings of 'samsara' and 'nirvana', that would help to take us back to the experiences that we have associated with these concepts: for instance, the degree of integration allowing us to move from rigid dichotomized models to more flexible provisional ones. To avoid the framing of the dichotomized model of 'samsara' and 'nirvana', it is not enough to merely state their identity and reduce that relationship to paradox: we need to be able to use *different* framing that captures the meaning of those concepts in more immediate relationship to wider meaning and practice. The Five Principles of Middle Way Philosophy attempt to do just that.

The same kind of subtilization slope can also be found in Western philosophy in relation to all the common metaphysical dualisms: for instance mind v body, absolute v relative, ideal v real, theism v atheism, freewill v determinism. Philosophical discussion of these remains fixated on defining ever more subtle metaphysical positions, rather than on recognizing that no metaphysical position on such topics can ever be justified. A philosopher of mind convinced that dual aspect monism is the solution to all the debates, or a philosopher of freewill and determinism preaching compatibilism, are making the same basic mistake of maintaining an idealized model as the final solution to such debates, rather than recognizing that the meanings that relate to our experience in them need to be continually recast in relation to practical judgement.[5] The focus on changing beliefs without changing the underlying meaning that composes those beliefs first is analogous to trying to cut a hard cord with a cheap disposable plastic knife, and then, when it snaps, substituting another such knife, without recognizing that the material from which the knife is made is unsuited to the task.

Another term that I have used in the past to describe the effects of representation blindness on our beliefs is the *ontological obsession*.[6] We remain obsessed, it seems, with describing how things are, rather than the process of judging them, regardless of the theoretical caveats with which we may sometimes surround our beliefs. That obsession appears to depend on representation blindness, because we remain unaware of it being an obsession at all: in the manner of absolutization, we assume that it is simply necessary, or how things are, and that there are no alternatives. Perhaps the strongest indication of this in the Buddhist tradition is the definition of the Middle Way itself in terms of ontology – that is, as the Middle Way between 'existence' and 'non-existence'.[7] The subtilization slope has perhaps reached its furthest point here, but it is the point from which we need to jump off ontological framing (and thus representationalism) altogether. Beliefs about 'existence' and 'non-existence' are *examples* of the opposing absolutes between which the Middle Way can try to navigate, but the Middle Way itself cannot be helpfully understood as long as we remain in the framing of an idealized model of 'existence', as opposed to ceasing to idealize the model.

---

5   See VI.
6   Ellis (2019) 4.b.
7   In early Buddhism: *Nidanasamyutta, Samyutta Nikaya* 12.15; Bodhi (2000) p. 544. This framing is then taken up by later sources in the Buddhist tradition such as Nagarjuna.

3. Taking Embodied Meaning Seriously

3.a. The Lack of Need for 'Sense-making'

> The idea of 'sense-making' involves filling in gaps of our understanding of a given context. This might be helpfully applied to the integration of belief using Vervaeke's 'relevance realization', but is also seriously undermined by its failure to distinguish meaning from belief. Meaning alone cannot fill gaps in adaptive belief, though it does provide important resources. Moreover, we do not generally suffer from a loss of meaning, but a fragmentation of the meaning we already have.

I hope the previous section of the book has given a clear idea of the profound difficulties created by representationalism, but my critique is not done yet. So far is it entrenched into our culture and its assumptions, that a deeper examination of some of the unrecognized impacts of representationalism is needed.

During the last decade or so, I have become increasingly dismayed and disappointed by what has happened to the initial impetus of embodied meaning, as it was laid out by Lakoff and Johnson. Although some of the work done subsequently seems to have genuinely developed what they achieved, much of it has not. Rather it has contributed to a grand missing-of-the-point, a bypassing of the radical challenges posed by embodied meaning, to incorporate it back into the existing representationalist framework whilst presenting a superficial appearance of change. Even some of those who have in some respects started to apply embodied meaning to practical issues have, in my view, thoroughly misunderstood it. Embodied meaning is not business as usual. We need to face it: embodied meaning challenges representationalism, and by challenging representationalism it challenges metaphysics. Those who continue to interpret embodied meaning in implicitly representationalist terms, then, such as those who think it is compatible with the Wittgensteinian reduction of meaning to communication, have missed the point (as discussed in 2.d). Those who think it is a kind of 'cognition' are also still implicitly representationalist (as discussed in 2.e), even if they are in other respects using a systems-based approach. Those who use some metaphysical framework (perhaps because they also believe that metaphysics is inevitable[1]) such as a naturalistic one, and consider embodied meaning to be subject to this, are also missing the point. Metaphysics, explicit or implicit, is impossible if you take embodied meaning seriously. Of course, the wide mass of people require time to adapt to new ways of thinking, but what hope do they have if even the supposed theoreticians of embodied approaches cannot think outside the box?

Some of my complaints about this situation have already been made in the course of presenting the trouble with representationalism in general in the previous section. However, there are further common ways of not taking embodied meaning seriously that I will need to address in this section. These will begin in this chapter with the increasingly popular idea of 'sense-making' – which blurs the boundaries between meaning and belief, and thus takes us back to representationalism by the back door. Another way is to fail to appreciate archetypal meaning as distinct from belief, which still dominates approaches to religion, and which I will tackle in 3.b. Attitudes to ineffability provide a further source of confusion (3.c), in which people fail to face up to the lack of determinate boundaries in embodied meaning, and thus that 'ineffability' can no longer be a helpful idea. Approaches to non-linguistic symbols will also need some discussion, so as to stop sidelining the role of art and music in our appreciation of meaning (3.d). Finally in this section, I will also make a wider survey of the extensive impact of representationalism in religion, philosophy, and politics. Without considering its impact more widely, we may be tempted to only stay in a relatively abstract realm of meaning theory, and not see the full radical implications of a different approach to meaning.

A review of the literature on 'sense-making' by Turner et al.[2] identifies 'sense-making' primarily as the process of filling in gaps in our understanding and response to a particular context. When we are puzzled by what we encounter, we construct 'bridges' from the resources available to us, potentially using both familiar and new sources of information. Either as individuals or as groups, we are actively involved in an autonomous process of filling those 'gaps'.

---

1 See I.4.e.
2 Turner, Allen, & Hawamdeh (2023).

The academic study of sense-making moves from the mere analysis of this process to the actual design of 'practices and frameworks that are meaningful and contextual'.[3] One of the most interesting potentially practical applications of 'sense-making' in this sense is the 'relevance realization' of John Vervaeke et al. – that is, the way in which our sense-making can be honed to find the optimal balance between different priorities, such as pursuing goals versus exploration.[4] Superficially, at least, 'relevance realization' has much in common with the Middle Way – but since it depends on the conceptualization of 'sense-making', we need to examine its prior assumptions.

The apparently unrecognized big difficulty with 'sense-making' as a concept is that it systematically fails to distinguish between meaning and belief. This point can be confirmed from Turner et al.'s comprehensive summaries of the literature on sense-making:[5] all the approaches to it are seen to *combine* functions of meaning, such as understanding and interpretation, with functions of belief, such as communication and action. Since belief constantly draws on and depends upon meaning, this would be fair enough if 'sense-making' was explicitly a discussion of how we form beliefs. However, it instead masquerades as a discussion of how we form meaning, explicitly using the language of 'meaning' or 'sense' as its primary descriptor. In this, then, it is bound to contribute further to the topsy-turvy assumption of representationalism – that is, that meaning is dependent on belief, rather than the other way round – and to divert our thinking away from the appreciation of meaning and the conditions for it in its own right.

Perhaps it is worth reviewing here, at the risk of some repetition, exactly why it is so vital to be able to separate meaning from belief. If we understand meaning in an embodied way, it is formed from associative experience over time and accumulates as neural links, through basic level categorization, embodied schemas, and metaphorical extension. This meaning can be used in ways that *do not* immediately affect belief, although they provide a long-term fund of resources from which new beliefs can be assembled. Meaning can be associated with discrete sounds, words, phrases, and images, but beliefs, when they are formally expressed, are propositional. These

3   Ibid.
4   Vervaeke, Lillicrap, & Richards (2012).
5   Op. cit.

meaning associations can also have a long-term emotional impact on us that is not simply built on our implicit beliefs.

If we insist on understanding meaning in terms of belief, then, in the very structure of the terminological vocabulary we use, we rule out clear understanding of the use of meaning without belief. In the process we rule out any understanding of the provisional use of the imagination, of the operation of archetypal inspiration, and of the role of the arts in stimulating that inspiration. One possible explanation (and I do not want to make this into any kind of *ad hominem* accusation) for this massive blind spot in 'sense-making' is that it has been created by people who work in social science or cognitive science alone, who do not think seriously enough about religion or the arts.

If *meaning* is interpreted strictly in the terms I have outlined so far in this book, however, we do not need any 'sense-making'. That is, in order to fill gaps in our coherent beliefs about the world, we do not need meaning: meaning alone cannot do that job, as it tells us nothing about those gaps. Perhaps sometimes we need new terms or vocabulary to help us to develop new and more adequate *beliefs* about the world, to address those gaps, but this is very much an indirect process, not the prime activity that is presented as 'sense-making', which is that of considering new possible beliefs and judging between them (the process of *weighing up* as discussed in *The Five Principles*[6]). The research into 'relevance realization' as a honing of 'sense-making' may have much to contribute to our understanding of that process of making provisional judgements – which we could more easily appreciate if it was not presented in ways that unhelpfully confuse the basic terminology.

Particularly, here, I suspect the confusion of *fragmented meaning* with a *lack of meaning*. The fragmentation of meaning will be explored systematically in the next section, but in brief it consists in the non-availability to us of the meaning resources we need to understand a particular context. These resources may not be available to us for a variety of psychological reasons, but they are separated over time in our experience rather than necessarily absent. An integration process is needed to mobilize meaning resources when we need them to construct new beliefs adequate to a new situation, making sure that we synthesize the associations we have already made sufficiently to

6   II.2.g.

apply them in that situation. We do not need to 'make' that meaning in most cases, as it is already there, although we will indeed occasionally seek out new symbols or concepts to use in understanding a new situation. The concept of 'sense-making' thus seems to have been developed on the assumption of a single permanent perspective in an individual, rather than taking into account our variation over time and its effects in creating conflict between meaning or belief that is absolutized at one time. What has been described as 'sense-making' may thus be better described first of all as an integration of meaning and an integration of belief.

Given that meaning is built up from an ever more complex layering of new associations on top of previous ones, it is doubtful if we ever 'make' meaning in any remotely pure way. To 'make sense' of a new abstract idea like incorporation in business, for instance, the etymology tells us that we probably combine the container schema with the object schema, to form the idea of putting a smaller 'body' (corpus) *into* a larger one. Confronted with a new situation involving incorporation, then, do we 'make sense' of it? At best, the idea of 'making sense' blurs two separable processes: the understanding of 'incorporation' (and any other new concepts) by association with our previous meaningful symbols, and the development of beliefs about the situation involving a specific case of incorporation and how to respond to it. The process of association re-uses and complexifies our previous associations rather than forming entirely new ones. We could also do this without forming new beliefs, withholding judgement for a while.

So, despite its association with some approaches and techniques that parallel aspects of the Middle Way, 'sense-making' is shaped by too many unexamined representationalist assumptions to provide a helpful approach to meaning. Meaning is largely *made* in the initial differentiation of infancy, not by the adult process of developing more adaptive beliefs. It is the *integration* of meaning, as we will see, that needs to be the basis of the adult quest.

3.b. Archetypal Meaning, not Metaphysics

> Representationalism undermines helpful archetypal responses to religious or other inspired experience. An account of archetypes as sources of inspiration can be based on embodied meaning, and avoids the unnecessary but entrenched metaphysical interpretation of inspirational and integrative experience. Archetypes need to be separated from their specific symbols and from their projection as beliefs, but none of their power needs to be lost in an agnostic attitude to their 'reality'.

An extremely widespread and entrenched confusion of meaning with belief is also found in the tendency to assume that archetypal experiences of meaning are experiences of metaphysical 'truth': for instance, that religious experiences are sources of revelation from God or insight into 'reality' rather than profound experiences of *meaning*. I have said little about archetypal meaning so far in this book, because I have more deeply explored it in my previous book *Archetypes in Religion and Beyond*.[1] However, the topic forms an important part of any exploration of the implications of embodied meaning in relation to the Middle Way, so I need here to at least summarize some of the case I made in that book. There I have argued that Jungian archetypes can be readily interpreted in terms of embodied meaning, and that the immediate association of archetypal experience with metaphysical belief is an unhelpful shortcut, created by projection as a dimension of absolutization.

Archetypal symbols are meaningful to us in exactly the same way as any other symbols – through basic categorization, schema, and metaphor. Where they differ is that archetypal symbols have an archetypal function – fulfilling our need to maintain inspiration *over time* and thus counteract internal conflict and forgetfulness. As I argued in the earlier book, there is no need for the theoretical Jungian construction of the 'collective unconscious', nor for any beliefs about its supposed relationship to Platonic Forms (both of which are often interpreted metaphysically), to understand archetypes and their value from a practical and phenomenological point of view.[2] Archetypal symbols can be seen as schematic, because they relate general areas of experience to types of symbols: for instance, the heroic schema associates the experience of overcoming difficulties

---

1 Ellis (2022).
2 Ibid. 1.e & f.

through persistence over time with symbolic figures – whether these are Hercules, Harry Potter, Marie Curie, or your grandma.[3] The relationship between this general function and any one given heroic symbol is obviously then one of metaphorical extension.[4]

I have analysed four main archetypal functions, corresponding to four main overall types of archetype: the *heroic* function, which helps us persevere in fulfilling goals over time; the *shadow* function, which helps us avoid long-term threats; the *anima/animus* function, which helps us relate to the attractive other; and the *God* function, which keeps us in touch with an overall wider potential beyond what we currently identify with.[5] These do correspond to what Jung at times emphasized as the most important archetypes, but they need to be carefully distinguished from specific symbols – for instance, the God archetype is an overall convenient label for the function that could operate for us in a wide variety of symbols, including Buddha, nature, truth, or even the concepts of rationality or democracy as sources of inspiration, and should not be confused with God as a specific symbol.

By 'inspiration', here, I am talking about meaningful recollection that helps us to put this moment's feelings and motives in the wider context of the ones we have previously marked as most helpful to us in the long term. I am not talking about any necessary beliefs associated with the symbol, apart from practical ones that are immediately associated with our own motives and actions. Thus, for instance, being inspired by God as an archetypal symbol implies that we have a practical belief that the inspiration of this symbol is likely to be beneficial to our deeper motivations. It does not imply any belief that God 'exists', or created the universe, or provided revelatory truths, or any other such metaphysics – beliefs that can only be held absolutely or not at all.

The association of these sources of inspiration with metaphysics seems to have arisen, like all forms of absolutization, as a shortcut used in socio-political contexts – a way of motivating the tribe. The sharing of absolute beliefs, expressed invariantly in particular forms of language, allows very quick and effective mass copying, which can be highly beneficial to a group of organisms that can exploit it in

---

3   Ibid. 1.c.
4   Ibid. 1.d.
5   Ibid. 1.a & 4.a–f.

relatively stable environmental conditions.⁶ In human contexts, this is what makes metaphysical belief a tool of power and a method for rapid group-binding. To command an army quickly and effectively, for instance, one does not trouble to make sure that every soldier is genuinely inspired to fight in the long term. Instead one employs absolute beliefs (often nationalistic ones in this case) to give every soldier an immediate motive of group conformity based on a shared model. If we fail to accept the absolute belief that dominates our group, we then risk losing its vital support.⁷ We can get a quick motivation from an archetypal symbol (such as God) in this way, but one that short-circuits the process of taking responsibility for it or of being aware of our own engagement with it. The inspiration that results is thus short-lived, fragile,⁸ and highly dependent on constant group reinforcement.

That shortcut can also be understood as projection of the archetype.⁹ Rather than recognizing that the archetype has a function in our own experience, we treat it as present in the symbol. Frequently, that means treating another person who has strong symbolic power for us as though their meaning in our embodied experience provided us with a true representational account of who they really or 'essentially' are. Thus, the man whose efforts inspire us, say, in facing up to pain, is treated as courageous in every respect and generally faultless. The beautiful woman who creates an ecstatic response in a man is worshipped as though her beauty set every aspect of her character, not as a source for an inspired response *in him*. The shadow is treated not just as a reminder of possible threats for us, but demonized as intrinsically evil. The God archetype is treated not as a symbolic reminder of the vast, awe-inspiring potential we may glimpse in religious experience, but as a supernatural entity that controls the universe. These projections rely strongly on the assumptions of representationalism: that the symbol's meaning must be based on the 'truths' it tells us rather than the associative effects it has on us.

Archetypal projection is often such an entrenched, habitual response that there are few cultural resources to help us question or contextualize it. Rather, cultural and religious models are idealized

6   III.1.h.
7   I.5.e.
8   I.2.c.
9   I.5.b; Ellis (2022) section 2.

into metaphysical 'necessities', so that we are unable to avoid reifying God, just as we 'objectify' the people we have relationships with, and literalize or allegorize artistic symbols. It becomes a matter of course that we should want to possess someone we fall in love with, because we assume that we have fallen in love with something separate from our own experience of their meaning, and that we can somehow then incorporate that new possession into ourselves. We also cannot appreciate that the evil of a Hitler or a Putin is found in their judgements at each moment, constantly amplified by the further subservient judgement of others in the socio-political systems they have bent to their own purposes. Or if we can no longer regard Hitler as wholly evil, we may alternatively rush to the conclusion that there is no evil at all.

The unhelpful assumption that inspired or integrative experiences must come from a metaphysical source is thus not at all confined to the delusions of literalized theism (the belief in God's 'existence') in religion. However, that is probably its most obvious and far-reaching manifestation. When inspiration is thus reduced to completely abstracted beliefs set in an idealized model, we no longer have any responsibility for placing them in the context of experience. The infinite scope of those beliefs[10] then allows any amount of rationalization to be attached to the appeal made to a special religious experience, used to justify beliefs or actions far beyond the positive state that may have been glimpsed in that experience. The experiences of the prophets justify war against their enemies, or the words of the book said to have been received through revelation are wielded to justify any kind of repression against those who deny that revelation, as infidels. These are not problems with the specific metaphysical beliefs held by these theistic groups, but problems with metaphysics itself – and thus in turn problems of representationalism. For instance, the Bible can only give you a moral imperative to commit genocide against your foes when you believe its words are capable of representing 'reality'.

The alternative of responding to archetypal meaning *as meaning only* in no way diminishes its power, nor is it reductive in any way. God remains just as powerful for us – if we have had a response to symbols of him in the first place – when viewed as meaning as when viewed in terms of belief. That power is not the projected power

---

10 I.4.d.

of being able to smite demonic foes, but the power of raising our own levels of awareness through ever-stronger connections with the associations of inspired experience. That inspiration makes us capable of contextualizing our beliefs more effectively, and thus gives us the power of transforming our judgements and actions in practice. Despite the claims to the contrary in the metaphysics of the traditional ontological argument for God's existence,[11] an imagined God is not 'lesser' than a 'real' God. Rather there are arguments that a solely meaningful God has a much more clearly beneficial effect than one who is the object of absolutized belief. That is because a meaningful God can be separated from maladaptive projections. There is no 'just' or 'merely' about a symbolic God, just as there is not about a love for a symbolically powerful person.

The use of a psychological explanation to help understand the impact of that symbolic archetype also in no way implies that our view of the archetype is 'just' psychological. We have *added* another perspective to provide us with more contextual awareness as compared with any account without such a psychological perspective, not taken any awareness away. A psychological account including the role of archetypes as phenomena gives us a provisional basis of belief with which to reconcile our experience of archetypal inspiration with all our other provisional beliefs about the world around us. The psychological account, however does not have to offer any speculations about the supposed nature of archetypes themselves, or of any 'realities' behind them, being concerned only with how we interact with what we experience. Remaining agnostic about any claims concerning the archetypes themselves, we are then free to appreciate them as meaning, recognizing the impact of that meaning in our experience. The relationship of that meaning to belief is then indirect, not the mere unreflective reduction of meaning to belief we get in traditional religious metaphysics.

---

11   VI.5.c. The ontological argument is found in St Anselm's *Proslogion* and Descartes' *Meditations*, and summarized in any introduction to the philosophy of religion.

3.c. The Tapering of Ineffability

> The concept of ineffability is a negative application of representationalism to assert that we can't represent profound experiences – an assertion that assumes we can represent more normal experiences. Mystics can and do discuss profound experience, even if communication or expression of it gets incrementally harder, because our ability to do so depends on association rather than representation. An embodied approach to our experiences allows us to take responsibility for our interpretation of them.

The failure to properly understand embodied meaning and its implications has also created another structural problem in the framing of discussion around profound experience of any kind – such as religious experience, deep meditation experience, or sublime artistic experience. Such experiences often continue to be considered 'ineffable', that is, beyond description. The counter-dependence here between the whole concept of ineffability and that of representational describability ('effability') is often missed, with once again the framing of the models we use being driven by belief, rather than by the practical need to create the conditions for provisional judgement through the use of alternative models for the *meaning* of what we are discussing. Ineffability often interacts with the subtilization slope already discussed in 2.h, to oddly produce more and more elaborate verbal formulations for things we are theoretically unable to talk about. The Zen Buddhist tradition is particularly prone to this. According to Zen, the words we use are merely fingers pointing towards the moon (the object itself), not to be confused with the moon itself,[1] yet at the same time Zen produces voluminous paradoxical discussions of that very 'moon', all of which is intended to stimulate us into a discontinuous leap of realization.

Let us be clear that if meaning is embodied, then there is no representation beyond a specific practical context: but if there is no representation, there is no ineffability either. The failure of representationalism does not imply that we should react against it to assert the opposite (that nothing can be represented) in certain instances of 'ineffable' experience, because we cannot do this without a constant implicit assumption that 'normal' experiences are, by contrast, effable or representable. Our language is a complex

1   Shigetsu (1961).

pattern of associations built on our experience, and we can make those associations with the most profound and mysterious experiences, just as we can with the most everyday practical ones, or with the discussion of 'facts' based on what seem to be widely shared models. It may be *harder* to frame what we experience as more profound and far-reaching experiences in ways that we judge to be adequate, whether for the purposes of communication or of expression, but that is a difficulty in finding shared models, not a lack of any possible model that we can try to use. We constantly mistake this difficulty in finding appropriate shared models to communicate such meaning with the loss of a representation that we never had in the first place.

It is clearly not the case that we 'cannot talk about' profound mystical experience. Mystics claim not to be able to talk about it, but then they do talk about it, often at very great length. What they are doing when they talk (or write) about it is usually sharing symbols that they have associated with deeply inspiring experience, often using the metaphors that have developed into idealized spiritual models in a particular tradition of mystical practice. For example, in Christianity they are likely to use symbols of God, which are associated with experiences of open potential going beyond previous assumptions or identifications, and helping us to access awe, wonder, and expansive emotion.[2] In Buddhism they may discuss enlightenment, drawing on an archetypal function that is similar (the God archetype), even if the surrounding philosophical models used to interpret it are totally different.[3] Alternatively, in Buddhism, the *jhanas* are described as a series of increasingly integrated temporary states, where mindful awareness, concentration, and positive emotion reach extraordinary levels of intensity.[4] Far from not being able to describe such states, Buddhist tradition offers ways of describing them that are of enormous value, especially for people from other traditions who have yet to engage with the models that tradition offers. However, both the states themselves and the descriptions of them have readily acknowledged limitations. These limitations are not in any way 'intrinsically' different from the ones we might face when trying to describe a mug in front of us, or the experience of seeing a bird fly between two trees. Either way, words

2   Ellis (2018) 7.b.
3   Ellis (2022) 4.f.
4   Ellis (2019) pp. 30–4.

always fail us in the sense that we cannot represent that experience fully. However, they do not fail us in the sense that we cannot associate symbols with that experience, and try to communicate it by sharing those symbols. With sufficient shared models, sympathy, and receptivity, what we manage to share may sometimes be very powerful for others. The special claims of ineffability applied to particular special experiences, then, are no more than the general conditions applied to the symbolization of any experience whatsoever.

Buddhist, Christian, and also Hindu spiritual traditions have often fallen back on what is known as the *via negativa* when discussing mystical experience.[5] We cannot talk positively about God or about enlightenment, they say, but we can say what it is *not*: it is not the world or the ego, nor any other of our projections. This approach can help us to disengage from positive representationalism, but it still leaves us with the basic framing of expectation that representation is the model of meaning we should use when discussing mystical experience. The limitations of the *via negativa* as a source of inspiration have also long been noted by Christians who prefer to talk positively about God: we cannot associate meaning very strongly with abstract negations, because they are too far removed from right-hemisphere experience of meaning. If we can shift that model of meaning, the *via negativa*, or any other paradoxical model, should become unnecessary. Instead we should be able to talk positively about that experience, using whatever models we wish, but with an awareness of the provisionality of those models.

An attenuation of meaning is required as we enter the increasingly abstract realms required to discuss agnostic stances on metaphysical claims around religious experiences – though not necessarily required to positively symbolize religious experiences themselves (poetry may convey this more directly). This attenuation of meaning is a product of the increasingly effortful processing that we need to go through to comprehend abstraction, working back down the tree of meaning via models and metaphors to make links with more immediate associative experience. When negation is added to an abstract model, yet another layer is added to that effortful processing, as it is harder for us to maintain a sense of the complement of an idea (what it is not) than of what it is.[6] The difficulties in grasping

---

5   Ellis (2018) pp. 164–6.
6   Darley, Kent, & Kazanina (2020).

negations are hardly surprising when we consider how much wider a reference they normally have within the terms of a particular model: for instance, there are a great many more non-ravens than there are ravens, and the complex idea of non-ravens include boots, corporations, crows, ants, and many other things that we can only encompass very abstractly in one go.

This effortful processing can, of course, be reduced through training and practice, which is why academics or other highly-trained people can often move through the abstractions of their specialism with apparently greater ease than they can through concrete ideas. The same point, then, applies to discussion of 'ineffable' experiences: the symbols we have adopted to discuss them can come to seem easy and natural with sufficient practice, so that we can even eventually substitute theological abstractions for religious experience itself. 'Ineffability', however, is merely a theological abstraction. The addition of a negative element to try to categorize profound experience makes it ever harder to recall the experience itself with the immediacy that is required for it to fulfil its archetypal function.

The concept of ineffability also takes us ever further from the responsibility we need to feel for our experiences and their interpretation. If we believe that the experience we had is almost beyond us, at best that we can relate to it with the tips of our fingers, we are hardly likely to be able to relate to the idea of taking responsibility for it. This point is reinforced by the most common academic accounts of mystical experience – for instance William James' idea that mystical experience is *noetic*, providing mysterious knowledge which is completely non-negotiable, imposing itself on us from without.[7] It is this idea of religious or mystical experience as beyond us, however, that bypasses our awareness of the uncertainty with which we engage with it, and leads us instead to substitute entirely abstracted false certainties – that God has spoken to us, or that we have grasped the intrinsic secrets of the universe. Before we jump to these interpretations, we need to start by acknowledging that *we have to interpret* what we have experienced, and that it could be interpreted in a variety of ways. The concept of ineffability only reduces our ability to do this, by reinforcing an absolutized model in which we either have complete control or none at all – not an experienced, stretchable degree of control.

7   James (1902) p. 380.

The concept of ineffability, then, is parasitic on that of representationalism, and should be re-examined along with representationalism. People often mistake it for a recognition of uncertainty or an open-mindedness in the face of the infinite – but actually it is a dogmatic view of the meaning of the language we use when trying to process or communicate profound experiences. It has done a lot of damage through its constant reinforcement of the false dichotomies that are often imposed on our experiences of inspiring meaning, leading us away from more concrete (and thus meaningful) ways of understanding our experience and taking responsibility for it. We would do much better to substitute incremental ways of talking about the difficulties we may have with discussing and understanding profound experiences, and of nevertheless talking about them – though with full provisionality.

3.d. Non-linguistic Symbols and Beauty

> Representationalists tend to see non-linguistic symbols as either 'subjective' because non-propositional, or 'objective' by indirect means – but neither is applicable to embodied meaning. Instead, non-linguistic symbols are meaningful through schemas and metaphors like linguistic ones, though with some further schemas specific to the visual arts and music. They differ from linguistic symbols in offering more direct access to aesthetic forms of beauty, that stimulate attention in direct response to sensual experience.

If we are to take embodied meaning seriously, this also implies a distinct change in the dominant attitude to meaning, where linguistic meaning has been taken to be the norm. Representationalism defines meaning in solely linguistic terms, since other kinds of symbols are not propositional, and thus cannot gain their meaning from any potential representation of 'reality'.

By 'other kinds of symbols', I mean for instance significant objects, visual art, icons, music, or other significant sensory experience. A significant object could be a tree on your daily walk, or an ornament on your mantelpiece. Visual art might mean the visual image in a painting, or the significant design of a pot. Icons are simplified and standardized instances of visual art, whether used on shrines or on computer screens. Music can be understood as meaningful tunes, rhythms, chords, or phrases. Other symbolic sensory experiences might include associations of touch (like disgust on touching a cold, clammy object like a slug) or associations of scent or taste (the welcome of the smell of baking bread, or Proust's chain of memories set off by eating madeleine cake). We could interpret any of these using propositions, but they are not themselves propositional: rather they carry meaning for us through the links we have developed with them in the course of our lives.

The meaning of non-linguistic symbols has to be accounted for by representationalists in a secondary way, either by arguing that non-linguistic meaning is 'subjective' (and thus second-class when compared with the 'objective'), or by identifying those symbols with the 'objective' information they can be claimed to indirectly offer. Either of these approaches maintains a false dichotomy between representation and its absence, along with a confusion of meaning with belief. Non-linguistic meaning can be readily understood without any of these issues, if we simply account for all meaning in the same associative and embodied way.

The supposed 'subjectivity' of non-linguistic meaning arises from the ways in which we obviously have different responses to it. A picture that for one person is a duck is for another a rabbit. A Beethoven sonata that for one person is a sublime experience of subtle pleasure, for another is a dreary piece of overdone pomposity. This 'subjectivity', however, is present in all meaning whatsoever, including the meanings of words and of propositions, because, as I explained in section 1, meaning is dependent on individual experience of symbols. The idea that any symbol is 'subjective', then, tells us nothing whatsoever distinctive either about the symbol or about the way it is meaningful, and clearly does not help us distinguish between one kind of symbol that is 'subjective' and another that is not. At most, there are meanings that are more or less widely shared, as I discussed above in 2.d. Those shared meanings are clearly present just as much in our responses to non-linguistic symbols as in linguistic ones. For instance, we are likely to have some commonality as well as some difference in our experiences of a picture of a hungry dog, just as we are to the meaning of the word 'dog', or the proposition 'the dog is hungry'.

On the other hand, those who are already convinced of the profound value of the visual arts and music may try to justify them as 'objective' in their meaning in some sense, maintaining the subjective v objective framework but merely flipping the polarities. They may argue, for instance, that aesthetic experience or artistic symbols can give us access to 'reality'; a claim that parallels the approach to religious experience discussed in the previous chapter, and makes exactly the same unnecessary assumptions. This access to 'reality' may be thought of in a Neoplatonic way, as inherent in the universe but accessed through understanding of its form, or even in the process by which the artist encounters its form.[1] Alternatively, they may argue that the value of non-linguistic symbols can be intellectually translated or reduced, perhaps with the aid of psychological or neuroscientific evidence, so that their meaning becomes

1   This approach originates in Plotinus's *anima mundi*, which in turn makes use of Plato's view of the Forms of the universe as subject to intelligible and essential laws revealing metaphysical truths – forms that can be revealed by the arts in intuitive ways as well as by mathematics. In more recent writing it can be found in Fideler (2014), and (unfortunately) in McGilchrist (2021).

representationally apparent.² Perhaps the arts challenge us to reconsider our beliefs, or perhaps they are judged to have a function of maintaining social conformity or social adaptation. Such arguments may offer some (one-sided) insights into the functions of the arts for us, but cannot offer the whole story, and of course ignore the individuality of meaning for each person.

These arguments about the arts and their 'objective' functions can also be seen as founded on assumptions about beauty, an area that deserves the more detailed discussion which I will make in volume VII of this series.³ In brief, I would argue that there is more than one kind of beauty, and thus more than one way that non-linguistic symbols can be meaningful to us and stretch our awareness. With a variety of forms of beauty, the meaning of any given experience of it will vary between individuals, even whilst beauty may preserve a similar overall value that we can try to describe in provisional universal terms. I will say a little more about the different forms of beauty below. However, the framing that understands this meaning as 'objective' is mistaken from the start, and is the result of importing representationalist assumptions, even when used by people who see themselves as going beyond representationalism.

To try to understand meaning as 'subjective' or 'objective' is to continue to confuse meaning with belief, as well as to impose an unnecessary dichotomy. In our practical judgements we need to distinguish between beliefs that are justified and thus provisionally accepted as the basis of action, and ones that are not and thus rejected as a basis of action. Such beliefs clearly have to be propositionally framed when made explicit, even though they are often implicit (we may not think 'this drowning child needs saving', but we believe it and act accordingly). The qualities that we may associate with 'objectivity', such as taking account of new information, thus need to be incrementally applied to our judgements about possible beliefs, not absolutely between 'subjectivity' and 'objectivity'. Meaning, however, only offers us the potential materials from which such beliefs may be assembled. The concepts of 'subjectivity' and 'objectivity' do not apply to meaning, even indirectly or obliquely. Where non-linguistic symbols are concerned, then, it is doubly inappropriate to unthinkingly adopt a framework of

---

2   This is 'aesthetic cognitivism': see Christensen, Cardillo, & Chatterjee (2023).
3   VII.1, 2, & 3.

'subjectivity' or 'objectivity'. Non-linguistic symbols cannot even be assembled into propositions used to form beliefs, let alone become the basis on which we could justify or reject those beliefs.

Representationalist approaches to the meaning of non-linguistic symbols thus unavoidably founder on this dichotomy. To instead offer an adequate account of the meaning of non-linguistic symbols in embodied terms, we need to take account both of their similarities to language and of their distinctive non-linguistic features. They are similar to language in being basically associative, and in the schematic and often metaphorical basis of their meaning for us. They are different, however, in their capacity to bypass left-hemisphere processing and to be overwhelmingly processed in the right hemisphere. The separation they offer from the conceptual models we often rely on in linguistic meaning also means that non-linguistic symbols can have a hotline to our integrated attention (and even help to develop that attention). That's a hotline that linguistic propositions are less likely to have, impeded as they are by a further level of left-hemisphere processing. That hotline to our integrated attention is *beauty*.

Mark Johnson offers an excellent summary of the role of schemas and metaphors in the meaning of non-linguistic symbols. Indeed, it could be said that schematic features, developed through prototyping, are even more obviously a feature of non-linguistic symbols than of linguistic ones. Drawing on the work of Rudolf Arnheim, Johnson shows how we search for prototypical features in any sensory experience – indeed that those prototypical features *shape* the experience itself. Far from having an experience of an object and then categorizing it intellectually, our perceptual experience is itself already in a *gestalt* form. For instance, given a pattern of dots, we fill in the gaps between them during the process of perception to *see* a continuous object, eliding and simplifying any ambiguities in the pattern.[4]

Our embodied experience creates close associations between objects, verbally defined qualities, and visual or other sensory properties. For instance, a jagged line in a drawing or painting could not be described as 'smooth' or 'relaxing' – instead it is associated with anxiety, nervousness, and discontinuity. A similar object depicted with jagged lines or smooth lines will thus have a very different

---

4   Johnson (2007) pp. 226 ff.

meaning for us,[5] not because of words we are applying to it, but because of the associative meaning with which we experience the visual image itself. In the same way, everything we engage with in a work of visual art, from its subject to its form, technique, and medium, can contribute to a meaning directly experienced in that work of art.

Works of visual art can be shaped directly by many of the schemas listed in 1.g, for instance:

- source-path-goal, as we trace a visual path through a picture
- container, as we focus our attention on what is inside a particular visual frame and distinguish it from what is beyond that frame
- centre-periphery, as we focus more directly on an object in the centre of a picture and less on the remainder
- balance, which helps to create a sense of geometric harmony when symmetrical features of a painting offer equal weight, even when there is variation in their form
- perspective (a schema that seems to be specific to visual art): the meaning that we get from a work of art having a standpoint parallel to the one we have outside the work of art

Any of these schemas can offer us a positive impetus to integrated attention on a work of visual art – or the opposite, as our expectations of beauty are broken and we experience ugliness instead. Symmetrical balance and strong contrasts are particular sources of beauty to us, reflecting the shaping of the balance and container schemas on our attention.

When it comes to musical symbols, we similarly have associations between the auditory properties of a piece of music and other, verbally defined, qualities, with the difference that those auditory properties need to be experienced in relation to each other over a short time period. Rhythm and melody, which I mentioned as likely schemas for music in 1.g, both require us to relate sounds to each other over time, as they form patterns in our perception. Both of these schemas are highly meaningful and impactful on us because of their direct relationships to heartbeat or pulse (in the case of rhythm) and emotional expression in the voice (in the case of melody).[6] A fast

---

5   Ibid. p. 224.
6   Johnson (2007) p. 237, drawing on Sessions (1941).

rhythm thus has strong associations with increase in heart-rate, and thus with excitement, a slower one with relaxation. The voice has strong associations with emotional bonding and reassurance, going back to our experience of the mother's voice in infancy. Linked to these schemas specific to music are also ones that are shared with linguistic meaning, such as these:

- iteration: music often achieves its effects through repetition, but with slight variations to maintain interest.
- cycle: the movement of a piece from a 'home' key to a different but related key, then back to the home key, or the variation of a melody followed by a return to the original melody, form a cyclic basis of meaning familiar to musicians.
- balance: the balancing of musical phrases and the experiences of harmonies (which metaphorically 'balance' different notes) also feed into the rich mixture that makes music so meaningful, and often beautiful, to us.

Any schema that helps to structure our attention can form the basis of an experience of beauty, as previously isolated sources of interest and energy are drawn together or integrated. We can experience beauty directly in the way our attention is shaped, or from the energies brought together in symbolic association. This forms the basis of the distinction that I will explore in greater depth in volume VII of this series – namely that between *aesthetic beauty* and *symbolic beauty*. Both kinds of beauty arise from the integrative shaping of our attention by meaning, but in the case of aesthetic beauty, this is from meaning formed directly from a sensual experience, whilst in the case of symbolic beauty, it is from meaning we import from prior association with symbols (whether linguistic or non-linguistic) *applied* to a new sensual experience.

To experience this distinction, imagine the difference between the beauty of a Zen garden and the beauty of a Renaissance Annunciation painting. The Zen garden primarily makes an impression on us because of the clear contrasts and balance in the visual experience of the garden itself (not because of the associations of the garden with Zen, although these may also be present). The Annunciation scene, on the other hand, is beautiful primarily because of what the figures of the angel and of Mary mean by association, in a rich cultural context combining religion with artistic tradition. If I viewed the scene without understanding of the world-shaking significance attached to what the angel is telling her about the potential within her, the scene would lack much of the power and meaning that I would otherwise attribute to it. There may also be further aesthetic beauty in the composition of the Annunciation scene – for instance in the spacing of the figures in relation to each other, or in the lapis lazuli blue of Mary's robe: but if you focus only on this, you will miss the central source of its beauty in the way it renews and draws upon our symbolic associations.

The distinctive potential of non-linguistic symbols can be found in their great potential to augment symbolic beauty with aesthetic beauty. The meaning of words comes overwhelmingly from their symbolic associations – though even here, aesthetic beauty may also be present in more formal features of the use of words, of the kind that are most obvious in poetry. The arrangement of words into rhythms, rhymes, assonances or consonances, or perhaps onomatopoeic features of the words themselves (e.g. growl, trill) can add the power of aesthetic beauty by focusing our attention on their meaning, and at the same time broadening that meaning. However, in most cases the meaning of the words is still symbolic. If we compare this to the effect of a non-linguistic symbol, such as a painting or a passage of music, though, the scope for aesthetic beauty greatly increases, and may often be the dominant feature. In the case of entirely instrumental music, we may not be aware of any particular symbolic meaning at all, but rather respond immediately to the aesthetic features of its rhythm, melody, and harmony.

The distinctiveness of non-linguistic symbols, then, is very much a matter of degree. We cannot separate them absolutely from linguistic symbols in the way that representationalism has typically done. Instead, we need to realize that all symbols have an embodied meaning dependent on association, and cease to privilege what we think of as representational language beyond that. The non-linguistic symbols of the visual arts, ritual, and music then begin to take much more of their rightful place in a fuller experience of meaning – one in which beauty can continue to inspire us without being reduced to mere representation.

3.e. Representationalism and Religion

> The representationalist dominance of religious traditions is not inevitable or essential, but nevertheless an overwhelmingly evident fact. This dominance is explicitly evident in beliefs about the revelation of the Qur'an in Islam, the dogmatic pronouncements of the Catholic Church, and the tradition of *Buddhavacana* in Buddhism, even though this needs to be offset against the more marginal mystical and liberal elements in all these traditions.

In the final three chapters of this section, I will be concerned with tracing the effects of representationalism more fully in three different cultural spheres where it has had an especially damaging impact: religion, philosophy, and politics. If we are to take embodied meaning seriously, it will mean disentangling our view of these spheres from various entrenched representationalist assumptions that in many ways may have come to seem essential or necessary to them. This is far from an easy task. In the process, I will also be beginning to introduce the concept of *fragmentation* of meaning – that is, the lack of a basis for mutual understanding that representationalism (whether explicit or implicit) creates. Fragmentation is defined and explored more fully in section 4 of the book.

I am starting with religion, because religion seems to provide the earliest evidence of representationalist assumptions. These assumptions arise from revelatory belief, which applies a cognitive model in which representationalism is a required frame, just as the model for 'Tuesday' requires a seven-day week.

In *A Systemic History* I wrote about the ways that we do *not* have to assume metaphysical belief (with its attendant representationalism) for the earliest forms of religion, despite the habits of scholars who interpret the earliest religious symbols (such as red ochre markings on caves) in these entrenched terms.[1] In *Archetypes in Religion and Beyond* I also distinguished between practical and dogmatic forms of religion, following Jung's view that religion has a valuable human function in human integration, through the inspirational relationship with archetypes that it develops.[2] So I begin from a point that challenges the widespread ways that representationalism has dominated our view of religion. The purpose of this

1   III.3.c & III.4.a.
2   Ellis (2022) 1.g.

chapter, though, is the more critical one of tracing that domination and its effects.

However one may wish to helpfully channel religious tradition, it cannot be denied that for the majority of religious groups, apart from a highly-educated liberal fringe, religion is based on propositional revelation. That means that propositions with absolute metaphysical status are claimed to be derived from God – or perhaps from Nature, or some impersonal source of the essential truths of the universe, or from those with religious experiences that give them access to universal truths. Revelatory beliefs assume that there is an absolute source of truth, which is then encountered in the world in the form of propositions that represent it. Even groups that may start off with a more mystical approach to religion can still end up in practice believing in propositional revelation, because of the habitual metaphysical forms that they use to express shared intuitions. Whatever their source, if they are to bear this kind of 'truth', these propositions must be interpreted in terms of a meaning that is separate from the interpreter – the non-divine human being receiving the divine truth. This divine revelation either represents divine truth as a separate object, or an idea of divine truth in human beings.

Any recognition that meaning is created metaphorically by individual human beings, that meaning is not essentially propositional, and that the meanings of the same symbols vary between different people would be fatal for the authority of propositional revelation. Hence the focus for all religious groups that believe in it must remain closely on the propositions themselves and their relationship with the divine truths they are said to refer to. Varying individual interpretations must be strongly discouraged, because they detract from the authority of the representational text. Theological strategies have to be developed to maintain the authority of the text.

I will briefly survey the three great universal religions here, to give more idea of the evidence for representationalism in these religions, and also to assess its extent.

The first is in Islam, which in many ways offers the clearest available example of a fairly uniform belief in propositional revelation.[3] According to Islamic belief, the words of the Qur'an were given to Muhammad in the Cave of Hira by God. The angel Jibreel told Muhammad to *recite* and the words sprang to his lips. Muhammad

3   See Ellis (2022) 5.k & l for a slightly more detailed and slightly more positive discussion of the role of archetypes and their projection in Islam.

received *wahi* (inspiration) or *tanzil* (descending truth) from God, described by Farid Esack as 'A letter from God, written by God and read out by the Prophet'.[4] According to tradition, the text of the different *suras* of the Qur'an was then remembered by Muhammad, recited to others at different times, and written down on various objects that were stored in a chest, later to be compiled into the book of the Qur'an.

In this way, the belief is maintained that the words of God are directly transmitted into the Qur'an. This emphasis on the words themselves is maintained particularly by recitation of the Qur'an from memory by Muslims around the world in the original classical Arabic, coupled with the belief that the only true Qur'an is the Arabic Qur'an. Children are first taught to recite the Qur'an by rote in *madrassahs* (Qur'an schools), a procedure which it is assumed must precede any attempt to understand, interpret, or appreciate it.[5] This can only be based on a major misunderstanding of the meaning of the Qur'an for those children, for whom the Qur'an could only serve any function through an imaginative relationship with the meaning of its words. Instead of developing that relationship, children taught in this way are constantly forced into a purely goal-driven memorization of text in the left hemisphere, because of the representational relationship with truth this text is said to have for others. Children taught in this way are being inculcated with representationalism of a particularly extreme and alienating kind from a very early age. Of course such approaches are by no means unique to Islam, and resemble the way that Latin grammar was taught in Europe in earlier ages, but Islamic *madrassah* education offers a particularly regressive bastion representing the extreme effects of unquestioned representationalism in the world today.

The other stratagem for avoiding questions of interpretation in Islam is the legalization and professionalization of interpretation. Although there is no priesthood, and Muslims pride themselves on the direct relationship of all believers to Allah and to his text, interpretative questions are in practice handled by the *ulema*, the community of Qur'anic scholars. This scholarly community predominantly handles interpretative issues not in a philosophical or literary way, but in a legalistic way in which the consensual tradition

4   Esack (2002).
5   Riaz (2008) p. 13.

of previous rulings *(ijma)* is an important guide, third in authority only to the Qur'an itself and the sayings of the Prophet *(Sunnah)*.[6] In the Shi'a tradition, the *mujtahids*, or rightly guided leading scholars, are believed to have contact with the hidden imam, who provides ongoing divine revelation in addition to the Qur'an.[7] At no point, in practice, is it open to a practising Muslim – apart from those living in modern liberal societies – to interpret the Qur'an in a way that is substantially different from tradition. Not only is the Qur'an itself handled in a way that allows for it to have only one divine meaning, but every other aspect of life must be understood in accordance with the meaning of the Qur'an. More than anything else, this is imposed by the religious discipline of prayer five times daily, using a prescribed formula that reinforces Qur'anic teaching: an exercise that, when fully practised, may exert such a profound cultural conditioning as to almost annihilate the emotional meaning of alternative perspectives.

To say that this text-obsessed religious approach has had a fragmenting effect on the world would be an understatement, for at times it has torn that world apart. It has done this, not just by being associated with different beliefs from those of other groups, but also by maintaining a highly disciplined communal imposition of the meaning of these beliefs. The degree of linguistic and cultural unity which has resulted from this within Islam is impressive, but this has come at the expense of repression of all contrary meaning in individual Muslims, and profound fragmentation between Islam and other groups. The much-debated intolerance of Islam is not so much a matter of certain potentially justificatory verses in the Qur'an (such as the 'Sword verse', 9:5) as not being able to understand perspectives that lie beyond its representational framework. Even if the Qur'an itself consistently instructed all Muslims to always be peaceable and tolerant (which is in any case debatable), this would be constantly undermined by the insistence on uniformity of meaning, which, by repressing alternative meanings, in turn undermines the very basis of integration between people that could create peace and tolerance. Such uniformity can be potentially dispelled by the recognition that the meaning of the Qur'an lies in the bodily experience of its readers and auditors, not in its equivalence to anything

6 Doi (1984) pp. 6–8.
7 Momen (1985) pp. 189–91.

beyond them, so Muslim traditionalists must fiercely resist any such recognition.

Apart from the ways in which Muslim representationalism provides a key condition of literalistic interpretation of the Qur'an that can be used by some to justify war and terrorism, there is perhaps no better illustration of the clash between religious representationalism and metaphorical meaning than the Salman Rushdie affair (that is, the controversy created by the publication of *The Satanic Verses* in 1988). The possibility that a novel using some elements from the life of Muhammad might be primarily significant in terms of its meanings rather than in terms of represented beliefs was clearly not one available to the large groups of Muslims worldwide who burned copies of the *Satanic Verses*, and supported the Iranian *fatwa* calling for its author's death. This response also showed a widespread identification by Muslims of cultural meaning with other aspects of values and identity, so that they felt insulted by a writer daring to play with Muhammad's story.

Another example of a religious group reliant on propositional revelation in a slightly different way is the Roman Catholic Church. Catholicism makes substantial use of the Bible, but does not expect its correct meaning to be available to the lay reader unassisted. The role of the RC Church, represented by its priesthood and headed by the Pope, is thus much more formally important. Like the Islamic *ulema*, the Catholic Church interprets sacred scripture, but in this case the scripture does not even formally stand by itself, but only in partnership with the Church's interpretation. To make this point without any ambiguity, the Catholic version of the Bible is preceded by the Church's *Dogmatic Constitution on Divine Revelation*, which affirms that

> *The task of giving an authentic interpretation of the word of God, whether in its written form or in the form of tradition, has been entrusted to the living teaching office of the church alone.*[8]

This despite the fact that

> *To compose the sacred books, God chose certain men who, all the while he employed them in this task, made full use of their powers and faculties so that, though he acted in them and by them, it was as true authors that they consigned to writing whatever he wanted written, and no more.*[9]

8   Paul VI (1965) ch. 1.
9   Ibid. ch. 2.

So, although the Bible (unlike the Qur'an) is admitted to have been composed by human beings, these human beings are nevertheless asserted to have been fulfilling the will of God. There must thus be a single divine meaning for scripture which was somehow communicated through the Biblical writers. They wrote according to the conventions of their time, but (it is asserted) what their symbols represented was a divine meaning. Lest this divine meaning should not be immediately apparent to the reader, the Church is there to interpret the text for her and ensure that the divine meaning is the one understood.

This mediating role of the Church is again re-created in the eucharist or mass, the central symbolic ritual of the Catholic as of other Christian churches. However, in the Catholic mass it is the Church, represented by the priest, who turns the bread and wine into essentially the body and blood of Christ, and it is participating in the mass that represents the salvation of Christ's redemption, bestowed not directly by Christ but through the mediating role of the Church.[10] The symbolic power of this ritual is reinforced by the other sacraments (baptism, confirmation, confession, marriage, ordination, and extreme unction), which again can only be bestowed by the Church. These rituals may well have all kinds of potent meanings for those who participate in them – meanings that in practice help to motivate people in continuing to practise them, but for the dogmas of the Church they have only one true meaning that is represented by them and can be given an equivalent in words.

Catholic representationalism thus depends not only on the Bible, but on the Church with its papal proclamations and its formal role in ritual. There is only one admissible meaning to scripture, that defined by the Church, and the Church's teaching as defined by the Pope. As in Islam, this authority is constantly reinforced through the communal discipline of ritual.

It is the Church's representationalism that supports its dogmatism, and its dogmatism that has supported its metaphysical teachings through the ages. This has involved not just the repression of alternative beliefs and the conflict between Catholic beliefs and other beliefs – represented classically by the Crusades and the Inquisition

---

10 See 'The Real Presence of Christ in the Eucharist' from *Catholic Encyclopedia*: http://www.newadvent.org/cathen/05573a.htm

– but the repression of alternative meanings in the mind of the individual believer, who even today is not allowed to interpret the Bible in a way not sanctioned by the *curia*. The doctrine of papal infallibility firmly sets not only the beliefs of the Church, but also the meanings within which these beliefs are expressed. In 1979 the theologian Hans Küng was stripped of his permission to teach theology by the Vatican for questioning papal infallibility.[11] Until 1966 the Vatican even still maintained a list of forbidden books: a strong indication that, like Ayatollah Khomeini who issued the Rushdie *fatwa*, the Pope did not understand the role of meaning as play.

The fragmenting effects of representationalism in Islam and Catholicism should be set against other movements within those broad religious groups that have maintained a larger base of meaning alongside its impoverishment at the top. The Sufi movement in Islam had a crucial role in maintaining popular allegiance to the formal Sunni Islam of the sultan during the earlier years of the Ottoman Empire.[12] It did this by providing a wider range of symbols whereby people could make links between Islam and common experience – for example through the veneration of saints, frowned upon in formal Islam, and through the cultivation of mystical experience, which allowed people to relate to the *meaning* of God in a much more ambiguous framework separated from beliefs. The same can be said of popular and mystical forms of Catholicism, such as the veneration of Irish saints. Widespread support for the austerity of representationalism can only be maintained in the long term if the right hemisphere is to some extent catered for rather than merely repressed.

Traditional Theravada Buddhism, too, appears to adopt propositional revelatory ideas through its belief that the words of the Buddha are recorded in the Tipitaka (Pali Canon). Texts that are accorded the status of *Buddhavacana* (word of the Buddha) are unquestionable sources of authority.[13] Here the revelatory element comes, not from God, but from the Buddha's access to the state of enlightenment revealing universal truths, also extended to the similar access attributed to other enlightened figures, or leading

11 https://www.washingtonpost.com/archive/politics/1979/12/19/vatican-rules-kung-guilty-of-heresy/fa2c354f-7379-49b6-bea5-3db7689480d2/ (accessed 2023).
12 Lewis (1963) pp. 152 ff.
13 Lamotte (1983).

disciples that were in contact with the Buddha. We find the same devotion to the texts themselves, as they are memorized and recited by specialist scholar-monks, and the books even put on shrines as objects of veneration. We even find the belief that the Buddha's true meaning can be better understood in the original Pali.[14] The same term, *dhamma*, is also used to conflate the ideas of universally true teachings, Buddhist teachings, and the books of the Pali Canon.[15]

However, in general the Buddhist tradition has a much better record on creating and tolerating a wide range of meanings than, say, Islam. Buddhist teachings have gone through major processes of reform at the beginnings of the Mahayana and Vajrayana which opened them up to completely new interpretations: particularly in the case of the Tantra, these meanings could be startlingly different from the previously accepted ones. The meaning of 'Buddha' for a Tantric might be an antinomian symbolic figure who breaks the monastic rules rather than following them. Even in the monasteries, there has also always been a diversity of philosophical interpretation in Buddhism: particularly in early Buddhism, followers of a rival school might practice and debate side by side in the same monasteries. There has not been any central dogmatic authority equivalent to the pope. The doctrines of *anatta* (non-essentialism) and emptiness help to discourage absolutization of propositions, though they may not always succeed in preventing it in practice. The variety of symbolic forms used in Mahayana Buddhism, particularly Tibetan Buddhism, is bewildering, and probably good evidence that the diversity of interpretation consistent with embodied meaning has been more widely practised in Buddhism than in other religions.[16]

In contrast to the clearly enforced representationalism dominant in Islam and Catholicism, then, Buddhism offers a much more mixed picture. There is often a formal recognition that words do not ultimately reflect realities, yet this attitude conflicts directly with a reverence for texts and the notion that the Buddha's words are conveyed directly by texts.

In Protestant Christianity, a much greater emphasis on the direct relationship between the individual and the Bible might seem at first to have a less fragmenting effect than Catholicism. Although

14   The Original Language Fallacy: see V.2.h.
15   Ellis (2019) 6.f.
16   See Ellis (2022) 5.c on the archetypal value of these symbolic forms.

Protestant sects have (in an organizational and belief-based sense) fragmented, this very fissiparousness indicates a richer climate of competing interpretations of the Bible. More liberal Protestant churches even recognize the value of a variety of interpretations of the Bible.

However, at the same time the puritanical disapproval of art and the narrow emphasis on the written word in Protestantism (particularly early Protestantism) has made it highly representational. McGilchrist provides evidence for how far early Protestantism was dominated by left-hemisphere processing, reflected in its preferences for unambiguous certainty, for word over image, and for abstraction over physicality.[17] More fundamentalist Protestants have often proceeded on the assumption that there was only one representationally correct interpretation of the Bible, even if it was up to individuals to discover that correct interpretation. Today, US fundamentalism is one of the most politically influential sources for the cultural entrenchment of unquestionable representationalism.

Representationalism generally, then, is associated with the overwhelmingly dominant dogmatic aspects of the major religious traditions. Against this tendency we can set the physicality of meditative and mystical traditions in all three universal religions, and the recent opening to a variety of interpretation in the liberal wing of the Protestant tradition. However, the slightest explicit challenge to representationalism itself has come only from a few marginal liberal commentators in recent religious history. McGilchrist complains that in early Protestantism,

> In essence the cardinal tenet of Christianity – the Word is made Flesh – becomes reversed, and the Flesh is made Word.[18]

However, this ironic reversal could also be seen as much more widely applicable to religion as a whole. A process that may begin with intensely meaningful religious experience in individuals, taking over their entire physical experience, rapidly degrades into a set of dead metaphors which then have to be socially imposed through power structures to compensate for the alienation they create. A general requirement for this process of degradation in religion is an overwhelming implicit representationalism whereby the words themselves come to enshrine meaning rather than the experience

---

17 McGilchrist (2009) pp. 314–23.
18 Ibid. p. 323.

of those who hear or read those words. That this is not inevitable, and that embodied meaning could be applied in the sphere of religion, is evident not only from the application of modern theories of embodied meaning, but also from the mystical traditions of all three universal religions.

3.f. Representationalism and Philosophy

> Representationalism has dominated Western philosophy since the theories of Forms and the soul in Plato. Empiricist challenges to Plato still assumed a universal source of meaning distinct from the body, as did the Kantian mediation of rationalism and empiricism. Wittgenstein offered some challenges, but turned to a social reduction of meaning. This dominance has disastrously imposed a polarized metaphysical model on both science and ethics, undermining any incrementality in justification because meaning remained absolutized.

The history of Western philosophy is a history of representationalism. Until at least the middle of the twentieth century, no alternative seems to have been seriously considered. For most of that history, too, representationalism has not been explicit. However, the animating questions have always been ones like 'What is knowledge?', 'What is truth?', 'What is goodness?', and 'What is beauty?': questions that assumed abstract objects of investigation with a meaning distinct from the immediate bodily experience of the investigator. Whether or not in the end the *existence* of such objects beyond ourselves was affirmed or denied, the question was still assumed to be one of a kind of existence that was *represented* by words.

Why this should be the case is clearly brought out in McGilchrist's history of Western thought in terms of left and right hemispheres.[1] Philosophy has always been overwhelmingly the activity by which the left hemisphere has tried to create a coherent representation of the world, even in areas that are more normally handled intuitively by the right hemisphere. The left hemisphere thinks solely in terms of objects of representation. For it to do otherwise requires frequent correctives from the right hemisphere – of a kind which philosophy has often made an effort to exclude, perceiving them as interfering with the purity of its rational representation.

Given this general approach in Western philosophy, then, it is unsurprising if the same assumptions were made about meaning as about other objects of thought. Plato's doctrine of the Forms is probably the earliest piece of Western philosophy that offers us anything like a theory of meaning, and it does this by claiming a rational basis for categories in Forms that can only be known by reason, not through the senses. For example, the meaning of a categorial

1 McGilchrist (2009) pp. 257–427.

term like *horse* is known, not by observing horses, but from a rational Form of the Horse. This provides a criterion for judging whether what we observe is a horse or not. The resemblance of an observed horse to the ideal horse could only be incremental, which was exactly the reason why Plato thought we could not have got the absolute rational form of the horse from experience.[2]

Subsequent philosophers have criticized the essentialism of Plato's theory of meaning, and the assumption that we must have categories prior to the observations where we apply those categories. However, Plato's underlying assumption here that the meaning of 'horse' or any other term is something separate from ourselves remained unquestioned. The debate about whether meaning was based on reason or experience became an important one, but in many ways this obscured the more important debate that should have been going on, as to whether meaning was created within individual experience or had some sort of existence beyond that. Although the empiricists who challenged Plato's rationalism thought that meaning (and thus belief and knowledge) were based on experience, they still assumed that the relevant experience was one that constructed meaning cognitively from information coming from beyond itself.

An early empiricist alternative to Plato can be represented by the theory of ideas and impressions, developed in slightly differing forms by Locke and Hume. For these philosophers, 'ideas' were effectively what is meant by 'meaning'. In Hume's version, ideas are said to be entirely empirical, paler and feebler versions of impressions (which are raw sense-perceptions).[3] Hume apparently denied any role (except that of passive recipient) to the mind in piecing together our perceptions into meaningful ideas. In his eagerness to create a clear alternative to rationalist *a priori* claims about meaning, he completely ignored the constructing and confabulating role of the left hemisphere. To justify scientific knowledge, he thought that meaning must be coming from beyond our bodies. The debate was only about the source of the mental picture – not whether there was a mental picture in the first place.

Whilst the debate about meaning in earlier forms of Western philosophy was thus only that between two forms of

---

2 The theory of Forms can be found in any of Plato's dialogues – especially *Meno, Theaetetus,* and the *Republic.* See VI.2.b for more detail.
3 VI.2.f; Hume 1975 (1777) Sect. 2; Hume 1978 (1740) Part 1.

representationalism, at the same time a debate about the self offered another set of conditions in which representationalism remained unquestioned. Again, Plato set the agenda here with the immortal and rational soul, a soul entirely separate from the body and capable of knowing the Forms. This soul in a sense contained meaning within itself in its rational capacities, but only at the expense of its separation from the body. The rational soul was separated from the appetitive and spirited souls, so that meaning was not based upon, but rather necessarily separated from, energy and physical experience.[4] This model of the rational self possessing meaning was also implicitly followed by the modern rationalist tradition after Descartes.

Hume was the first empiricist philosopher to deny this tradition of understanding the self. He did this, however, by arguing that there was no self as an object of internal (or external) perception, only a bundle of associated mental contents that we assumed to be a self.[5] As in his theory of ideas and impressions, he did this by effectively ignoring the need for a processor of meaning. What made the observing non-self's denial of its own existence meaningful? Hume punctured a few rationalist assumptions here, without really creating a coherent alternative.

It was left to Kant to first recognize that a framework of coherent meaning was one of the schematic prior conditions for meaningful experience as we know it.[6] This did involve a sort of self, but only the self of apperception – that is, a framing set of assumptions giving coherence to experience, along with other schematic frameworks such as time, space, substance, causality, etc. However, Kant assumed that apperception followed a similar pattern in all cases: that is, that we all use the same schematic framework, not directly shared but nevertheless reproduced in each individual human experience. Meaning for Kant was thus assumed to be universal still, even though it was part of the way we understood things rather than the way they were in themselves. Categorization was an intrinsic way in which we ordered the world, which we would all do in the same way as long as we were following consistent rational principles.[7]

4   VI.4.b; Plato (1941) 434D–445B.
5   Hume 1978 (1740) pp. 251 ff.
6   Kant 1929 (1787).
7   VI.2.h.

It is Kant's assumption of a single rational framework, together with the empiricism of Hume, which shaped the development of analytic philosophy from the end of the nineteenth century. The rational framework was increasingly represented by the development of mathematics, and the empirical one by the development of science, whilst one of the prime jobs of philosophy was seen as explaining the nature of the relationship between them. It is this which led to explicit truth-dependent theories of meaning, in which the problem of the relationship between the rational framework and empirical experience was resolved by hypothesizing the former and abstracting the latter: the conditions for meaning (rational framework) are fulfilled *if* (hypothesis) the conditions for truth or falsity can be specified (abstract of empirical experience).

The empirical experience on which meaning is theoretically based here is not one attended by the usual conditions of that experience (i.e. the conditions of the body), but rather an imagined possible empirical experience which merely checks for the presence or absence of the conditions specified by the rational framework. The 'meaning' specified by this theory is neither empirically adequate (since it neglects most of the empirical conditions that accompany experience) nor schematically adequate (since it assumes that a single rational framework *must* be the basis of meaning, as Kant and Plato do). At the most basic theoretical level, we cannot prove that there is only one 'schema' (i.e. idealized model) in which the categories of language must be placed: a paper by Körner has even shown this in the terms of rational argument alone.[8] In terms of the empirical basis of meaning, the idea that a *hypothesis* is an adequate basis on which to base meaning is rather bizarre, given that hypothesis is just one rather abstracted corner of experienced meaning with little connection to most of what we experience as meaningful. I presume, then, that the truth-conditional theory of meaning has been popular for so long only because it appears to bind maths and science together, but it hardly even does this in a satisfactory fashion.

The (implied) theories of the later Wittgenstein, based particularly on the *Philosophical Investigations*,[9] do challenge both the rationalist and empiricist traditions in some ways, as well as the false synthesis of those traditions in the truth-conditional theory. Wittgenstein

8   Körner (1967).
9   Wittgenstein (1967).

attacks the 'picture' theory of meaning, with its claim that meaning consists of a picture of the world built up in a private mind. However, in its place he appears to offer a behaviourist criterion of meaning: that a term is meaningful when it obeys socially constructed rules for the use of that term in its specific context. Whilst this challenges the narrowness of the truth-conditional theory, it does not challenge representationalism, but merely substitutes socially constructed rules for the previous criteria. Wittgenstein ignores meaning experienced by individuals beyond these socially constructed rules, just as Plato ignored experience of meaning beyond rational Forms and Hume ignored constructed individual meaning beyond incoming impressions.

The fragmenting effects of this philosophical tradition of representationalism are substantial, and not confined to the academic world. One basic source of division that I have already noted (see 2.e) is the entrenched distinction between cognitive and emotional forms of meaning, with emotional forms unable to be given recognition under this representationalist regime. Whilst analytic philosophers and linguists regard this as merely a useful distinction, its practical effect has been to shape and direct discussion of semantics in a different direction from that of pragmatics, and to prevent consideration of their interdependencies in basic experience.

However, the effects of philosophical representationalism go far beyond this, given that the truth-conditional theory is the assumed basis of nearly all philosophical discussion about epistemology, metaphysics, ethics, or any other branch of philosophy. Given that philosophy also interacts with other disciplines, this also means that sciences, social sciences, and humanities have adopted truth-conditional assumptions with regard to the status of the theoretical assertions made in those disciplines. In reaction to this, only the arts have remained as a context for non-representational understandings of meaning (of a kind that are almost never made explicit).

Representationalism is assumed in all metaphysical ways of thinking, because it has to be assumed that the absolute realities affirmed or denied in metaphysical propositions gain their meaning from a correspondence with the state of affairs they describe, whether true or false.[10] On an embodied meaning account, by contrast, the

---

10 I.3.a.

meaning of any symbol, propositional or not, metaphysical or not, is always formed from associated experience. Metaphysical propositions understood in embodied terms thus have to be interpreted in terms of experience, in which case they are no longer intrinsically metaphysical, only through absolutizing assertion. The presence of idealized models which apply left-hemisphere judgement within an embodied meaning framework does not fully explain the *meaning* of those metaphysical propositions.

This relationship between representationalism and metaphysics thus accounts for the way in which metaphysics has continued to flourish in all sorts of contexts. Early twentieth century thinkers such as Ayer and Popper were opposed to metaphysics because they perceived it to be incompatible with the use of experience as the test of claims, yet because they maintained representationalism, and failed to identify the denial of metaphysical claims as being equally metaphysical, their philosophies continued to be fertile ground for metaphysics, particularly in the form of naturalism.[11] Analytic epistemologies turned their back on global scepticism because they rightly perceived scepticism as denying all representational claims. The relevance of epistemology to dealing with our experience of doubt then disappeared, as it became uselessly devoted to merely analysing its own conventionally acceptable terms.

Scientific naturalists, on the other hand, have applied scepticism selectively, adopting convenient sceptical arguments in order to attack 'supernatural' claims, whilst ignoring others. They have maintained representationalist assumptions either explicitly in the truth-conditional theory, or implicitly in the belief that scientific theory can represent 'nature'. As a result of representationalism, then, we lost the capacity to apply rigorous and consistent epistemological criteria to science, because these would have to start with the recognition that the meaning of scientific claims can only be incrementally shared, through models that have an embodied schematic and metaphorical basis. If one holds out for the absolute truth or falsity of the conditions for understanding scientific claims, it becomes impossible to apply incremental justification in practice. On the one hand, if scientific theories are consistent with a naturalistic account, they will be assumed as true even when the evidence for them is limited, and on the other hand, if they are not consistent with a

---

11   I.4.a (pp. 93–5).

naturalistic account, they will be assumed to be false on the basis of similarly limited evidence. This helps to account for the short shrift often given to scientists who continue with scientific enquiry but dare to use unorthodox models, such as Rupert Sheldrake.[12] This resistance to incrementalism may not exist in theory, but operates in practice because of the meaning that scientific theory is assumed to have.

The whole justification of science and of scientific theories is thrown into confusion by this philosophical basis. On the one hand sciences are seen as factual according to representationalism, and on the other as incrementally justified according to experience and scientific evidence. Some people then assume that because science is not absolutely justified, it is 'only theory' and give equal justification to all theories, whilst others assert the 'naturalistic' or factual basis of science despite the evidence of its merely incremental justification. Both of these approaches repress the sense of science as incrementally justifiable. The only way to provide clear lines of justification for science is to drop the representationalist assumptions with which it is being interpreted. Justification can then be based on the processes of probabilizing and weighing up that I discussed in *The Five Principles*,[13] used to support provisional beliefs that are entirely compatible with embodied meaning.

If the philosophical basis of science has been thrown into disarray by representationalism, the effect of representationalism on ethics has been even worse. For representationalism applied to ethics immediately implies the fact-value distinction: the meaning of facts is distinct from the meaning of values because facts can be judged to be true or false in terms of representation, whereas values cannot. This distinction makes no sense in embodied meaning terms, because we will experience a degree of meaning for both facts and values. The acceptance of degrees of meaning also implies degrees of justification, rather than an insistence on absolute 'justification or bust' dependent on an isomorphic relationship with hypostatized reality.

The effect of representationalism on views of ethics has again been widespread confusion across society. On the one hand, representationalism insists that the meaning of ethical claims must lie in

---

12 Sheldrake (2012).
13 II.2.f & g.

their potential truth or falsity in relation to a state of affairs, but on the other hand experience suggests that ethics does not make sense in this way, but rather has a degree of justification in experience. Again, this results in polarized views of ethics, either as 'subjective' or as 'true'. As in the case of science, we need an incremental account of *meaning* to deal with the most basic issues in the justification of ethics and thus be more effective in promoting ethical life.[14]

It would be no exaggeration, then, to say that representationalism in philosophy has been a major disaster for Western civilization. What we have achieved has come mainly through incrementalism of belief rather than through considering the more basic conditions of meaning. If we try to incrementalize belief without incrementalizing meaning, we are constantly straining against the gravitational pull of a set of founding assumptions that work against incrementality. Unfortunately, too, the power of representationalism is still entrenched. If there is anyone with a responsibility to change this situation, it is philosophers. But whilst any advancement in a philosophical career depends on engagement with an existing representationalist tradition, academic philosophers have a major disincentive against changing this situation.

---

14 The implications of this argument are developed in VIII.

3.g. Representationalism and Politics

> The effect of implicit representationalism on politics is often to make voters choose from simplistic propositions in which abstract concepts of political ideology are central, but with these concepts understood prototypically and detached from the complexity of their practical application. Concepts like 'tradition', 'justice', and 'freedom', which are interdependent in an embodied context, are separated from that context, thus resulting in much less adequate policy propositions when judged representationally in terms of supposed 'realities'.

Many of the effects of representationalism on politics follow from those on philosophy. The confusion that representationalism creates about the justification of science, by presenting it as a description of reality, also creates confusion about the justification of public policy based on scientific evidence. The confusion that representationalism creates about ethics, by presenting good as a represented element in the universe, also creates confusion about the values that should inform politics.

Political ideology is focused around certain key concepts, which represent values. A useful basic list of such values, grounded in empirical evidence of their usage, can be found in Jonathan Haidt's work,[1] where there are six: authority, loyalty, purity, justice, freedom, and care. The meaning of any such concepts for key values, or of any other important political concepts, is decontextualized by the assumption of representationalism. For instance, we understand issues of justice in isolation from their relationship to freedom (and vice-versa), because we take 'justice' to represent a quality in the world, rather than recognizing its meaning in relation to our bodily experience of approving or disapproving 'fair' or 'unfair' judgements. If we can start to take responsibility for finding things fair or unfair, we can just as easily take responsibility for finding things free or constraining, authoritative or lacking authority, caring or brutal. These are our responses, justifiable to a greater or lesser extent, and carved out of our experience of relating to others in a complex sociopolitical system. Representationalism, on the other hand, helps us to absolutize 'justice', or 'authority', by insisting that their meaning depends on only a relationship with an abstract 'truth' in which alternative values may not appear at all.

1   Haidt (2012).

Whilst these concepts may be better integrated when they are discussed more fully, one of the effects of democracy is to force voters to make judgements about them based on an unintegrated grasp of only one aspect of the meaning of the terms. The politicians' own use of them, for their part, may often not be much better contextualized. Ideological concepts in political discourse, both in fulfilment of Western philosophical tradition and in pursuit of popular accessibility, have to refer to something that is assumed to be true or false, rather than a set of metaphors that may be shared to varying degrees.

These representationalist assumptions are not particularly due to the direct influence of linguistic philosophy over political rhetoric, but rather due to the ways that both are the products of a wider culture of implicit representationalist interpretation. Politics assumes a shared model of implicit representationalism, both amongst politicians and voters, that fragments political discourse. I will focus here on three key concepts that can illustrate this fragmentation: tradition, justice, and freedom.

The underlying ideological rationale for conservatism can offer a strong case for the value of tradition. Tradition, after all, offers proven and tested practice. Ways of thinking and acting that have worked over centuries in the past could be said to have a much stronger basis in experience than innovations. One can add to this the positive case against innovation. New ideas that have been developed only in left-hemisphere representation, rather than in the whole of experience, tend to be naive: there are bound to be many conditions that they fail to address. If there are to be changes, they should be slow and organic, left to society itself to develop in its own time rather than pushed through by political masters.

Thus goes the case for conservatism, often repeated in some form or other against a wide range of proposed reforms, from schools to electoral systems to defence. The trouble is that, interpreted in a representationalist fashion, this argument lacks incrementality. The meaning of 'tradition' in representationalist terms is that of a fixed quantum of habit and custom as it has been practised in the past. However, this time-blind left-hemisphere representation is incapable of taking account of the fact that 'the past' is itself a highly varied thing. As McGilchrist has pointed out, the left hemisphere can sequence points in a represented time, but cannot appreciate the changes in the experience of time itself.[2] It is only if we bring the right hemisphere into an appreciation of a term like 'tradition', that it loses its monolithic significance.

In embodied terms, though, 'tradition' is a concept that we establish through a web of metaphors in relation to our own experience, and which also has its prototype effects. These metaphors relate to a bodily experience which includes that of time actually passing, and which allows us to recognize its variability. This allows us to see tradition incrementally, as no more than a degree of continuity between practices, that, after all, have been in the process of changing in the past as well. At least, it allows us to do this as long as we adopt a model that does not override it by imposing a left-hemisphere representation.

The prototype effects in the meaning of 'tradition' indicate that we all envisage it in different ways and would identify different phenomena as good examples of it. English tradition, for instance, may stereotypically be thought of in terms of cricket matches on summer afternoons and warm beer. For others, though, it may mean getting drunk and sunburnt on a beach in Ibiza, or putting criminals in the stocks. The values identified by Haidt as distinctively conservative (authority, loyalty, and purity) may thus be represented quite inconsistently in our prototypical imaginings of 'tradition'. For example, George Lakoff identifies 'strict father morality' as a common prototype for conservative values, in which the role of the state is understood according to the metaphor of a father who enforces moral behaviour.[3] This clearly emphasizes authority over other values, and moreover highlights only those aspects of authority that are dependent on repression, not those accepted on the basis of mutual recognition of expertise or mutual benefit. Our ideas of tradition are not adequate to even a given tradition as a whole, but have merely appropriated the idea of that whole: generally, instead, they focus on a small selection from that tradition interpreted in a particular limited way.

The three distinctively conservative values may also be supplemented by the 'progressive' values of justice, freedom, and care, but applied in a 'traditional' way. 'Justice' understood traditionally thus may mean giving criminals their just deserts, but not

---

2   McGilchrist (2009) pp. 75–7.
3   Lakoff (2002) ch. 5.

redistributing wealth. Whatever we identify as tradition, even when it incorporates very one-sided versions of various values, becomes the basis of 'conservative' judgements, because these prototypes are taken to represent the reality that absolutely justifies the value. Unlike other kinds of symbols dependent on prototypes (for instance, a species of animal such as 'cat'), we do not have a readily accessible or widely agreed definition of such a term with which to challenge over-reliance on a prototype. It is only more or less in the realm of political philosophy that a person's underlying assumptions about a concept such as 'tradition' are likely to be challenged – not, for instance, in most normal political debate.

The prototype effects that apply to tradition make us ask 'Whose tradition?', 'What tradition?'. In Europe as a whole, for example, compulsory identity cards are quite traditional, whereas in Britain they are not. A Conservative objection to identity cards thus appears to be based specifically on an identification with *British* tradition, which, being the tradition of a smaller area than Europe as a whole, presumably means that the argument that tradition encapsulates experience should apply more strongly in favour of identity cards.

An appreciation of the value of tradition interpreted in embodied terms, then, turns out in practical policy to mean nothing much more than a degree of continuity, together with a degree of caution about new innovations, and does not necessarily involve the rejection of innovations that have been proven through experience elsewhere. Arguably, 'a degree of continuity' is about all any Conservative Party in the world manages to put into practice of Conservative ideology in a rapidly changing world. Yet the meaning of tradition for those who vote for it is likely to be quite different from this. Encouraged by the rhetoric of Conservative politicians who advocate (for instance) 'Victorian values', 'Back to Basics', or 'Matrons cycling to church in the morning mist',[4] the meaning of tradition is likely to be fragmented between its representation as selective nostalgia and its much more compromised meaning when it is applied in any practical context. In other words, we do not follow through what the nostalgia would imply if it was made the basis of a consistent policy, because they are not even linked together in our understanding, let alone in our beliefs. As with much political

---

4   These are all phrases used by John Major, Conservative UK Prime Minister 1991–7, the third one taken from George Orwell.

fragmentation, the gap between these ideas contributes to disillusionment and general cynicism about politics.

Having established some of the basic issues with this first example, I will be briefer in discussing the other two. 'Justice' (or 'fairness') is a term that can be analysed in a whole host of ways – retributively (just deserts), commutatively (fair trade), and distributively. Distributive justice in turn can be understood in terms of equality, desert, or need, with a variety of interpretations even of these. I will not go into the details of this analysis, which can be found in most textbooks of political philosophy. This degree of ambiguity about the meaning of 'justice' alone is enough to cause a good deal of fragmentation, as well as related confusion and conflict. However, more problems arise when even one of these senses of justice is used representationally.

Let's take the example of the arguments made by Nick Clegg, leader of the UK Liberal Democrats in 2013, in favour of a 'mansion tax' – that is, a property tax on high value property. Clegg called this 'the politics of fairness'.[5] Such a tax would be 'fair' in terms of equality: redistributing wealth to a small extent from those who are rich enough to own a large asset to help those who are poorer. However, this will still leave some people in large and luxurious houses whilst others live in bedsits or are homeless, so it would hardly be 'fair' in any complete sense in terms of bringing about equality.

'Fairness', again, turns out to be a matter of degree and a matter of context. According to representationalism, 'fairness' must get its meaning from a state of affairs that could either be true or false. Representationalism could consistently distinguish between different senses of 'fairness' that could be true or false: for example it could specify equality as the relevant sense of fairness. However, 'fairness' to the voter in practice means an idealized, prototypical equality that is then applied even to cases of very marginal changes in the direction of equality, like the mansion tax. A tax that in some ways leaves inequality untouched and takes it for granted, thus misleadingly takes on the mantle of something more radical that actually produces more substantial equality.

If instead the voter interpreted fairness in a way that relied only on her experience of adjusting judgements that take into account

---

5   http://www.theguardian.com/commentisfree/2013/feb/23/nick-clegg-conservatives-politics-fairness (accessed 2023).

discrepancies of resources, she might be able to understand it as making marginal changes to a largely 'unfair' status quo, and indeed as depending on the attitudes of the beneficiary: should the poor be grateful for a bit more welfare made possible by a mansion tax, or rail against the inequality that is taken for granted in the institution of the tax? If Clegg was not delivering his argument in a context of overwhelming representationalism, it might not be misleading to describe the mansion tax as 'the politics of fairness', but in the actual context, almost any use of an ideological term like this creates fragmentation between the politician's pragmatic world and the voter's idealized one.

My final example is freedom: a political value appealed to by ideologues of almost every type. Like tradition, freedom is likely to show prototype effects, and be applied more to some cases than others. Being let out of jail or being freed from slavery might be in our minds when the term 'freedom' is used rhetorically by politicians. The representationalist model commonly applied in understanding such rhetoric will see it as a state that can either be true or false: you're either free or you're not. Yet 'freedom' notoriously depends on the attitudes of the free, whose mental states could be unbounded as they sit in a prison cell, or alternatively imprisoned in deep hatred or craving as they roam the open plains or spend millions of dollars. Can you be free if you're a billionaire in a country with a 75% tax rate? Well, maybe, to a degree, because it depends on your assumptions and the degree of impact 'freedom' has on you in what way. The US is 'The Land of the Free', a phrase that could at best be interpreted as 'The land where some people have relatively less interference in their lives from authorities than other people, on average, depending on their mental states and thus what they consider to be undesirable forms of interference'. The gap between ordinary people's idealizations of freedom and what it means in political reality is again a hugely fragmenting one, perhaps contributing to the widespread development of extreme libertarianism in the US (a development that may in turn contribute to the fragmentation).

What may appear bizarre about this account of political representationalism, I am aware, is that the more complex concepts that I have used, like the complex paraphrase immediately above, to indicate more adequate or embodied meanings (as opposed to left-hemisphere simplifications) are the ones that we commonly regard as more 'rational'. If ordinary people interpret political concepts in an unsophisticated, less 'rational' way, it might be objected, surely this is just a condition we have to get used to, that neither politicians nor other commentators can do much about? What I am suggesting, however, is that the over-simplification of political concepts has little to do with 'rationality', and much more to do with the interference of a socially-supported left-hemisphere dominated model on these concepts. If we merely allowed an understanding of terms like 'tradition' or 'freedom' to emerge out of the interaction of education with experience of these concepts in practical operation, they would be far less over-simplified. One of the unfortunate effects of democracy, however, is that every citizen – or at least those who bother to vote – is forced, often prematurely, into an evaluation of political claims using concepts that are understood in strong dependence on the left hemisphere (conveyed through superficial media discussion), while the right still has insufficient experience on which to create a more sophisticated sense of them. I am not suggesting that there is necessarily a better system of democracy available than one that effectively forces voters' choices in this way, but that given voters' responsibilities, they need a better education in the meanings they work with.

Representationalism has a fragmenting effect on politics, then, by creating the expectation of a single final and correct meaning for key political concepts that have actually developed in a complex field of experience. Whilst politics in practice always depends on compromise and incremental change, our understanding of political concepts constantly undermines this political process by supporting absolute models against which real political change will always be unsuccessfully measured. Far from needing politicians that stick to their principles, we need pragmatic politicians who recognize that moral objectivity does not always arise from principles.

4. The Fragmentation of Meaning

4.a. What are the Fragmentation and Integration of Meaning?

> Meaning is not subject to conflict in the way that desire and belief are, but is subject to fragmentation, which is a lack of connection between different meanings in our experience (and/or in our neural network). Integration of meaning, which connects separated meaningful symbols wherever relevant, reduces the conditions for conflict in a way that is indirect but also still important. Integration of meaning roughly differs from meaning in general in being mainly developed through individual awareness rather than cultural expectations.

So far, this book has been largely focused on contrasting the embodied approach to meaning with representationalism, and making clear the implications of each. To integrate this perspective into Middle Way Philosophy, however, the practical and moral purposes of the embodied approach over the representationalist one need to be highlighted. That means that we need to start focusing more on what we *do* – that is, how we respond to challenges of embodied meaning – rather than only on accounts of how embodied meaning and representationalism operate. The second half of this book, then, will be organized around two concepts that help me to structure that response and to relate it to other strands in Middle Way Philosophy – namely the concepts of fragmentation and integration of meaning. The account of fragmentation of meaning in this section is accompanied by a mind map **[diagram 5]**.

Integration overcomes conflict. The concept of conflict was introduced in *Absolutization* as offering an important psychological perspective on why absolutization is so damaging: that is, that as long as we hold absolute beliefs capable of infinite rationalization, experience cannot have any impact in making us modify our opposing beliefs to make them more compatible (either with those of others, or with our own at different times).[1] Conflict, however, is a feature of opposing desires and beliefs, not of meaning, because meaning

1   I.5.a.

only offers a range of possibilities. As long as we refrain from confusing meaning with belief, no meaning ever conflicts with another meaning. Nevertheless, background conditions of meaning can have a decisive impact on the development of conflict, when the *associations on which embodied meaning is based do not connect with each other to provide a basis of mutual understanding*. This is why we need a concept of *fragmentation of meaning* as distinct from one that tries to apply the concept of conflict more directly to meaning.

Some initial examples to illustrate the fragmentation of meaning could be drawn from a wide range of situations in which humans fail to understand each other. I could hear a Japanese couple speaking to each other in Japanese (a language of which I am ignorant) and fail to understand them. I could try explaining Middle Way Philosophy to a high-school student, and, even if I offered glosses of the terminology, he would probably not understand me. A mother could fail to understand why her teenage son spends five hours a day playing video games. A liberal could fail to understand why a conservative apparently lacks compassion in her attitude to refugees who are desperately seeking refuge in her country, even though the rest of her life is apparently not at all devoid of compassion.

Of course, lack of connection is everywhere, but it is only in particular circumstances that it becomes relevant. Lack of connection as an embodied property is always subject to a relevance criterion that can save us from fruitless concern with speculative hypotheses about things we don't connect with simply because we don't encounter them. The complete meaninglessness of most Chinese characters to me, for instance, is not normally a matter of fragmentation, because it is not relevant in the environment I normally inhabit, where Chinese characters are rarely encountered. The fact that I have no connections or associations to give those characters meaning is thus not an issue, and not a potential source of conflict: however, if I were to move to China, it might start to become one. On the other hand, a parent's failure to understand the relationship between the words of their teenaged son and the emotional states that they are communicating, through a failure to 'connect' with those words, is of obvious relevance to that parent's situation, even if the parent is dismissive and does not regard what the son says as 'relevant' at the time.

The Fragmentation of Meaning 151

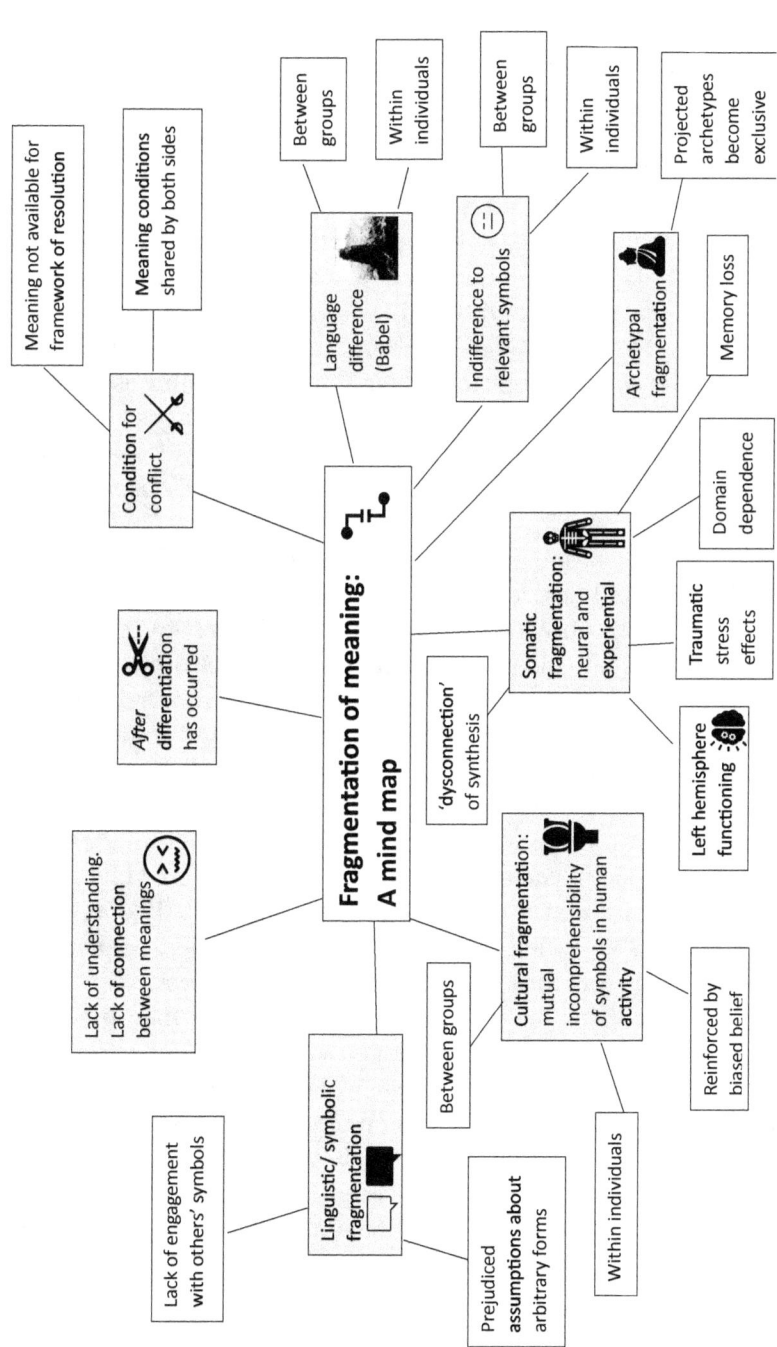

Diagram 5. Fragmentation of meaning: A mind map.

I have already discussed in 1.c how fragmentation differs from differentiation. Differentiation is the separating-out of associations in infancy, to allow discrete associations for the meaning of each symbol. That separating-out of symbols occurs rapidly as a child learns, driven by the need for basic meaning with which the child participates in his/her society. Strong cultural expectations encourage differentiation at every step of the way. Fragmentation, on the other hand, is not a separation that allows new meaning, but rather a gap that frustrates it. It begins at the point (vaguely defined though it may be) where exploration takes over from socio-cultural expectation, and where individual awareness starts to supplement group habit. My guess is that children cannot really experience the fragmentation of meaning until their sense of meaning is already differentiated to a fair degree, and their net of meaning is becoming more distinctively individual: perhaps at what Robert Kegan called the 'imperial' stage of development, which commonly occurs from seven or eight years old.[2]

Fragmentation of meaning can be considered at both an individual and a socio-political level. For instance, beliefs fuelled by hatred that maintain the conflict between groups (such as between Israelis and Palestinians) are also dependent on simple lack of understanding of members of the other group, and can often be reduced by meeting and engaging with people in the other group, and hearing them talk about their needs. The lack of connection between groups at a political level is that lack in individual brains and bodies, with the added complexity of being multiplied many times as it is reproduced in each individual, and then reinforced by group processes that influence individuals.[3] Our individual representations of groups and their demands, however, are left-hemisphere based,[4] and it is this that gives conflict of belief a more direct role in the creation of fragmentation of meaning (rather than the other way round) at the socio-political level. We fail to connect beyond our group partly because of the particular cravings and fears our group membership prompts, given our constant dependence on the approval of others. We *believe* that we should maintain the approval of others in our group, and in some cases this can actively prevent us from learning to understand others beyond our group: for instance,

2   III.2.d.
3   I.5.e; II.5.e.
4   This goes back to an earlier phase of evolution: see III.1.h.

a white supremacist is unlikely to develop an interest in black history. The complex relationship between group biases, meaning, and belief will need much further discussion, and this will be found in the next volume of this series.[5]

Staying with the concept of meaning fragmentation in general, though, much further clarification will still be needed in the next few chapters. The ways that fragmented meaning can provide a condition for conflict will need to be explained in more detail (4.b). The ways that fragmentation of meaning can be understood in relation to *both* the sorts of meaning normally regarded as 'cognitive' and those regarded as 'emotive' will need to be explained (4.c & d). Linguistic, cultural, and archetypal forms of fragmentation will also need to be distinguished (4.e, f, & g). The underlying idea throughout, though, will be *lack of connection*, whether this is seen experientially or neurally.

The *integration* of meaning is the resolution of this fragmentation through connection. Whatever processes create greater meaning association, then, can contribute towards the integration of meaning. At the most basic level, then, integration of meaning is indistinguishable from meaning itself, because meaning is connection. Meaning keeps growing with our organic experience (discussed further in 5.a), even though it may also need pruning as part of the process of growth (5.b). The *absorptive* way in which we develop meaning in childhood and subsequently may provide ways of overcoming fragmentation of meaning seemingly without any particular practical effort (5.c). However, we then develop communicative, expressive, and perhaps even meditative ways of overcoming fragmentation of meaning (5.d, e, & f). For instance, we can overcome conditions of conflict by communicating our feelings, and thus encouraging an empathic response that takes those feelings into account. We can also make contextual connections in our experience, to boost awareness, by finding new ways to express our feelings and ideas. In this way the arts can make a vital contribution to reducing the conditions for conflict.

To clarify the nature of the integration of meaning, I will also be exploring three further concepts towards the end of section 5. *Ambiguity* is a feature of meaning that we can expect as a basic implication of embodied meaning: one that only becomes a problem

5   V.1.

when we have to clarify our beliefs as the basis of judgement. The acceptance of ambiguity before that point (for instance, through humour) can thus be a helpful aspect of meaning integration practice (5.g). The integration of meaning also includes synthesis, a concept already discussed in *The Five Principles*[6] and that can be applied both at the level of meaning and that of belief (5.h). Temporary states of heightened integration of meaning can give rise to experiences of *sublimity*, which we can compare helpfully to other aspects of temporary integration (5.i).

Integration of meaning, like other forms of integration, is not defined backwards in terms of an end-point (such as enlightenment), but is an incremental process. However, the *idea* of an end-point or fulfilment of the integration of meaning can still be important to us as a source of inspiration. That will be the final topic of 5.j.

In the broadest terms, then, the fragmentation of meaning can be seen as a disconnection between symbol and experience, when a connection may be relevant. The integration of meaning is then a corresponding connection or re-connection that potentially reduces the conditions for conflict. The practice of the integration of meaning has a less direct effect on reducing conflict itself than does that of the integration of desire or of belief, but this should not lead us to underestimate its importance. As we shall see, it is often too late to resolve conflict by adjusting beliefs when the meaning context for those beliefs has already been set. If the work of the world's mediators often seems to be in vain, that is because the conditions for conflict are often so entrenched in meaning terms. It is by working at the level of meaning that we might stand much more chance of loosening those entrenched sources of conflict, both within and beyond ourselves.

---

6   II.2.d.

4.b. Fragmentation of Meaning as a Condition for Conflict

> Fragmentation of meaning is a condition for conflict because the alternative meanings needed to integrate a conflict are unavailable to us in the model being used. This limiting model may be shared and defended by both sides. This fragmentation is usually implicit, but can also happen within an explicit framework, where the explicitness is selective. Not all fragmentation necessarily causes conflict, because it depends on the obscured meanings becoming (unpredictably) relevant.

In practice, it is often difficult to differentiate *not understanding* from *disagreeing*, and we often use similar language for both. For example, if a campaigner says 'I don't understand how people can deny the obvious evidence of global heating', they may mean either that it is not sufficiently meaningful to them how people can deny it, or that they do find it sufficiently meaningful, but that they disagree with it. As often, here, meaning and belief are frequently confused. Yet the distinction is important: if we already find someone's view highly meaningful yet disagree with it, there is no way of addressing that conflict other than at the belief level – namely, reframing the terms of the conflicting beliefs. If, however, we merely fail to understand (or fail to understand *sufficiently*), then greater understanding (that is greater meaning) can resolve the issue. A little more listening, a little more empathy, or an openness to new language may enable such greater understanding. This situation is by far the most common situation of conflict.

At the belief level, conflict consists in incompatible *beliefs* linked to opposing *desires*. Each of those beliefs, however, is dependent on the continuing life of models, metaphors, schemas and basic-level categories that form a superstructure of meaning for that belief. Our conflicting beliefs remain incompatible (in relevant situations where they might be challenged) because of their absolutization, and that absolutization involves the rejection of alternative meaning beyond that of the two absolutized alternatives (for and against one's beliefs).[1] One of the key insights of the Middle Way approach is the recognition that *this rejection of alternative meaning is shared in cases of conflict*. Despite being diametrically opposed, desires and beliefs that are in conflict share an idealized model of the nature

1   I.5.a.

of the discussion. At times, the shared defence of this idealized model may take precedence over the polarized conflict within it, resulting in an *unholy alliance* (a phenomenon discussed in *The Five Principles*).[2] The strategy for defending an unholy alliance involves *dismissal* of alternative possibilities as meaningless, rather than a serious engagement with them as opponents on the same level. See, for instance, how the atheist Richard Dawkins approves the muscular theistic dismissal of agnostics as 'namby-pamby, mushy pap, weak-tea, weedy, pallid fence-sitters'.[3]

We cannot be in conflict without *assuming* shared meaning through our idealized model, and we generally do this by assuming representationalism about that model. However, the conflict is created by the gap between this assumption of shared meaning and the fragmentation of the embodied meaning that is the basis of our experience. In other words, we think or feel that we understand each other, and that the 'other' with whom we are conflicting wilfully holds a different view that is 'wrong', 'false', 'irrational', etc. In practice, though, our responsibility for conflict depends on the way in which we interpret the words that are used to express our own or others' beliefs – a responsibility that is always more or less ambiguous, given that our interpretation depends on our bodily experience. We can pay more or less attention to that interpretation, making it possible to allow in new meaning, and in the process allow alternative meaning to enter our awareness. A simple example of this would be that of feeling insulted by the 'tone' of what someone has written online (even though written words have no tone!). Perhaps they made a slightly challenging observation that was meant kindly, but your interpretation (which you take to be 'true') is that they are attacking you. The embodied experience of meaning for a person offering a kindly challenge is completely different, though associated with the same words, as that of a person feeling attacked, with the former assuming a reassuring context of social connection and the latter a threatening context with a dualistic model.

The fragmentation of meaning, then, may contribute to conflict in two different ways: it may give rise to conflict that is due to incomprehension, with an *implicitly assumed* shared framing that

2 II.4.f.
3 Dawkins (2006) p. 69.

The Fragmentation of Meaning 157

we are not actually justified in assuming, or it may occur *within* an explicitly shared framework. The former case is far more common in normal life than the latter, as it is typically only in more 'academic' or 'philosophical' discussions that frameworks of meaning get explicitly clarified – for instance, through the definition of terms. Even in more academic discussions, we are likely to assume that most of the meaning we are using is shared and representational without having to explicitly discuss the meanings of the terms we are using. However, I will return to the case of more explicit discussions below.

An implicitly assumed representationalist framework creates conflict by repressing alternative meaning. For instance, if I believe that what Marx really offered was a comprehensive insight into the true socio-economic causes of class conflict, then I am likely to categorize all alternatives as not Marxian. Appropriation and lumping will be applied to make sure that all alternatives are re-framed to fit the dualistic framework.[4] There is thus taken to be a true Marxian teaching, and a false Marxian teaching: the latter being condemned along with all non-Marxist beliefs. Alternative interpretations of the meaning of statements about Marx or of the topics of his teaching (such as the nature of capitalism) cannot be considered. We can see this as a rigid ideological belief about Marx, but we can also see it as a representationalist assumption about the *meaning* of Marxian teaching. Alternative meanings to the two options categorized as 'true' or 'false' are repressed, so we are not allowed to consider, for instance, that what Marx wrote was uncertain either in theory or application, that he might have been undecided, or that some elements of his theory may be practically helpful and others unhelpful. In effect, we are not allowed to engage with his teaching as meaningful in relation to our own embodied situation, but must only engage with it as it is believed to be in itself, with this belief dictating our approach to meaning. Raising such possible approaches is likely to result in dismissal. Small wonder, then, that Marxist groups are well-known for their fissiparousness (their tendency to split easily).

If the conversation about Marx does ever turn to issues of meaning, an *explicit* basis for representationalism will be readily found in the materialist basis of Marxist philosophy. If the physical world determines all, it must clearly determine our language too, through

4   II.4.d.

a representational relationship between states of affairs in the world and linguistic propositions. As Marx revealingly wrote:

> *The only intelligible language that we speak to one another consists in our objects in their relationships to one another. We would not understand a human speech and it would remain ineffective....*[5]

If Marx (in some undeveloped way) did hold open the possibility of a 'human' embodied meaning here, he did not regard it as a possible basis of communication, presumably because, like all the representationalist thinkers before or after him, he did not allow for any distinction between meaning and belief, or for psychologically provisional ways of using meaning without absolute belief. This offers just one of many such representationalist positions made more or less explicit. What these have in common is the same emphasis on the 'objects' of meaning, rather than on the experience of a human system in relation to them, and as a result the continuation of conflict whenever our representations of these objects are incompatible.

Explicit conflict about beliefs, in which both sides have a good understanding of each other's positions, is usually likely to focus only on explicit discussion of one aspect of the conflict, rather than in a synthetic perspective that links all the relevant interdependent assumptions together. There are obvious reasons for this: it is hard to maintain so much complexity in our minds at the same time. 'Explicit', then, only generally means explicit in one respect, with other aspects remaining implicit. Nevertheless, such explicitness can help us to reframe a conflict by contextualizing it in relation to alternative models, and at least sometimes it is necessary to be synthetically explicit in order to avoid potentially absolutizing some beliefs even whilst other possible beliefs remain accessible. This is why synthetic philosophy is needed, to compare the products of different traditions of thought or different disciplines explicitly in relation to each other. Where the conflict only involves implicit models that clash, without any further context of awareness being given to those models, the illusion of linguistic transparency helps to maintain our implicit representationalism and limit our awareness.

Conflict can thus be seen as the outcome of fragmentation of meaning, because fragmentation of meaning is the repression of alternative meanings, and the repression of alternative meanings is the means by which beliefs are absolutized. Not all fragmentation

5   Marx (1977) p. 121.

The Fragmentation of Meaning

of meaning practically results in conflict, however, because not all possible beliefs are relevant in practice, and not all are incompatible with opposing beliefs. We can fail to understand others, or even fail to understand our own past perspective, without this impacting relevant beliefs in the circumstances. However, since we never know what meaning may be relevant in uncertain future circumstances, fragmentation of meaning is a constant limitation that needs to be addressed and worked with.

4.c. Babel: The Fragmentation of 'Cognitive' Understanding

> The 'cognitiveness' of meaning fragmentation is always a matter of degree, given the constant interdependence of 'cognitive' and 'emotive' elements. Relatively 'cognitive' fragmentation includes many types of language difference, from whole languages to jargon. It can include fragmentation within an individual over time as well as between groups. Such fragmentation is more likely when we lack motives to overcome it – an indifference that can be culturally reinforced.

One aspect of fragmentation of meaning can be readily symbolized by a well-known story in the book of Genesis of the Hebrew Bible.

There was a time when all the world spoke a single language and used the same words. As people journeyed in the East, they came upon a plain...and settled there....Then they said, 'Let us build ourselves a city and a tower with its top in the heavens and make a name for ourselves, or we shall be dispersed over the earth'. The Lord came down to see the city and tower which they had built, and he said 'Here they are, one people with a single language, and now they have started to do this; from now on nothing they have a mind to do will be beyond their reach. Come, let us go down there and confuse their language, so they will not understand what they say to each other'. So the Lord dispersed them from there all over the earth, and they left off building the city. That is why it is called Babel, because there the Lord made a babble of the language of the whole world. It was from that place that the Lord scattered people over the face of the earth.[1]

This has often been interpreted shallowly, as an aetiological myth that attempted to explain the facts of language difference. However, its deeper symbolic significance for us can be seen as lying in the ways that it suggests our own responsibility for the fragmentation of meaning.[2] The story links a narrow left-hemisphere based pursuit of goals with the assumption (or imposition) of a single language. However, this is then disrupted by 'the Lord', who can here be read as symbolizing the wider right-hemisphere based connectivity on which meaning is in practice based. When meaning is embodied, our fantasies of perfect representation underlying perfect wish-fulfilment are constantly frustrated by a lack of mutual understanding – often a lack of mutual understanding between

---

1   Genesis 11:1-9 (Revised English Bible).
2   This is not a scholarly interpretation of the 'true meaning' of the text or of its origins, but a practical suggestion for how we can use the story to help recall an insight about fragmentation.

groups, but also between individuals, and within one individual over time. The more we try to build the tower that reaches 'the heavens' of absolute understanding, the more fragmentation 'disperses' our efforts. God here personifies both of those aspects of conditions in contradiction to each other, illustrating how our understanding of others cannot be achieved through shortcuts, but only through accepting and working with fragmentation.

If language difference is understood in representationalist terms, it is the use of different symbols by different groups to represent the same objects. However, language difference is not itself significant or problematic without fragmentation of meaning – that is, without gaps in our understanding of one another (or of ourselves). These gaps are found on a continuum from total incomprehension to total comprehension, in which neither of the extremes can occur in a pure form, and in which 'cognitive' elements are always in practice completely interdependent with 'emotive' ones. A failure to understand someone's language can be much mitigated by emotional engagement with them, just as a theoretical understanding of the words someone is using can be greatly undermined by the lack of such engagement. Explorers meeting uncontacted tribes may be able to communicate more effectively, in a few cases, than members of the same family can with each other.

If we see 'lack of understanding' as inextricably *both* 'cognitive' *and* 'emotive', we can also simultaneously acknowledge the weighting that is likely to occur in one direction or another in any given case of fragmentation of meaning. My inability to understand the speech of a group of Chinese tourists speaking Chinese to each other in my own country is not particularly due to lack of engagement with them. However welcoming and communicative I may be, I will still probably not even get the gist of what they are saying, and may even misinterpret culturally-shaped paralinguistic features such as head movements or tonal expression. However, the more relevant their communication becomes to me, the more I am likely to focus my efforts on communicating by whatever means are available – whether that is the use of impromptu sign language, or an effort to stretch the usage of the few symbols we may share.

The more abstracted and decontextualized the symbols are, the more purely 'cognitive' their comprehension may seem to be, but also the more restricted their practical relevance is likely to be. At the extreme end of the spectrum of 'cognitiveness' may be symbols that we think of as entirely comprehensible, but which we have no particular motive for paying any attention to. Tiresome, repetitious bureaucratic language is a common instance of this, such as safety warnings that have to be given for legal reasons, but which serve no function in making their targets aware of new relevant risks. The safety announcements in aircraft are likely to be experienced in that way by frequent flyers – cognitively entirely meaningful, but emotively nearly meaningless.

At the relatively more 'cognitive' end of fragmentation of meaning are not only differences between what we conventionally regard as 'languages', but also many differences within a given 'language': accent, dialect, professional jargon, idiolect (private words), 'errors' that depart from standard usage, misprints, mishearings, or culturally-influenced misinterpretation can all contribute to not understanding others' symbols. One modern maintainer of Babel is over-specialization, which I have previously discussed in *Absolutization*,[3] drawing on the image of the Buddha's parable of the blind men and the elephant. Over-specialization not only fosters limiting assumptions within professional or study groups, but also specialized vocabulary, the meaning of which may overlap with that used by other specialized groups in unacknowledged ways. For example, when psychologists talk about 'personal development', when religionists talk about 'spirituality', and when philosophers talk about 'ethics', generally completely different habitual vocabularies are applied, helping to foster completely different assumptions, and the huge contribution made by specialisms other than one's own favoured one is likely to be ignored.

However, if the relatively 'cognitive' fragmentation resulting from differing language from others seems reasonably obvious, we also need to recall the less obvious fragmentation of meaning within ourselves over time. This occurs when we do not understand the symbols used by ourselves in the past – not only because of relative alienation from ourselves in the past, but also because we have forgotten the significance of the language or other symbols we used. I have a fairly clear example of this from my own life based on my study of Prakrit (one of a range of ancient Indian languages that evolved from the more ancient Sanskrit) in my early twenties as part of my BA degree. On studying a Prakrit text, I noted

3   I.6.a.

down a striking verse in the language (without any translation) in a notebook, and then rediscovered this notebook about thirty years later. By that time I had not the faintest idea what the verse meant, having only a vague recollection of the sentence structure and a few isolated words of vocabulary, but nowhere near enough to piece together any sense of the meaning of the verse, even though it was written in my own handwriting.

In any such cases, though, of course, the interaction of 'cognitive' and 'emotive' elements will be especially obvious. I did not maintain my understanding of Prakrit because I had no use for it, and no motive for doing so once I had completed my degree. When the symbols that we used in childhood or youth are still valuable to us, of course we are very likely to understand them, perhaps even recalling vivid memories that accompany their importance. Our capacity to lose understanding that we had in the past is a function of how far we cease to care about its symbols – ones that were already probably caught up in some degree of conflict during that past. See 5.b for more about the process of forgetting meaning.

The 'cognitive' fragmentation of meaning within individuals also shadows that occurring at a social level. If I no longer understood a Prakrit verse, this also reflects my social circumstances, which are not ones in which understanding of Prakrit is ever valued or reinforced. It is rare to study dead languages and relatively rare to study culturally distant languages, let alone culturally distant dead languages. My own lack of understanding of the language I once studied thus reflects that in my society, where only a handful of highly specialized scholars in practice maintain understanding of the language.

Such fragmentation at a social level also obviously translates into political and economic effects. Political decision-makers are most unlikely to give priority to funding the study of Prakrit, like that of any other topic that voters are unlikely to understand the value of. The only countervailing political force to this is the liberal ideal of the university as a context for the cultivation of as wide a range of understanding (normally misunderstood as 'knowledge') as possible:[4] an ideal that has been established in the past, but subsequently undermined by the absolutized assumptions both of economic instrumentalism and of bureaucratization. Absolutized

---

4   An ideal wonderfully encapsulated in Oakeshott (1989).

beliefs about value prioritization in society are constantly interdependent with such prioritizations in the individual ego, and these simultaneously appear as co-dependent meaning fragmentations.

4.d. Planetary Indifference: The Fragmentation of 'Emotive' Understanding

> The 'emotive' aspects of understanding become fragmented when we fail to pay enough attention to some relevant symbols – even ones of which we have a full 'cognitive' grasp. This is often due to habitual responses to immediate sources of meaning, reinforced by culture. Planetary indifference to global warming is a good example where over-cognitive understanding fails to move us sufficiently. In contrast, aesthetic attention such as mindfulness can engage emotive meaning without any immediate symbolic ('cognitive') content.

Just as lack of 'cognitive' understanding is constantly reinforced by the 'emotive' issue of where and how much we bestow our attention, a lack of 'emotive' understanding is constantly reinforced by 'cognitive' fragmentation. When we fail to engage with someone else (or a part of ourselves) we simultaneously fail to connect the symbols being used to associations that make them meaningful. Imagine that a couple is quarrelling, and one of them says to the other 'I hate it when you don't listen to me'. This is apparently all about emotive engagement, and follows a typical pattern in many marriages between men and women, in which the male partner may seem to lack emotional engagement and attention. But if he is not listening, does he understand what she is saying when she talks about the unfair burdens she feels she is carrying? Obviously not. Attention is simply a necessary condition for any associative process. It is not that he could not ascribe a meaning to the words she is using, but that the overall pattern of those words fails to communicate new meaning to him. In this case, then, a lack of emotive understanding also affects cognitive grasp.

However, there are obvious cases where we do pay attention to experiences without symbolic meaning being present: this is what I would call *aesthetic attention*, and is the distinctive feature of mindfulness. In a mindful state, we pay attention to the sensual detail of, for instance, the colour of an object, or of a pattern that has no other particular significance (like the grain of wood), or of the experience of the breath as it comes in and out of the body. Aesthetic attention seems to consist in 'emotive' understanding without 'cognitive', but, as always, it is not quite as simple as that. It is more that the cognitive associations when we are in aesthetic attention are at a wider and more instantaneous level – a direct right-hemisphere significance rather than one that needs to be mediated by the left hemisphere. So we have associations, but they don't have to be formed into propositions, and are thus free of mental proliferation. We will still be aware of our longer-term intentions. Over-simplifications of mindfulness thus tend to involve statements like that we 'stop thinking' when we are mindful: but it would be much more accurate to say that we stop thinking in a decontextualized way, with the 'cognitive' meaning subjugated to the 'emotive'.

The fragmentation of 'emotive' meaning thus happens when we *lose* this attentional context. Aesthetic attention can provide one such context, but reflective thinking and creativity can offer others. If the man who doesn't listen to his wife did some meditation it might help indirectly, but probably the most immediate remedy would be to start putting her language in a wider context by reflecting on her needs and feelings as part of the conditions – what's often seen as working with compassion. This is a primarily a process of extending *meaning*, although beliefs about her are also a necessary part of the background. The lack of understanding between them comes from a lack of attention of various possible kinds, but all of them with an emotional impact: aesthetic, symbolic, compassionate, or intellectual.

The fragmentation of meaning towards this end of the spectrum is perhaps most obvious in personal relationships where we might expect a relatively high level of understanding and engagement, but it is absent or diminished: for instance, parents who don't understand their children, or old couples who are yoked together by habit but have lost all interest in each other. However, we can also find it in a range of other important and far-reaching contexts. These include economic relationships, responses to the environment, and the absolutization of religious or ideological beliefs into dogmas. In all of these types of examples, we can 'know intellectually' (to use the common expression, even though we don't 'know' anything in practice), even when we can't 'absorb it emotionally'. The lack of such absorption is an issue of fragmented meaning long before it becomes one of unjustified belief.

The first of these examples is the alienation of economic relationships, where meaning is often limited to what can be reduced to economic benefit. The meaning of a T-shirt that I might buy cheaply in a chain store in the UK is likely to be limited to immediate considerations of appearance and price, not extending to the history of the production of the cotton from which it is made, or of the conditions in which it was manufactured by low-paid workers in Bangladesh. The meaning of commodities can be limited to those that align with our relatively narrow goals, and even people themselves can be treated as commodities in the same way (as in the employment market, or in pornography). We often do not lack 'cognitive' understanding of these wider conditions surrounding our economic transactions, but goal-orientated left-hemisphere attention is reinforced by cultural convention to allow us to constantly limit our 'emotive' understanding, and thus our habitual range of attention in relation to both the goods we buy and the people we trade with. Of course, stress responses may also continually inhibit our ability to extend that awareness.

This narrowness of economic meaning can be linked in turn to the wider issue of our response to the environment. We can find global warming, the biodiversity crisis, and other major planet-wide threats 'intellectually' meaningful, and yet give them low priority in even our personal decision-making, let alone our political choices. We give them low priority because, although there are accessible neural channels through which we can reflect on these phenomena, they are far smaller and less developed channels than the ones we have already developed to deal with nearer and smaller issues. The use of cars or flights is initially more important to us than reducing CO_2 in the atmosphere, just because cars and flights are so meaningful. There is the car, a constant symbol of convenience, freedom, and utility, standing in front of the house as a constant reminder – how could an intellectual abstraction about levels of greenhouse gases possibly become more significant than that? Before we get even to considering the *belief* that we should reduce or end our car use, the very subject has to become meaningful enough for us to even consider such a belief. It is the gap in understanding (the fragmentation of meaning) that prevents us from recognizing the importance of the issue.

Planetary indifference is thus perhaps the most striking and damaging instance of the fragmentation of meaning today. As discussed in 4.b, that fragmentation is a major condition for conflict, without itself consisting in conflict. Any major condition of this kind, that is on too big a scale or too remote to be highly meaningful to us, struggles to reach our attention by comparison with more immediate symbols – whether those symbols are those of accustomed language, group identity, or familiar objects. We do not sufficiently *understand* the planetary perspective because it is not sufficiently meaningful to us. Its lack of meaning is overwhelmingly towards the emotive rather than the cognitive end of the spectrum.

The third example is the absolutization of religious or other ideologies into dogmas. Again, we usually think of this in terms of belief, but the alternatives to dogmatic belief have to become meaningful enough to us before they can become objects of (provisional) belief. When God *means* a set of abstract belief statements (or even theological rationalizations of those statements), we are hardly in a position to cross the gulf in understanding from those who experience the God archetype more directly without that projection. The importance of mystical movements in the major religions thus lies, not in the beliefs they put forward (which are typically varied and inconsistent, whether orthodox or unorthodox), but in the way in which they treat experience of God as meaningful, and thus allow us to engage with it directly rather than via abstract absolutizations.

I have continued to enclose 'cognitive' and 'emotive' in scare quotes, because the key implication of embodied meaning is that the fragmentation of either is the same kind of process. When I fail to understand (in any immediate and relevant sense), then I am failing to understand the structure of embodied meaning in the other. To some extent I do not share the 'other's' schemas, basic level categories, and metaphors, even when the 'other' is myself at a different time. Whether that difference in experiential meaning construction is primarily because I have not learned to recognize the symbols being used, or because I am not sufficiently interested in the symbols being used, is at best a matter of emphasis. The integrative solutions, which will be discussed in section 5, always involve the interdependent working with both 'cognitive' and 'emotive' elements.

A much more effective way of analyzing fragmentation, then, is not in terms of 'cognition' and 'emotion' at all, but in ways that preserve the unity between these aspects. In the remainder of this section of the book I will thus be approaching fragmentation from a rather different direction, focusing on some of the relatively distinct social and psychological levels at which fragmentation along the whole spectrum can emerge. This will begin with *linguistic fragmentation* – that is, lack of understanding due to the use of differing language. Language, however, nests within a cultural context that transmits that language, and some fragmentation is thus *cultural fragmentation*, shaped and often entrenched by the social groups that use the language. These cultural factors then interact with our psychological need for inspiration in *archetypal fragmentation*, where we fail to understand because the drives created by our deepest needs as individuals have been diverted away from the conditions for their own long-term fulfilment. Finally, *somatic fragmentation* is the conditions in our bodies themselves that prevent understanding: these are not to be seen dogmatically as determined because they are in the body, but they are nevertheless a key element of the reasons we don't understand.

4.e. Linguistic and other Symbolic Fragmentation

> Fragmentation in the understanding of language or other symbols depends on lack of engagement with symbols used by others. These are often reinforced by prejudicial beliefs about the status of their linguistic or symbolic forms. These beliefs lack justification, as differences in linguistic form are arbitrary, and they are not inevitable. They can be separated from fragmentation of meaning, even though they are often interdependent with it.

Linguistic fragmentation of meaning is the lack of mutual understanding due to the use of differing linguistic forms: that is, different languages, dialects, pronunciations, spelling conventions, specialized languages, and idiolects. It is in many ways the most obvious form of fragmentation of meaning, because it is clearly 'cognitive' (as already discussed in 4.c) – for instance the mutual incomprehension of speakers of different native languages who have not learned any of each other's languages.

However, it is not only the forms themselves, but our differing responses to the forms, that produce the fragmentation, and the differing forms would entirely lack relevance if there was no encounter of any kind between the different meanings, leading to any kind of response. Our differing responses to varied linguistic forms are, of course, more strongly 'emotive'.

We prefer some kinds of symbols to others, even if we have some degree of meaningful association with all of them, so we will thus engage more with some symbols than others. Where language is concerned, we are likely to associate some kinds of language with the in-group (or with higher status within that group) and other language as the preserve of the out-group. Such associations often develop into explicit discriminating beliefs that are the basis of accepting one kind of language and rejecting another, but even if we don't do this, more or less favourable implicit values can easily accompany the meaning of the language.

The study of sociolinguistics provides evidence of these ensuing beliefs, by showing that language with high social status or 'in-group' status tends to be seen as more pure, beautiful, correct, precise, or useful. For example, the use of Standard English with Received Pronunciation is often assumed to have morally superior status when compared to localized dialects of English with lower social status.[1] Amongst those with that lower social status, though, in-group reactions may lead in turn to the denigration of Standard English.

That these kinds of belief-reactions are not a necessary part of the meaning of the language can also be seen if we recall our experience of getting used to and accepting differing language that we may have previously rejected – for instance, in this series I personally adopted '-ize' endings (as in 'absolutization'), that are associated with American usage, over my previous use of '-ise' endings, at the time of the publication of 'Absolutization', to fit my publisher's preferences. Now I 'have no problem' with -ize endings: they have become normalized. If I previously had an implicit belief that '-ise' endings were somehow morally superior to '-ize' endings, I have now followed through my recognition that the difference is arbitrary. Any fragmentation that may have occurred because of my previous rejection of '-ize' endings is thus over.

The arbitrariness of the association between a linguistic form and its meaning is one that is widely accepted in linguistics, and is helpful to reflect on to show the unnecessary nature of linguistic fragmentation. For instance, there is nothing about either the sound or the spelling of 'dog' that makes it intrinsically any better than 'cat' to represent *Canis familiaris*. Hypothetically, if we completely reversed all the associations of 'dog' and 'cat', so that 'dog' meant cat and 'cat' meant dog, we would be no worse off. This arbitrariness does not appear to be affected by embodied meaning by comparison with representationalism. It is, of course, possible to concoct speculative theories about the 'intrinsic' meaning of particular sounds, letters, or combinations (for instance, metaphysical claims about the significance of mantra sounds). There may also be a few cases of sounds that are either easier to produce in a certain context where they become meaningful (as in a baby's 'mama') or are onomatopoeic (Crash! Hiss!), but even these are very far from determining any fixed relationship between linguistic forms and meaning beyond the one we have created through association.

Nevertheless, our biased judgements as we respond to differences in language completely ignore this arbitrariness of linguistic form. Of course, differences in language may raise other issues: they may cause confusion or equivocation, which may have practical

---

1   Trudgill (1995) pp. 7 ff.

effects. Linguistic fragmentation can thus contribute to conflict in the way outlined in 4.b. However, most often the sources of conflict in differences of arbitrary linguistic form are entirely unnecessary, and our concern with them is extremely silly. No, it doesn't matter if you and I pronounce 'tomato' differently, nor does it matter if you can't manage to spell *onomatopoeia* without errors, nor does it matter if you refer to *la mort* when I refer to 'death'. In none of these cases does the difference by itself need to create either confusion or equivocation, so there is no justification for preferring one form of language over the other. A clearer understanding of meaning here can help us to work with our biases.[2]

These points about linguistic fragmentation can also be applied equally to other kinds of (non-linguistic) symbols, which we get attached to in the same ways, despite the similar appearance of arbitrariness in many symbols. For instance, we may identify strongly with a particular tune, which we associate with particular emotional connections: think of the way that the *Marseillaise* means France, not only because of its words but because of its musical form. However, to hum the *Marseillaise* out of tune, or to change a few of its notes to the 'wrong' ones whilst the whole remains recognizable, would strike many French (and indeed other) people as offensive, or at least distasteful. This is despite the overwhelmingly arbitrary nature of the relationship between this particular sequence of notes and France. Symbolic fragmentation would be the effect of one person singing the *Marseillaise* out of tune, whilst failing to understand why that would be so offensive to someone else. This might obviously lead quickly to conflict involving opposing beliefs.

In some cases, other symbols may seem rather less arbitrary than language. For instance, the cross as a symbol of Christianity does not seem arbitrary, because of its origins in the story of Jesus' crucifixion. However, the cross as a wider symbol for religion or for spiritual practice would gain increasingly arbitrary features: it would be metonymic, taking one tradition of practical religion as symbolic of all in the same way that 'The White House' is only one feature of US government, but can stand for all of it. The selection of one feature rather than another as the basis of the metonymy, though, begins to involve arbitrariness: why should we choose the cross as a symbol of religious practice rather than the Buddha? Or why should we

2   V.2.

choose the Buddha rather than the cross? If the answer to that question is only that we belong to one religious tradition and reject the other, then it can reasonably be asked why we only select the tradition that we belong to. Embodied meaning does demand that we go through a prototype process (as discussed in 1.e), associating a symbol with a narrower range of experience before we broaden that association to a wider meaning. But prototyping does not justify us in maintaining a narrower meaning when we have the capacity to broaden it. Thus fragmentation can also be created by a failure to understand the limitations of the way we are using a symbol, even if that use is not entirely arbitrary.

In both the cases of linguistic fragmentation and of other kinds of symbolic fragmentation, it's important to distinguish fragmentation itself from the conflicts of belief that it makes possible. At the point where fragmentation begins to become relevant in a practical situation,[3] we merely fail to understand because of differences in language or symbol, whether these are predominantly 'cognitive' or 'emotive'. That failure to understand can be addressed by integration of meaning, using the imagination to extend what we understand, before it becomes a matter of conflict. When it has become a matter of conflict, though, we are likely to need to work at the level of belief, examining our biases in relation to the beliefs we assume about what is meaningful, in order to address that conflict.

3   I.7.

4.f. Cultural Fragmentation

> Cultural fragmentation is the wider context for linguistic fragmentation, and consists of the mutual incomprehensibility of habitual symbols and accompanying actions across every field of human activity, including religion and the arts. Whilst most obvious between larger groups, this fragmentation is also found within individual meaning over time, especially when we move between social contexts with contrasting values. It is reinforced by belief, but not reducible to it.

Linguistic and symbolic forms do not operate in isolation, but are embedded in cultural contexts. Obviously, the reason one language is separated from another is because it is used by separated groups of people, and generally the more those people have been separated, the more their language will diverge. Geographically proximate groups in Papua New Guinea, for instance, nevertheless have highly divergent languages because of the presence of mountains that make contact between those groups very difficult, whilst on the other hand geographically highly dispersed groups speaking English across the modern world have maintained some degree of commonality (as well as some divergence) because of modern communications. This linguistic divergence is also cultural divergence, and affects a great many other aspects of human life: for instance, customs, rituals, art, clothes, the design of artefacts, the use and preparation of favoured foods, the conduct of relationships, the dominant socio-political values, and the political structure. Very often, we do not understand each other's language or symbols because we do not understand each other's cultural context. Within ourselves as individuals over time, too, we may experience cultural change (especially if we move between groups), and fail to understand our past or future selves.

Culture not only provides a context for meaningful symbols, but it *is* meaningful symbols. All the human forms we live amongst are meaningful to us, precisely because they are so familiar to us and because they reflect our values. From the reason why a particular traditional culture has a certain style of bone knife, to the type of car favoured by a particular modern family, to the form of a coming-of-age ritual such as a *bar mitzvah*, the reason for the continuity of these forms is dependent on their meaning to those who use them. In our particular, embodied circumstances, we have associated the

The Fragmentation of Meaning 175

meaning of all these forms with their context: so that, for instance, it seems right to fry aubergines rather than to boil them, or to bow in front of the statue of a god. The embodied meaning of associated actions is part of the meaning of an object or a person.

Cultural fragmentation is thus our attachment to mutually incomprehensible symbols between individuals or groups or over time. It is largely a difference in the 'emotive' meaning attached to symbols, but of course also has an unavoidable 'cognitive' component. If we think of a particularly powerful example of cultural fragmentation – that of religious division between, say, Christians and Muslims – the main cause of fragmentation is the differing emotional impact of both linguistic and non-linguistic symbols on the different groups. The cross, or the word 'Christ', will have a much more profound, and generally more positive, emotional effect on the Christian than on the Muslim, and vice-versa for the crescent or the word 'Muhammad'. At the same time, however, there are varying degrees to which Christians do not understand the cognitive sense of 'Muhammad' to Muslims, because of the culturally complex web of metaphors through which it is understood, or vice-versa for Muslims and 'Christ'. Once we accept the metaphorical basis of meanings that are not immediate gestalts, it is not enough to claim to know what 'Muhammad' means through reading religious studies textbooks and being familiar with the facts about his life, contexts, and place in Muslim belief. These facts do not necessarily give us full access to the meaning of 'Muhammad' in the fully embodied and enculturated experience of a Muslim (although they may take us some of the way).

This bigger example could be set beside a relatively trivial one. If my daughter likes and appreciates a popular song that I neither like nor appreciate, this is not merely a matter of 'taste', nor of 'the generation gap' – or at least there are further ways of understanding both. It is an example of fragmentation of meaning, because I lack her attachment to this cultural symbol, and the difference is relevant to our lives. Although I may understand the words of the song, I also fail to understand the positive significance she invests in it, through the metaphorical relationships between the song and her immediate experience. I may, however, also find it much harder to even hear the distinct words in the song than she does, because I am less familiar with differentiating the parts of this form. The meaning of the song probably has a complex relationship with other aspects of personal experience, such as different peer groups and different physical experience.

These last two examples illustrate how cultural fragmentation may be especially obvious in the spheres of religion and the arts. However, there is also a wide range of other aspects of our environment in which meanings differ: architecture, design, food, patterns of daily activity, attitudes to work and leisure, attitudes to animals, attitudes to the non-human environment, communication practices, gender roles, sexual practices, attitudes to sexuality, attitudes to age difference, social organization, conduct of trade, attitudes to law and government, political organization, rites of passage, attitudes to intoxicants, sports, forms of transport, clothes, cleanliness, toilet practices, medical practices, childcare customs, education, agricultural practices, and attitudes to violence. Doubtless this is not a complete list.

If we take the example of toilet practices, the Indian custom of cleaning the anus after defecation with water using the left hand, and of rejecting the Western habit of using toilet paper, is accorded significance by both sides. Even if the divergent customs were regarded as unimportant and treated quite flexibly they would still be significant, but given the degree of cultural attachment to each different approach, the fragmentation of meaning here is actually substantial. Obviously, when it becomes explicit, this difference in meaning becomes a divergence of belief – a possible basis of conflict, focusing mutual disgust in which one's own accustomed toilet practices are assumed to be the only 'clean' ones. However, the cultural fragmentation of meaning alone does not depend on any explicit language being used to discuss the divergent practices, or on any feelings of disgust or conflicting beliefs. We may simply fail to recognize the others' practices as being like our own, and be puzzled by them.

All such differences are obviously incremental. They are on the whole likely to be bigger between large and well-defined culture blocks, such as 'Western', 'Chinese', or 'Indian', or over substantial periods of time. Between closely related national or regional cultures, such as English and Irish, you might be able to find some slight differences in every category, but most of them would be of little importance. The English do not play Gaelic football, and they are less likely to attend mass, but on the other hand if you tried to analyse the average differences in style of clothes worn on the streets of Dublin from those of London, your results would probably not be detectable to the casual observer.

Given that we are dealing with habits of symbol-attachment, comparisons at the individual level would have to make allowances for averaging-out of individual habits over time. Perhaps I am wearing green today and you are wearing blue, but my wardrobe may actually contain more blue and yours more green. Nevertheless, these averaged-out habits can still change for one individual over time, sometimes dramatically, or in some cases different cultural meanings may be held simultaneously because they are associated with competing desires. Take the example of a young man who is struggling between twin ambitions to be a doctor and to be a poet. When the doctor ambition is uppermost, attitudes of brisk scientific detachment, with conventional dress and distanced manners, will have symbolic importance and be more or less consciously prioritized. When the poetic self comes to the fore, though, the poems of Rimbaud and Yeats become significant, the dress less conventional and the mode of interacting with others more personal and more intense. Cultural fragmentation, like conflicts of desire, is the fragmentation of meanings held by individuals which are not eternal or absolute selves.

Many children's early experience of fragmentation of meaning may come from that of very different norms dominant at home and at school. At school, the culture imposes uniformity, whether by pressure from teachers or peers. Cultural relationships to wider society may be imposed by teachers by the use of national or religious symbols, whilst the culture of the school itself may be promoted through uniform, ritual, and verbal formulae. In contrast, the home environment may either allow the child to develop more individual symbol-preferences, or may involve a family culture that differs substantially from the school one, because based more on specific class, religious, political, or professional cultures. Thus, from an early age, value conflicts for a child are associated with fragmentation of meaning.

The legacy of this perhaps for many adults is 'professionalism' – a set of cloaked moral beliefs about duties in a profession depending on the use of differing preferred symbols in work life to those used in private. These may reproduce a similar pattern of meaning fragmentation to the one imposed between school and home, or later inculcated through specific professional or job training. In a large company, for instance, 'professionalism' may involve adopting the 'mission statement' of the company, symbolized by its name, logo, and flagship products, and applied as a prioritization of its competitiveness. The meaningfulness of personal love and care for others, let alone openness to the values of rival companies, may be left at the office door. Again, the fragmentation of meaning between these rival groups does not necessarily require conflict in the sense of incompatible beliefs, but nevertheless sets up an exceptionally fertile field for such conflict.

Cultural fragmentation of this kind can often be entrenched by identification with the meanings of metaphysical propositions. These are particularly associated with religious and political groups. The belief that Christ saves us from our sins, for example, taken absolutely in accordance with the Christian doctrine of atonement, creates a sharply-defined cultural sphere in which 'saved' Christians (who believe in Christ's self-sacrificial act of salvation) are distinguished from the rest of humanity, who are still mired in sin. This is obviously a conflict of belief, but that conflict is also built on fragmentation between the cultural spheres of, say, the evangelical church compared to the club (even where some of the members overlap!). In the evangelical church, constant use of particular terms (Christ, sin, atonement, etc.) framed within certain models, creates a context of meaning that also supports the group's cultural separation – for instance in its rituals of baptism and the eucharist, its practices of petitionary prayer, bible study, hymn singing, etc.

Cultural fragmentation is an extremely complex phenomenon, uniting the disjunctions between cultures at the broadest level with the most specific cultural differences within local societies and within individuals. At the broadest level, we could make a case that it has decreased in recent history due to the impact of globalization. Not only trade, but accompanying language mobility and communications, have increased massively throughout the world, and also exert an integrating effect on political and educational expectations. However, at the same time new cultural fragmentations have emerged between those who face up to environmental conditions and those who do not, between rich and poor, and between the old whose remaining future is relatively secure and the young whose future is increasingly insecure.

4.g. Archetypal Fragmentation

> Archetypal fragmentation is the separation of our understanding of symbolic sources of inspiration from one another, so that we lose that inspiration. This is typically due to projection of the archetype, in which we cease to take responsibility for its role in our own experience, and assume it 'exists' out there in an object with that sole quality. Projected archetypes cannot be combined in a wider understanding in the way that integrated ones can.

Archetypes, as I described them in *Archetypes in Religion and Beyond*, are diachronic, schematic functions – that is, types of association that fulfil a particular need for humans *over time* (diachronically), through a wide association of symbols across different contexts (schematically).[1] The particular human needs fulfilled by archetypes are those of inspiration. Given that we often lose that inspiration due to our constantly changing states, and are distracted from its sources, we need ways of maintaining more consistent motives over time. Archetypes can be seen as a human adaptation needed to remind ourselves of those necessary sources of inspiration.[2]

Archetypes as I understand them, then, are basically integrative symbols. They have an associative meaning with the wide function of maintaining longer-term meaningfulness – a sort of meaning that acts like glue to bind other meaning together. This in turn can help us to overcome the fragmentation of meaning and the conflict that depends on it. A wide variety of possible symbols in different contexts can have these archetypal functions – whether they help us to remain engaged with the other, to persevere in our efforts, to imagine other possibilities or to beware of threats. Examples of such figures may include a hero in a story, a god figure, a beloved person in your life, or a villain who makes you aware of threats.[3]

The practical use of archetypes, then, can help us to overcome fragmentation in the longer term. However, like all such helpful adaptations, it is also itself subject to absolutization and fragmentation. In *A Systemic History*[4] I traced this 'hijacking' process in a whole range of integrative processes that start off as adaptations

---

1   Ellis (2022) pp. 3-4.
2   Ibid. 1.a.
3   Ibid. section 4.
4   III *passim*.

of some kind, only to become dominated by reinforcing feedback and thus to become 'ends in themselves' that disrupt the process of adaptation. In most cases we fail to understand as a condition for conflicting belief, but in the case of archetypes it is the other way round: the belief itself prevents us from understanding the symbol helpfully.

The hijacking belief that disrupts the integrative process in the function of archetypal symbols is that of *projection*. Projection is the assumption that an archetype actually 'exists' beyond our experience, and can help us in the same way as a person or object beyond us. The belief in the 'existence' of the symbol is also equivalent to the simplification of a complex object so that it is *only* symbolic and has no other functions that we can appreciate: our beloved, for instance, consists only in the beauty and other positive qualities that we respond to so passionately, whilst the demonized person that we reject has no redeeming features, but is assumed to be pure evil.[5] These simplified qualities are assumed to be intrinsically in the objects themselves, rather than being the effect our own experience of the object has on us.

Archetypal fragmentation, then, is the effect of this projection and absolutization of archetypal symbols. If we appreciate them as an aspect of our own experience, we can reach an understanding of them that is compatible with the understanding held by others – whether they are the objects of the archetypal inspiration or whether they are third parties. For instance, if we fall in love with someone who does not return our love, there is obviously a huge gap between the ways in which each of us understands the situation: for one person there is experience of a massive source of inspiration in the other, but in the experience of the other person, there is someone making a nuisance of themselves. This situation is not resolvable as long as we fail to take responsibility for our feelings as meaningful to *us* through our bodies, and persist in believing that the person we love themselves can solve all our problems. Differences in motive, of course, may even persist even when we do start taking that responsibility, which is closely associated with the embodied meaning perspective. However, a major source of fragmentation, blocking our understanding of each other, is removed when the person who has fallen in love succeeds in separating their

---

5   Ellis (2022) 2.a.

experience of the emotion from its object (even if incompletely). To acknowledge our own experience of archetypal symbols also enables us to acknowledge their absence in others, rather than feeling that the other should somehow share the same feeling because that is how things are.

Similar issues of archetypal fragmentation can occur when we demonize, projecting the shadow onto a complex person or persons – from the warlike leader of an opposing country to our ex-spouse after an acrimonious divorce. We may well have well-justified reasons for regarding these people as a threat, but their threatening aspects to us are not definitive to them as individuals – instead they are far more complex than that. It is our simplifying belief about them that limits their *meaning* in our experience, both cognitively and emotively. This narrowed meaning is then likely to be unnecessarily incompatible with those that do not share the motives that produced it – the compatriots of the warlike dictator or the ex's new partner.

It is archetypal fragmentation of the God archetype, however, that is probably the most damaging and far-reaching. Our beliefs about God – or about any other absolute concept that fulfils the same function, such as Nature, enlightenment, or rationality – traditionally shape our experience of the meaning of God, rather than the meaning preceding the belief. Our mutually exclusive narrowed meanings of God then block understanding between opposing groups – Christians and Muslims, theists and atheists, pagans and conventional religionists, theists and Buddhists, rationalists and intuitionists. If we build our understanding of God as embodied meaning up from its schematic role as an inspirational archetype, however (rather than idealizing a metaphorically-derived model), all the features that have become attached to that God archetype through its association with the beliefs of a particular group (for instance omnipotence, revelation through particular scriptures, literal creation of the world, cosmic justice, overall responsibility for both good and evil) become contingent. What we have left, that unites humans in potential understanding, is the experience of being inspired by new possibility.

The culturally entrenched representationalist tradition of substituting beliefs for meaning, then, is particularly damaging when it comes to the phenomena of archetypal fragmentation. We are prevented from understanding each other – or even sometimes ourselves – most of all on the things that matter to us most over the long term. Whilst more everyday forms of linguistic and cultural fragmentation may be overcome more easily when we apply a relatively small amount of compassionate awareness, in the case of archetypal fragmentation this is unlikely to suffice. A much deeper critical perspective is needed to avoid being swept up into the absolutizing beliefs that have hijacked the very symbols we have developed to integrate our experience, with long-term divisive effects. Here more than anywhere, then, we are likely to need a wide combination of different types of practice, working in the long term, to integrate what has been fragmented – as we will see in the next section of the book.

4.h. Somatic Fragmentation

> Somatic fragmentation is the gaps in understanding encountered at bodily level, as separation of webs of meaning (neural or experiential), interdependent with other types of fragmentation. These gaps can be understood in terms of left-hemisphere functioning, 'dysconnection' interfering with our synthetic processes, domain dependence, localized traumatic stress, or loss of memory. This fragmentation conditions our experience, but should not be interpreted as determining it.

Embodied meaning implies that all meaning needs to be understood in relation to what is happening in the body, as well as linguistically, culturally, or archetypally. In 1.a I explained how this could most basically be understood as a process of association that we can approach both from a neural and from an experiential point of view. When we create new meaning, we associate objects of experience, which means that we are more likely to experience a connection between them in the future, and a neural link is either initiated or strengthened. Fragmentation of meaning can also be understood at this basic level, from the asymmetries and irregularities of the process of association. Our connections clump or form partial webs, with some gaps where connections might be expected. Whenever we *fail to understand* in some respect, there is also a failure of association or a gap in our web of meaning, which becomes an instance of fragmentation when it is practically relevant.

Perhaps the most basic somatic basis of fragmentation is that of left-hemisphere representational construction. The left hemisphere without sufficient connection to the right can develop the belief that it has the whole story, but the more basic condition for thinking one has the whole story is a failure to understand any other story. That in turn involves a failure of the imagination, based in the right hemisphere's generation of alternative possibilities. One can thus distinguish fragmentation dependent on the left hemisphere from absolutized belief dependent on the left hemisphere, in the sense that the former is a necessary but not sufficient condition for the latter.

In neuroscience, what has been put forward as the 'dysconnection hypothesis' also helps to explain fragmentation[1] ('dys' being the

---

1 Friston et al. (2016).

Greek prefix for bad, although this overlaps in sense with the more common Latin prefix 'dis'). Applied particularly to help explain schizophrenia, dysconnection involves functional breaks in the hierarchy of increasingly abstract models we may use to account for new experience ('synaptic gain'): in other words, as I would interpret this, a failure of synthesis.[2] In schizophrenia, somatic (probably mainly genetic) causes interfere with the awareness applied when we connect specific experiences to abstract models, so that our higher-level awareness of uncertainty is bypassed, and we develop over-hasty and biased beliefs that fail to take into account the range of meaning models we could draw on. As Friston et al. explain this:

> *A failure of neuromodulatory mechanisms that control synaptic efficacy or post-synaptic gain corresponds, functionally, to an inability to augment (attend) or attenuate (ignore) the precision of sensory evidence, relative to the precision of beliefs about the causes of sensory cues. This can lead to false inference (e.g., hallucinations and delusions) that may reflect the brain's attempt to compensate for a pernicious and fundamental attentional failure.*[3]

Although the research was focused on schizophrenia, this explanation has wide implications for understanding the general role of bias – that is, a tendency for evidence to be interpreted only in terms of a particular narrow base of meaning. Bias becomes absolutization only when we assume that the bias (or alternatively our rejection of it) tells the whole story,[4] but up until that point it is fragmentation of meaning.

One can also understand fragmentation somatically in relation to the webs of meaning created in contexts at different times, which may have insufficient connection for us to associate them. We 'compartmentalize' or, in more formal psychological language, become 'domain dependent' in our meaning.[5] One common example of this is the gap in meaning association between professional and domestic contexts, 'on' and 'off' duty in the social role one may associate with one's profession or other role. Nassim Nicholas Taleb gives the example of a banker who got a porter to carry his suitcases for him, but then shortly afterwards went into a gym to lift kettlebells in a very similar training lift to the one he would have used

---

2 II.2.d.
3 Ibid.
4 V.1.a.
5 V.4.a.

if he had carried his own suitcases.⁶ There are also marriage guidance counsellors who can't keep their own relationships together, and decision theorists who make terrible decisions.⁷ One could, of course, attribute this to the beliefs that people have about appropriate ways of thinking and behaving in different circumstances, but domain dependence is a type of bias that particularly seems to be due to simply not 'making a connection' between two contexts, even when the connection seems highly relevant and obvious to others. Somatically, the distinct webs of meaning have formed separately around domain-dependent *models*. For example, the banker may have been using the *counterforce schema* and *object schema* differently to identify objects that provide the counterforce needed for weight training. Both of these schemas need application within a given context, according to a model of what is the right sort of object because it provides the right sort of counterforce. One can imagine the model used for gym training developing in a largely separate web of connections to the model used for carrying suitcases.

These webs of meaning can also be associated with different parts of the body in a way that more directly expresses fragmentation. For example, a tension in your shoulder can be associated with a particular traumatic event, suggesting that the activation of a particular web of meaning in the neural system (not only in the brain but throughout the body) also extends to the muscular and hormonal systems. This has been extensively discussed in Bessel Van der Kolk's well-known book *The Body Keeps the Score*.⁸ The remainder of the body may not understand this tension or its cause, as other associations are more dominant for it, which is why trauma may remain unaddressed as a potential source of conflict. Van der Kolk recommends that the development of a stronger integrative meaning in the rest of the body (challenging the helplessness and rage associated with the trauma in a particular part of the body) is the key to treatment of past trauma. The integration of trauma is likely to involve integration of our beliefs about the past in relation to the present, but the first step of the integration of belief is one of compassion – that is, of recognizing the emotional impact of past traumatic events on the meaning-associations created by the body, and connecting this with the wider significance we experience.

6   Taleb (2012) pp. 38-9.
7   Dobelli (2013) pp. 232-4.
8   Van der Kolk (2014).

The loss of memory due to bodily deterioration can also increase fragmentation. The relationship between meaning and memory will be discussed further in 5.a, but if we lose memory (for instance, due to dementia) it is clear that we also lose meaning. If we cannot recall past events, we cannot relate them to present events over time. Although some forms of memory loss may preserve semantic memory (abstract memory of words) without episodic memory (memory of events), in the absence of episodic memory, we will be unable to make the connections necessary to understand the general significance of words anew.

The somatic element of meaning is strongly associated with past conditioning – whether that is traumatic negative conditioning, or the more positive conditioning associated with personal development in a secure environment. However, it is a common and unnecessary error to interpret this conditioning deterministically. Applying sceptical insights to avoid metaphysical assumptions,[9] we can recognize that we have no way of predicting future events, and whether or not they will be in line with what we take to be the implications of past conditioning. From a practical, embodied, perspective, then, we will always be in some measure of doubt about how far we will be able to modify past conditioning. We can no more justifiably assume that we are helpless before it than we can assume that we are completely free of it. The body's participation in meaning does not make it determinate in implicit contrast to the 'rational mind', any more than linguistic or cultural fragmentation are determinate because they form a basis of social conditioning.

We should finish this account of different types of fragmentation with a reminder that they offer only an analysis to aid understanding of an interdependent complex phenomenon. Somatic fragmentation is, at one and the same time, also linguistic, symbolic, cultural, and archetypal fragmentation. If, for instance, a veteran holds a trauma in a part of the body, related to extreme stresses during past military service, that trauma is also associated with military language, symbols, and culture, reminders of which may help to trigger traumatic effects. Military service is also closely associated with the absolutization of heroic archetypes – the belief that we can overcome the enemy no matter what the cost. Military culture also strongly emphasizes the imposition of a left-hemisphere model, with strong

---

9 II.1.

rules and conceptions of duty, over the right-hemisphere awareness of other possible ways of operating.

At various points in discussing fragmentation, it has been necessary to introduce integration in contrast to it. Now, however, we need a fuller survey of how fragmentation of meaning can be overcome.

5. Integration of Meaning

5.a. The Growth of Meaning Resources

> Our resources of meaningful symbols can grow almost limitlessly with almost no cost, thus defying the trade-offs that affect most other human capacities. Growth in right-hemisphere meaning does not involve the alienating repetition of left, and is based on episodic, not semantic, memory. Research on memory engrams shows the separability of flexible linkage in memory from specific representational content. This growth is dependent on general development, and is boosted by education, with meaning (not 'knowledge') as education's function.

The integration of meaning overcomes the fragmentation of meaning, by creating understanding of relevant symbols (used by others, or oneself at a different time) that are otherwise not understood. I have already discussed the definition of integration of meaning in 4.a, in relation to the fragmentation that it overcomes through connection. This connection or understanding is a matter of degree, as it depends on strength of association. The case for it in this section is accompanied by a mind map **[diagram 6]**.

There is no absolute boundary between the integration of meaning and meaning in general (both involve learning), but the difference in usage is based on the way that integration of meaning overcomes fragmentation, whereas meaning in general begins long before fragmentation. As mentioned in 1.c, we can think of the earliest phase of learning in human life as 'differentiation' learning, but this is gradually taken over by 'integration' learning once a basic functional independence has been achieved.

Integration of meaning is created through practice, in the broadest sense – that is, by activity that may lie on a spectrum between passive absorption and active creation (always to some extent combining both), but that has the effect of extending our experience of meaning and our neural connections. This practice begins at birth (or perhaps before birth, in the womb), but can become increasingly focused and explicit as we develop into adulthood. In *The Five Principles*, I have already discussed some of the practices that can

Integration of Meaning 189

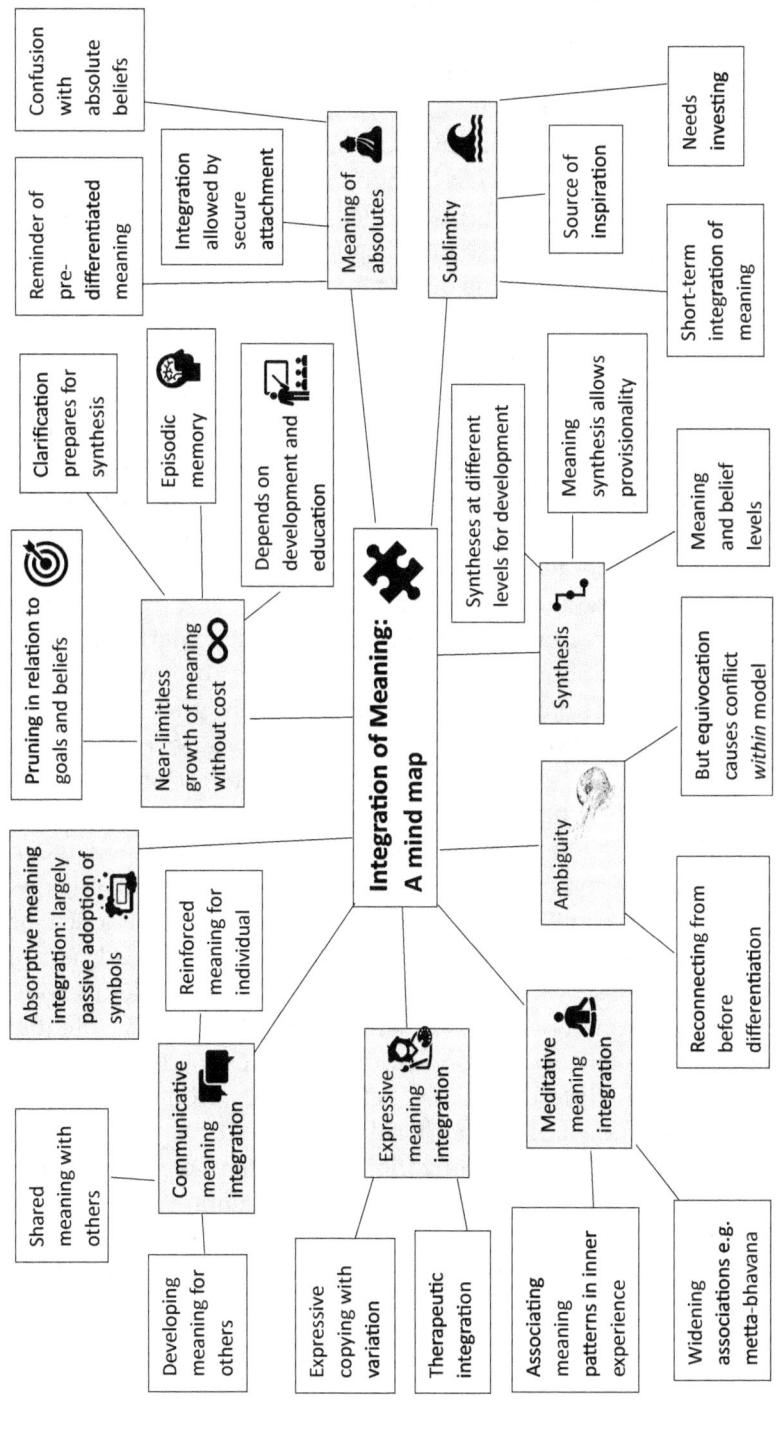

Diagram 6. Integration of meaning: A mind map.

contribute to integration of meaning, in the context of the practice of the Middle Way in general.[1] In 5.c to 5.f, I will be introducing an analysis of these practices into four types: absorptive, communicative, expressive, and meditative.

The creation of understanding depends primarily on the growth of meaning-resources, which is the topic of this chapter. The growth of meaning-resources is simply the learning of more symbols, so that they either begin to have meaning for us when they did not do so before, or their meaning is deepened, augmented, and enriched. However, this growth is also 'pruned' according to practical criteria in the contexts where it is used, as I will discuss in 5.b. This process of proliferating growth followed by cutting back is a feature of living systems, as I discussed them in my *Systemic History*.[2] Proliferating growth involves reinforcing feedback loops, whereby more and more of a particular feature is produced, as a response to its success in a particular context. The cutting back or pruning of growth involves balancing feedback, adjusting to a particular context. Balancing feedback is crucial for the adaptation of a living system to any given environment, and in humans it particularly takes the form of the adaptation of belief as opposed to its absolutization.

However, the astonishing thing about meaning lies in the way that it provides an exception to this normal importance of balancing and self-limitation in living systems. When we understand meaning as embodied rather than representational, *we cannot have too much of it*. We cannot have too big a vocabulary; we cannot have too wide or deep an appreciation of symbols; we cannot have too much engagement with others and their meanings. Meaning can, in practice, be left to grow indefinitely without any cutting, like the head hair of a traditionally observant Sikh. It is only when we consider meaning representationally that too much meaning becomes a potential impediment, so that we need to prune it. In this respect, meaning is fundamentally different from belief. Whilst the Middle Way normally implies the careful use of balancing feedback to avoid the reinforcing feedback of absolutization, then, where meaning is concerned we need much more of an abundance mentality.

Perhaps the best way of explaining this exception to the general pattern (of relationships between the Middle Way and feedback

---

1 II.6.e.
2 III.1.

Integration of Meaning 191

loops explored in this series) is in terms of the limited biological costs of meaning connections. Obviously the overall conditions that enable us humans to experience all this meaning – the size of our brains, the complexity of our culture, the long duration of our maturation – do impose many costs on us, in the sense that we have forgone other possible evolutionary advantages to develop them. For instance, big brains that can deal with lots of meaning create big heads, and thus problems in childbirth, whilst long maturation creates vulnerable early life and heavy responsibilities for parents. However, for us as individuals, inheriting these conditions, there is almost no further cost involved in using them to their fullest extent. Our trillions of neural connections do, of course, take energy and maintenance from the body, but not significantly more than our brains would require without them (at least, there does not seem to be any research suggesting that those with more complex mental development need significantly more energy input). Meaning alone also does not have any cost that arises from changing our behaviour in more demanding ways, as it is our beliefs that do that.

The integration of meaning through growth in meaning resources is thus – almost – a free lunch. We have almost nothing to lose by developing a capacity to imagine more, to consider a wider range of possibilities, to think and feel more deeply, to become aware of connections that others miss. To do this places us under no necessary obligation to behave differently – although of course in practice it probably will have that effect. Imagination alone does not make us more generous in our behaviour, or more critical in our beliefs – changes that obviously do bear costs. However, we do often behave differently, in a secondary way, because of imagination. The integration of belief may make us more likely to have beliefs that prioritize the value of the arts or other practices that integrate meaning, and these of course do bear some cost – though a worthwhile cost.[3] Any such costs then become increasingly justified the more we take a long-term perspective and the likelihood of changing conditions into account.[4]

To be understood helpfully, though, the growth in meaning must be seen in an embodied way as a development in connection, meaning that it is right-hemisphere meaning prior to formulation

---

3   See VII.6 for discussion of the aesthetics v ethics dilemmas involved in prioritizing integration of meaning.
4   I.7.d.

in propositions that is at stake. It is right-hemisphere meaning that is practically limitless, because it still consists in a range of potentials impacting our awareness, not in selected propositions that we become committed to. In a left-hemisphere representationalist way of thinking, the idea of there being more or less meaning will not 'make sense'. For representationalists, a symbol either 'makes sense', as potentially fitting into a coordinated picture parallel to a presumed reality, or it does not.

This distinction between these two different ways of understanding growth in meaning can be readily seen in the process of copying or repeating. Copying in the left hemisphere is a precise reproduction of (what is assumed to be) exactly the same meaning:[5] identical goods produced on a factory production line, or endless 'lines' written in school as a punishment ('I will not write on the furniture. I will not write on the furniture. I will not write on the furniture'). Writing 'lines' is *intended* to be a boring and alienating activity, because the repetition of symbols processed through the left hemisphere adds no further meaning. Repeating this disembodied 'meaning' does not increase it, but merely creates tautology. This takes us no further towards our goals, so we feel that our time is being wasted and become bored and alienated. However, *embodied* meaning increases with the weight of experience (and thus connection) we bring to it. Right-hemisphere meaning, by contrast, *depends* on our interest and attention, not just on some theoretical link with 'reality', and it grows as we devote more interest and attention to a given symbol. Repetition of 'the same' symbol, then, turns out to be full of new rich connections, subtleties, and associations. It is not 'the same' at all, because its meaning does not depend on the form of the symbol, but rather on our embodied experience of that symbol, and that embodied experience keeps changing. We can immediately experience this in mindfulness meditation, or in any kind of aesthetic contemplation of a work of art – we get interested in the richness of the process of breathing, or of the colour and texture of a painting – not in a conceptual reduction of these things. 'Copying' turns out to be something quite different in the right hemisphere, because of the different properties of embodied

---

5   McGilchrist (2009) section 7.

meaning from representationalist meaning. Meaning *grows* through creative copying, with small developments and variations, rather than being alienated.⁶

Meaning grows through connection with the existing meaning that is already present in our experience and neural network, much as a tree grows from its existing branches. There is thus always some degree of repetition involved in the development of embodied meaning, together with variation, because a new symbol needs an anchor point in the existing web to become meaningful to us. To make that association, we need to recapitulate the anchor point, as well as connecting it to a new experience.

The growth of meaning can also be understood in terms of another key everyday concept: that of memory. Memory is meaning: it is built up over time created by associative neural links. More specifically, meaning can be understood as what is referred to as 'episodic' or 'semantic' memory, which are two interdependent concepts. Episodic memory involves clusters of personal experiences from the past, though we will nevertheless only recall what we have paid attention to in the past and thus been able to meaningfully associate. Semantic memory includes memories of the meaning of words, symbols, and 'facts', which can be considered in abstraction from the context in which they were learnt. However, if we go back to the development of meaning in early childhood, we can readily see how basic level categories and embodied schemas are created from an accretion of individual experiences over time. As we develop propositional linguistic capacities, this meaning gets passed decisively to the left hemisphere, where its episodic relationship to specific experiences may be lost. The process of abstraction from specific experiences shows how memory, like meaning, is a single interdependent phenomenon – not one to be absolutely divided into completely separate sub-forms.⁷

The psychological and neuroscientific study of memory indeed offers a recognition that each memory has a neural presence, in the form of a 'memory engram'. A memory engram consists of a neural

---

6   In Ellis (2018) 4.a, I put forward an interpretation of the Judeo-Christian creation myth based on this view of creation, where divine creativity is interpreted in terms of the potential given us by right-hemisphere meaning.
7   Davis & Yee (2021) point out how semantic memory is inseparable from 'distributional' information about the cultural usage of words, because both are dependent on personal experience.

link or links, and there seems to be evidence that several such links may reinforce or substitute for each other.[8] Such an engram is clearly associative, but at the same time psychology is constantly impeded by a belief-based modelling of memory. Memory is said to 'encode' the 'information' of 'knowledge'. The concept of 'semantic memory' involves no distinction between remembering the meaning of a word and remembering a fact – e.g. remembering the meaning of 'uncle' and remembering that my uncle is on holiday in Croatia. Although the association with the 'fact' of his holiday in Croatia, or of other 'facts' about him, may make a small contribution to the meaning of this specific uncle, or even of 'uncle' in general, I do not have to believe this 'fact' to find 'uncle' meaningful. Instead, each episodic memory adds a new element to the semantic memory, gradually modifying the meaning of 'uncle', in my experience.

The extension of memory is thus an aspect of the integration of meaning. Any practices I can develop to help me strengthen associations will also be ways of improving understanding. Some such practices are quite common: the use of mnemonics to help us memorize a formula or a list, for instance, or the classical use of a 'memory palace' in which each room has associations that we can then recall by visiting the room in our imaginations. Tony Buzan has written in practical terms about such ways of developing and augmenting memory through deliberate development of association. For example, one can memorize a number by associating each digit with a thing (for instance through its shape), and then creating a story about the things. As he points out, the use of humour or sexuality can add a further power to our associations: for instance, you could associate the number 1 with a penis, 3 with a pair of breasts, and 5 with a pregnant woman.[9] So the number 135 could be easily remembered by associating it with a story about a sexual encounter and its results!

The growth of meaning resources, through our memory of experiences, depends only on the ways that we engage with our experience and reflect on it. To some extent this will happen even in the most restricted lives, and to some extent maturation will occur through the growth of meaning resources, integrating meaning to some extent regardless of our attitudes to practice. However, as I discussed in *A Systemic History*, many habitual adult judgements

8   Josselyn & Tonegawa (2020).
9   Buzan (1986) p. 54.

may not mature beyond the second or third stages identified by Robert Kegan: the interpersonal (third) stage (in which meaning comes predominantly from relationships with peers), or even the prior imperial (second) stage (in which meaning comes predominantly from an assumed concrete world). Central to progression to the ideological (fourth) stage is a process of consistent abstract modelling, which can only occur because the models used become sufficiently meaningful in the first place, whilst the interindividual (fifth) stage, when abstract modelling is questioned in a wider context, depends on alternative models becoming meaningful to us. Even beyond the impulsive stage of early childhood, where our learning is still largely differentiation learning, then, there is an element of the growth of meaning that we would expect to occur without conscious reflection or practice, but also an element that depends on it.

Clearly, the role of education in modern societies is crucial to the transition between maturation that is subject to the accidents of surrounding conditions, and that which is nurtured more systematically. Education systems, which of course can vary a good deal in their effectiveness, have in common the transitional use of socially-organized practice and reflection that can eventually promote more autonomous practice and reflection for each individual human being. This practice and reflection allows the *integration of meaning* (not 'knowledge') as the prime implicit goal of education. If education encourages its students to extend their neural networks, thus developing their adaptivity to a range of conditions, this is a matter of meaning, not of belief or knowledge. Whether or not the students come to believe any of the possible representations that have become meaningful to them, and whether or not any such representations are 'true', is entirely incidental to the key point of the practice – which is to grow meaning. Any further disciplines that we adopt as adults are then similarly 'education' in this sense, providing an initial structure for us to *understand* how we can judge differently.

5.b. The Pruning and Clarification of Meaning

> The exception to the limitless growth of meaning is that of pruning and clarification, but this needs to be seen as honing meaning in relation to goals and beliefs, not as limiting more basic meaning. At the neural level, synaptic pruning is a necessary aspect of learning. At the experiential level, clarification is the helpful limiting of meaning in relation to goals and beliefs through shared definition, analysis, or stipulation. This may be a necessary preparation for synthesis.

But surely, it may be objected, the integration of meaning is not simply a matter of adding endlessly to a cornucopia of connections? Surely we need to give these connections a haircut occasionally, otherwise impossible complexity and entanglement will result? Perhaps even 'Ockham's Razor' may be invoked! 'Do not multiply entities needlessly' say William of Ockham and his followers through the ages, in a principle often invoked in science and critical thinking. In other words, keep your theories as simple as possible, because simplicity allows clarity in the means by which you can test them or compare them to evidence.

At once, though, we must note that Ockham's Razor is a theory about *belief*, not about meaning. We can only test a theory (or even a hypothesis) on the basis of some degree of belief in it, however provisional, which then provides a basis of action that meaning by itself cannot provide. Even if we are engaged in a thought experiment as opposed to an actual experiment, the experimental approach requires that we clarify exactly what we are testing before we see how it matches up to conditions. The clarification of what we are testing involves propositions in a hypothetical form, such as 'lithium burns on contact with water' or 'rabbits like to eat carrot tops'. Ockham's Razor helps us to keep our beliefs in a practically testable form. It does apply to meaning, but only the meaning of a hypothesis specifically – not meaning in general.

If we are to prune and clarify our meaning, then, we have to do so *in relation to a purpose*, however provisional that envisaged purpose. That purpose could be the testing of a proposition, and it could also be the fulfilment of a personal goal: if we are clear about what we are seeking, we are likely to have a much better recognition of it when we find it. Our lives are full of such purposes, but these all involve attention to belief in relation to meaning, in constant interaction.

That is why pruning and clarification continue to influence meaning, and why assumed representation continues to play a role even in a thoroughly embodied model of meaning, but only in relation to beliefs and goals.

At the neural level, meaning is cut back through the process known as *synaptic pruning*. This consists in both the loss of some neurons, and the loss of some synaptic connections between neurons, which are pruned back in order to improve the efficiency of the brain when operating in its environment.[1] Synaptic pruning is thus part of the learning process, and is at its peak during the period of greatest learning in human life, from infancy through to the mid-twenties. The way in which it responds to the environment indicates that it offers a feedback mechanism for pruning back the meaning that would habitually be used to form practically interfering beliefs. It is not simply a matter of meaning being removed when it is not 'useful' in the immediate environment, because our inability to predict usefulness would then rapidly lead to a problem of 'catastrophic forgetting'[2] in which we would lack the meaning we need in new situations. The best way of understanding synaptic pruning, then, is surely one of removing meaning that actively contributes to practical interference, not of removing all 'useless' meaning. We still cannot have too much of that 'useless' meaning, *as long as* it doesn't actively interfere with vital belief.

Interference with practically important beliefs is maladaptation within the terms of a dominant model, preventing us from communicating or even thinking in ways that contribute to the fulfilment of our goals. Having failed in the current terms of the left hemisphere, a symbol may, of course, continue to be meaningful in the terms of the right. However, the phenomenon of synaptic pruning suggests that even right-hemisphere meaning may eventually be lost if it interferes with other meaning that we make frequent practical use of. Though I'm not aware of any specific evidence that links synaptic pruning to specific experienced meaning, the most coherent view of it would in my view be to see it as removing confusion in our meaning structures. In order to develop an understanding both of individual symbols and of the implications of symbols combined into propositions, we need many false starts and blind-alley trials

1 Chechik, Meilijson, & Ruppin (1999).
2 Riesenberg (2000).

through the course of our lives. Some of those trials, if their legacy remained, would make it more difficult to employ the meanings we subsequently rely on. Our ability to exemplify these failed trials, however, is subject to survivorship bias:[3] that is, if we remember any examples, they have obviously *not* been lost. One example of such a confusion (already mentioned in 1.c) that I recall from my own childhood was the assumption that 'sister' meant an older sibling of either sex, based on my own experience of having two older sisters and no brothers. Such a confusion, if it had endured in too prominent a form, would obviously confuse a basic function – that of being able to navigate family relationships with all the implicit social rules governing them. This example, of course, is an example that has survived in my memory, but one could also easily imagine it not surviving – my simply forgetting that I had ever had such a misconception, because the risk of it confusing my use of the word 'sister' in basic ways was too great a risk to be worthwhile.

More research seems to be needed in this area, that does not begin with the common assumption that meaning is a kind of belief, but rather follows through the implications of the two being separable and tests those implications. We cannot remember what we have pruned away, but the contents of what children have pruned away might potentially be detected by systematic testing from others, to determine whether previously present confused uses of words and symbols have been entirely forgotten, or whether they are maintained as meaning.

The process of *clarification*, however, forms a much more easily detectable process by which maladaptation of belief feeds back into meaning. In a process of clarification, we change our use of a symbol in relation to a particular purpose, by using feedback that often comes from others (based on the common usage of a term), or sometimes from our own experience and reflection on the problems that can arise when we use a term in a particular way. Most commonly, we need to use language in communication with others to achieve particular shared goals, and thus need to keep working on the clarity with which we use that language to make sure that the basis of our shared actions helps us to reach those shared goals as far as possible. For instance, the study of any subject or topic will often begin with an introduction to its technical terminology.

3   V.4.c.

Integration of Meaning 199

We would have trouble working to improve our nutrition without a reasonably well shared understanding of what a calorie is, or of proving a chemical formula without a shared understanding of a molecule. Although our socially derived definitions do not determine the whole of the meaning of a word or symbol for us, they can still substantially change that meaning.

Clarification can thus happen in a variety of ways. We can check the socially-accepted definition of a word using a dictionary, to try to align our usage with that of others. We can ask others for further information about 'what they mean' – that is, the meaning they experienced when they communicated with us using particular symbols. We can supply further information ourselves when we communicate to clarify our meaning, by distinguishing different senses and by stipulating the sense we are using. It's important to recognize here that the use of a dictionary for *clarification* is not an appeal to a dictionary as a source of authority: that is, a meaning is not 'right' because it is in a dictionary. However, it is more likely to be *shared* because it is in a dictionary.

As long as we recognize that we are working within a model, clarification allows that model to be sustained and applied consistently. To sustain our use of a model is often to integrate, as we continue to recall our intentions, along with the background assumptions with which they were framed, over time, despite constant changes in our mental and emotional states. Such clarification is often labelled 'reason' or 'rationality', but it is a process, not an abstract absolute, and its results can be integrative in one context but disintegrative in another. For instance, by being consistent in my use of a disciplinary rule with a child, I can nudge them towards awareness of the longer-term effects of, say, lying to a friend or stealing their toys. That consistency depends not only on a moral belief that I am applying, but also to a whole set of background models that format the meaning I and the child are both using – so that we both have some idea what 'lying' and 'stealing' mean. In another situation, though, the meaning of a traditional practice may be absolutized precisely because it is fixed over time and not responsive to new conditions – so that, for instance, we carry on with unnecessary flights and consumption of animal food in the face of global warming, because flights are part of the family holiday tradition and meat is part of our culinary tradition. Left-hemisphere meaning creates a coherent sphere for the use of a model that promotes integration within that sphere, but may also fragment meaning beyond it.

Analysis can be used as a tool of clarification, to ensure consistency within the use of a particular model. This is, indeed, the purpose not only of analysis in philosophy or other disciplines, but also of logic and mathematics, which examine the consistent properties of the models used to create propositional claims. Logical analysis of concepts in analytic philosophy, or mathematical modelling of theoretical positions in science, can be used to ensure that people researching using these theories and concepts do so consistently – which can, within limits, be integrative. The larger the volumes of data available, the more mathematical modelling can help us to handle that data consistently in accordance with a theory: so, for instance, the mathematical modelling of vaccine design has streamlined the process of the development of new vaccines. Like any kind of clarification, however, this should not be seen as an end in itself, but as a tool to be used within the terms of a particular useful model. As I have already argued in *The Five Principles*, analysis can also reinforce the models relied on in a specialized context, and thus also work against the synthesis required to integrate the perspective of that context to other contexts.[4]

The value of the practice of *stipulation* should also not be underestimated as an approach to clarifying meaning for particular purposes. It may be observed that this series of books is full of stipulation: it could not have been written at all if the meanings of the terms employed were restricted to those already habitually employed within particular specialisms or traditions. To be able to synthesize a model, we have to be able to expand its terms in ways that can be combined with those in other models, which means that we need to be able to state for ourselves what meaning we are using for the synthetic purpose we are engaged in. To insist on a narrower definition of the term when a stipulation is suggested is often simply to prevent synthetic thought from happening. That point can be illustrated from any of the major terms used in this book, most obviously meaning itself, but also belief, archetype, integration, and fragmentation. Middle Way Philosophy could be described as the creative and strategic outraging of specialists through stipulation.

4   II.2.d (pp. 77 ff).

Integration of Meaning

Three chapters later in this section (5.g–i) will explore in more detail how even clarified terms within a left-hemisphere dominated model then need to be reconnected in the creative interaction of the right, through ambiguity, synthesis, and sublimity. All of these processes may be seen as clouding the specific details of the meaning of a term that we may experience through clarification, but nevertheless they often cannot occur without some clarification as an earlier part of the process. Ambiguities involve the creative combination of meaning from different contexts, but not a loss of differentiation. They could not occur without prior differentiation leading us to associate a symbol with meaning in at least two different contexts that can then be united. Synthesis, similarly, could not take place without some analysis of what we are synthesizing in the contexts that we are synthesizing – the synthesis is never total (if it is, it is in danger of losing helpful meaning in an explosion of woolliness). Sublimity, that brief experience of intense integration of meaning, is also only possible because meaning is more habitually differentiated – creating a temporary power when it is recombined.

The value of pruning and clarification for the integration of meaning, then, should not cease to be appreciated: its 'rational' processes are necessary as an aspect of almost any integration of meaning process. However, they are also far from being an end in themselves. Integrating meaning is *primarily* a synthetic process, only secondarily an analytic process. Ockham's Razor only needs to be wielded in the specific circumstances that the matted, straggly hair of meaning's free growth is actually getting in our way – not out of any intrinsic principle of the rightness of barbering.

5.c. Absorptive Methods of Meaning Integration

> The most basic way of integrating fragmented meaning is in a relatively (but not absolutely) passive process of absorption. This can come through observing and associating new symbols (including vocabulary) in experience, or from activating wider grammatical structures to help us develop coherent models. Education offers many absorptive opportunities, as does learning foreign languages and travel. The arts can be absorptive, particularly as music or story, and fairy tales have a distinctive role in integrating meaning for children.

The processes by which we can integrate meaning lie on a scale between relatively active and relatively passive. None is entirely passive, nor on the other hand merely a matter of will. At one end of that spectrum, we 'absorb' new meaning mainly by being exposed to it – although of course receptivity is also needed. At the other end of the spectrum, we connect existing meanings through an active and creative process of synthesis – although there is still an adventitious passive element in the way we encountered these symbols and were stimulated to combine them. There is obviously a tendency for more active methods of meaning integration to take over from more passive ones as we grow older, as there become gradually fewer unfamiliar symbols in our environment, and as we gather more power to shape that environment. As we become more active, too, meaning integration gradually takes over from meaning differentiation, because we adopt a wider variety of meanings that fail to understand each other.

What I call 'absorptive' methods of meaning integration, then, are towards the passive end of the scale. We encounter new symbols through our senses, and, due to some motive of attention, these symbols 'make an impression' on us: that is, we form new neural links or associations that link a symbol with other experiences. The motive of attention (the active element) may be left-hemisphere driven (related to our goals) or right-hemisphere driven (dependent on general alertness), but it always needs to be present. Only a small part of what we could potentially experience through our senses is meaningful to us, because of this need for attention.

This absorption of meaning could occur at the level of merely observing and associating objects: for example, I go into a nearby wood and see an oak tree, so I associate the oak with the wood. Part of the *meaning* of 'oak' or 'that oak' then becomes its location in the wood and the whole atmosphere of the wood as I experienced it. A similar process can occur with a non-linguistic symbol such as a picture: that is, I associate the picture with the object (or type of object) and the meaning I have already developed for it.

When it comes to words, we likewise absorb new meaning by associating the word with a context that gives it meaning. When we see the new tree in the wood, perhaps our companion tells us that this is an 'oak', and we associate the word 'oak' both with the object and with the setting. We can do this, provided we have enough motive of attention, even if we never actively use the word, although our initial experience of meaning is still not devoid of enactive elements, dependent on the state of our bodies at the time we made the new connection. Of course, the word may be experienced in a spoken or a written form.

Many words, however, are not meaningful in isolation, but gain their meaning from a grammatical role in the construction of propositions. The way in which we learn the meaning of grammatical systems has long been the subject of debate in linguistics, with disagreement centring on how far our understanding of grammar is innate and how far it is learnt from experience. It is not necessary to take any position on that question in order to recognize that grammatical meaning is dependent on an interdependent system – a system comprising the cultural traditions of language, the biological potential for language, and the experiences of the individual linking these together. Experience is necessary for us to *activate* our grammatical abilities so that we can structure verbal meaning into propositions, whether that activation is of largely pre-existing or of largely newly-acquired capacities.

This activation of grammatical structure, however, is crucial to our development during childhood into the impulsive stage and then the imperial stage.[1] In this early period of life, we begin to move from the mere differentiation of meaning to the assembling of meaning into coherent models. At first these models are fragmentary, as we see in the difficulties four-year-olds may have in distinguishing 'fantasy' from 'reality'. However, even then, we understand sentences as the basis of the structure we are developing to try to represent the world around us for specific purposes. The more we can

1   III.2.c & d.

begin to compare these sentences with each other and make them consistent within a shared representational model, the more our grammatical structuring becomes meaningful. For instance, the use of the conjunctions 'and' and 'but' allow us to distinguish consistent and inconsistent representations: 'The cat is purring and affectionate, *but* she kills mice too'. In a language with the definite article ('the') such as English, even the seemingly insignificant grammatical function word can help us make important distinctions: 'He's not just any old mayor, he's *the* mayor of London'.

As we develop, then, we continually absorb symbolic associations with objects, with non-linguistic symbols, with words, and with phrases or propositions in which grammatical terms are used. We do not pay equal attention to all of this 'data' (which is why it may be misleading just to think of it as 'data'). Some of it may be rapidly forgotten, lost in synaptic pruning. Some of it may be adopted more actively for communicative, expressive, or meditative use, as I will discuss it in the next few chapters, and this usage considerably strengthens the neural links concerned. Some of it remains more or less passive, but familiar: perhaps I see a particular red car on the street outside my house every day, and I have no idea what model it is or who it belongs too, but nevertheless its appearance is constantly associated with the location where it is habitually parked. It is only if it moved and was parked somewhere else that I might start to pay more active attention to it.

All of this absorbed meaning provides us with a rich fund of resources that may have an integrative function, because it may help us to bridge gaps in understanding. When a detective questions me about my observations of the red car, I make new links of significance with it – perhaps it turns out to have been in regular use by some criminals. When I learn about the effects of climate change in Australia, adding to my overall understanding of climate change across the globe, I could not understand this without first having learnt what 'Australia' means, and making lots of associations between that word and its shape on a map, its climate, its wildlife, etc. When a mother fails to understand her teenaged son's obsession with video games, she begins her journey towards greater understanding just by recognizing that the terms he is using (such as 'Fortnite' or 'Call of Duty') are names of games, so these symbols are the focus of great value to him.

Obviously, one of the main contexts where we absorb new meaning in this way is education. The main value of education is clearly the way in which it makes an increasing range of symbols more meaningful, so that we can more readily understand whatever experiences we engage with in our later lives using those symbols. That is why education is education in meaning, not in 'knowledge'. Even when, for instance, a physics teacher acquaints us with a new formula showing us the relationship between mass and acceleration, the value of this lies in the way that we are able to apply it to understand events in the world around us, as part of a consistent and useful model of scientific explanation. It is not the 'factuality' or 'truth' of these formulae that makes them worth learning (they may be superseded by a new theory of physics in the future), but their meaning, which enables them to be used provisionally as a theoretical tool.

The breadth of meaning that we need is one of the best arguments for general education that is not prematurely specialized, and that this general element needs to continue throughout adult life. However, an education that focuses effectively on meaning rather than 'knowledge' needs to be organized and prioritized accordingly, in terms of the ways in which we encounter meaning rather than in terms of our idealized model of the world. I suggest that that requires a curriculum of deep generic skills rather than of areas of knowledge. In the educational curriculum as currently organized, however, we need to try to approach study in terms of the integration of meaning it can aid us in. This probably means that learning that is primarily absorptive is insufficient, and that the greater depth offered by communicative, expressive, and meditative integration of meaning needs to be maximized in the ways that we prioritize our use of education.

Learning foreign languages is one of the key absorptive forms of meaning integration available to us, because of the ways that it acquaints us with new models for the use of both vocabulary and grammar. Studies have shown that the use of a foreign language can help us to overcome a range of types of framing effects,[2] and that bilingual people can resolve conflicting cues more easily.[3] The use of a foreign language also makes our moral decision-making

2   Costa et al (2014a).
3   Bialystok (2009).

more flexible, so that we are more likely to consider alternative moral approaches to our earlier conditioned ones.[4] We are forced to become aware of varying boundaries in our use of terms, possible distinctions not made in our language, or the questioning of distinctions made in our language, so that eventually we can no longer merely translate directly from one term to another, but instead have to move between differing models.

Sometimes this movement between models in different languages can have an immediate impact on our belief-assumptions. For example, both French and German distinguish between terms for 'knowledge by acquaintance' (*connaitre*, *kennen*) and 'propositional knowledge' (*savoir*, *wissen*), which are all bundled together in the English 'know': a distinction that may obviously help to reinforce a difference in usage and assumptions. English, on the other hand, does make distinctions that French does not make, such as the distinction between 'bullock' and 'beef', where French has the single word *boeuf*. The distinction between an animal and its meat in English may well have the effect of decreasing our awareness of the origins of the meat in the living animal. Variations in grammatical structure may have even more profound effects in extending our awareness of meaning: for example, English has a complex range of tenses which allow subtle distinctions in time in relation to a speaker, that are not available in many other languages: 'I am going to eat', 'I will eat', 'I will be eating', 'I will have been eating', and 'I am about to eat' are all distinct.

Learning foreign languages is mainly absorptive because, although we learn faster when using language actively, it depends largely on being in a context where the language is used. Language teachers attempt to reproduce such an environment in a classroom, but this is only a limited substitute for the social environment where the language is routinely spoken in everyday life. In this respect, the integration of meaning through language learning closely follows that through travel. By immersing ourselves in a new and culturally different environment, we encounter new meanings that are not only linguistic, but also strongly offered by the symbolic power of all the objects around. In my own experience this is strongly exemplified by travelling to India: there, many of the more educated people spoke English, but the meaning of people and objects in the

---

4   Costa et al (2014b).

environment contributed to a massive extension of my cultural horizons: acrid-sweet smells, bicycle rickshaws, differently harmonized music, chaotic traffic, urban cows, rubbish heaps in the street, dirty temples, street sleeping, tiny shops selling multi-coloured powders.... These are all relatively superficial impressions, of course, before we get on to the study of the deeper motives that sustain all these phenomena, and that add to their meaning when they are understood. The development of meaning absorbed by such meaningful associations is multiplied by reflection that links them together with other meanings.

Absorptive approaches to meaning are also found in the arts, even though the most important use of the arts is expressive and creative. Mere exposure to the arts can not only make us aware of a range of different new symbols, but also raise the very possibility of creativity and synthesis. As already noted, however, such absorption depends on a degree of attention. It is possible to walk quickly through an art gallery and experience no interest in the exhibits – caught up, perhaps, in habitual superficiality and conceptual reduction. To absorb meaning from them, one needs to actively look at works of art, to explore them sensually and imaginatively with a degree of curiosity. With that relatively small degree of active engagement, however, the work of art yields a cornucopia of meaning, whether that was left there by the artist or developed entirely by our own associative experience with what they produced.

Absorptive effects are perhaps most obvious with music, because we can develop a sense of association with a tune even without very deliberately listening to it – as exemplified by our later recognition of it. As discussed in 3.d, a non-linguistic symbol like a tune can particularly extend meaning through its depth of embodied meaning, as it becomes associated with our experiences of heartbeat, pulse, and voice tones.

Absorptive meaning also readily comes from listening to, reading, or watching stories, which have a crucial role in the development of archetypal meaning. This is particularly due to the relationship between goals and inspiration in relation to the hero archetype, which fulfils the function of inspiring us to persevere towards goals (even when the goals, or the methods for reaching them, change). The shadow archetype also inspires us to be alert for threats that interfere with our well-being and pursuit of goals, whilst the anima/animus archetype inspires us in developing the relationships with others that we need, obviously also the object of goals.[5] A narrative typically involves a character or characters, with whom we identify, pursuing goals and overcoming difficulties in their pursuit, so that the experience of hearing or reading a story makes those goals and the methods used to pursue them increasingly meaningful for us. Even if the hero of a narrative is in a very different situation from us, we can still be inspired by the similarities in meaning between their situation and ours – similarities that are accentuated by skilful telling of the story. Inspiration works on us because of its diachronic aspects – that is, that it keeps offering meaning for us across time, and encourages us to integrate meaning through time. Thus, when a goal that we have started to pursue becomes less meaningful, reading any novel – from Jane Austen's *Emma* to Tolkien's *Lord of the Rings* – can help to rekindle it, not because of its precise fit with our own goals, but more because of its integration with wider meaning in a breadth of human experience. Similarly, after watching a film, we can leave the cinema in a state of inspiration, as the meaning of the characters and our identification with their progress has not only been presented in story, but often reinforced through imagery.

The traditional role of stories in early childhood tells us much about the importance of narrative in the psychological development of children – an importance explored as long ago as the 1970s by Bruno Bettelheim. Although he lacked a very precise account of meaning, in broad-brush terms Bettelheim identified how listening to fairy tales aided the helpful development of it in children:

> To find deeper meaning, one must be able to transcend the narrow confines of a self-centred existence and believe that one will make a significant contribution to life – if not right now, then at some future time. This feeling is necessary if a person is to be satisfied with himself and with what he is doing. In order not to be at the mercy of the vagaries of life, one must develop one's inner resources, so that one's emotions, imagination, and intellect mutually support and enrich one another. Our positive feelings give us the strength to develop our rationality; only hope for the future can sustain us in the adversities we unavoidably encounter.[6]

Though there are many vague and unexamined terms here ('self-centred', 'satisfied', 'vagaries of life', 'rationality', and 'hope'),

---

5   Ellis (2022) 1.a.
6   Bettelheim (1975) pp. 3–4.

Integration of Meaning

Bettelheim goes on to give a relatively precise account of how many specific fairy tales can go on to provide this development of meaning. This is a development that has a particular importance at the impulsive stage of development, when models are still fragmentary, but also continues into adulthood. If we no longer understand meaning in terms of belief, it becomes easier to explain how fairy tales provide us with *resources* that are used in increasingly coherent models (roughly what Bettelheim, and many others, insist on calling 'rationality'). These resources do not themselves have to fit into coherent beliefs to provide meaning: grandmothers do not turn into wolves, or coaches into pumpkins, in a coherent set of beliefs about the world. The inspirational meaning of fairy tales, however, gives us a sense of integrated values that can be applied across fragmentary models. The more those values (like the sense of an overall integrating good) can be applied in a wide range of imaginary conditions, the deeper they will go as values.

Our ability to absorb meaning through any of the arts, as through education or travel, though, is merely a prelude to more active engagement. All of these different ways of absorbing meaning have their more active communicative, expressive, and meditative counterparts, as we will see in the next few chapters.

5.d. Communicative Methods of Meaning Integration

> Although communication only contingently shares meaning, it can still integrate it (1) in its production, reinforcing meaning for the individual, (2) in the meaning shared with others, either implicitly or explicitly, which can also enable dialectical reframing, and (3) in the development of meaning resources for others, including in the patterns of meaning found in stories or theories. The Buddhist speech precepts offer some practical guidelines for everyday application of this.

The integration of meaning gathers pace as we grow old enough not only to absorb, but to communicate. As I discussed in 2.d, communication is not the basis of meaning, but the relative coincidence of meaning between two or more people. If you ask me what sort of pet I have, and I say 'a dog' to you, there is probably enough similarity in our different understandings of the word for us to communicate sufficiently for our purposes – at least, for you not to think that my pet is a rabbit or a canary, and to get roughly the right sort of animal, however differently we may feel about dogs, and however different our prototypical dogs may be. In many other cases, however, communication fails, because the words or other symbols I use to try to communicate do not have a similar enough meaning for us for the practically important message to be received. For instance, if I tell you that I have a dog because of the companionship it offers, but dogs have only ever been an experience of threat to you, you will at best have only a very abstracted understanding of what the companionship of a dog means, and may even interpret it wholly as a defensive function – a 'companion' as a guard.

Even in this situation in which communication has only a relative and contingent effectiveness, it can nevertheless have an integrative effect. Communication can integrate meaning in at least three different ways, both individual and socio-political. It can integrate meaning for me when I am trying to communicate, because I am actively using the symbols. It can integrate meaning between me and others whom I am communicating with, to the extent that understanding is spread and conveyed. In the process of spreading such understanding socio-politically, I may also be enriching the symbol resources for others, either at an individual or (where those new resources are shared) at a socio-political level.

Firstly, then, communication can integrate meaning for the individual because of the way that it reinforces the meaning of symbols for that individual. When we use a symbol actively in order to communicate using it, far more of our bodies and nervous systems are involved: not only drawing on understanding of a word, but on its appropriate grammatical combination with other words, in response to a live communicative situation where we need to adapt the words to the needs of the moment. To understand how to communicate, we need signals from the audience as well as an understanding of what we want to say, to adapt the language we use to their understanding. All this adaptation and connection is an active process for us that synthesizes a given word much more fully with the context around it, strengthening all the neural connections. It is a familiar truism for language teachers, for instance, that new language used actively is far more deeply learned than what is merely absorbed passively: they thus typically do not just introduce new vocabulary, but set their students a task in which they make use of that vocabulary.

The same points apply to the effect of using non-linguistic symbols for communication. The design of icons used on computers and phones, for instance, serve the communicative function of instant recognizability through simplicity and standardization. By designing such an icon to represent a meaning we want to communicate, we are reinforcing its meaning for ourselves. The same would apply when setting words to a song, adding musical communication to linguistic communication, and in the process making the language far more memorable both for ourselves and others.

Secondly, the act of communication integrates socio-politically. Obviously the main aim of communication is to share meaning. We do this only to the extent that the associative effects of the symbols we use coincide – which they do because of both similarities in human body structure, similarities in the cultural association of symbols, and similarities in mental state allowing mutual attunement. The similarities in human body structure can help us to communicate even in situations where we have no shared language: for instance, if someone points downwards into their mouth we are quite likely to understand that they are hungry, because of the universality of food being taken into the mouth and pointing indicating an object of importance. Cultural similarities obviously enable mutual understanding of words, but this also extends to non-linguistic symbols and gestures: Greeks understand each other to mean 'no' when they toss back their heads, in a way that confuses Western Europeans. It is mutual attunement at individual level, however, that enables the closest integration of meaning through communication. We get an indication of another's mental state, their emotions, and the direction of their attention from their bodily positions and movements – all the more so if they are well-known to us. This not only helps us to choose our words appropriately, but also sometimes to match our own 'body language' to theirs and thus make communication more effective: a skill developed in 'neuro-linguistic programming'.[1]

This sharing of meaning through communication is clearly a requirement for dialectic – that is, for the process by which opposing beliefs can be reconciled through reframing. The reframing of a belief first requires that we consider other possible models beyond the one we have been relying upon and that has created the conflict. Having considered other possible models, we are then able to recognize the ways in which they might serve our longer-term goals better and shift to them. The pictures of the two mules **[diagram 7]** illustrate this process effectively, including the communicative integration of meaning, despite the non-linguistic nature of the communication in this case.[2] In the fourth frame, the mules have changed their orientation so that they are facing each other, which is sufficient for the most basic universal communication to occur, also accompanied by some degree of personal attunement, despite the presumed absence of verbal communication. No words need necessarily be exchanged here for a dialectic to occur, then, but only a shift in attention to other possible models of the mules' goals in relation to the immediate situation. An important part of the communication is surely the mutual attunement of the mules as they implicitly recognize each other's presence and shared needs, no longer so narrowly focused only on their own individual needs.

This account of the integration of meaning in communication as a *precondition* for the integration of belief has some parallels in the theory of communicative action of Jürgen Habermas.[3] Habermas's approach to communicative action must be distinguished from his account of *meaning*, which reduces meaning to communication, and

1   Bandler & Grinder (1979).
2   II.2.d & 5.b.
3   Habermas (1984).

thus offers no advance on Wittgensteinian versions of representationalism. However, Habermas did much to develop a detailed understanding of the conditions in which we could engage in effective discourse, which he saw as the basis of universal morality and of democracy. For this he uses a concept of *validity* which is not merely logical validity – rather it lays the emphasis on a hearer's capacity to understand the reasons offered by a speaker. We do not have to share the reasons or accept the beliefs offered in order to allow the speaker entry into a dialectic or a field of discourse where the potential to resolve conflict then arises. Whilst concepts like 'rationality' and 'validity' in my view generally do more to obscure the issues here than to illuminate them (so are better avoided), it must be acknowledged that some sophisticated pragmatic philosophies, like that of Habermas, do apply the integration model to some extent (usually at a social rather than a psychological level), and do incorporate insights into the relationship between meaning and belief once the language is unpicked.

Diagram 7. The two mules.

Thirdly, the process of communication may also have an impact on the meaning resources available to others. It may introduce new symbols, or it may reinforce existing ones. Others may have symbols introduced or reinforced by absorbing what we are communicating (although to do this, they will still need a degree of engagement with it), or by more actively responding to us using the same symbols. Again, language teaching offers a convenient and obvious model here. When trying to introduce new language, the teacher aims firstly to create connections with what the student already understands, before then getting the student to use that language. This is a formalization of the model that applies to all of us when we learn new symbols, of whatever kind.

The active telling of a story offers a further instance of this kind of impact of meaning integration. By telling a story, we actively reinforce the archetypal meaning of the characters and events in it, both for ourselves (as mentioned in the previous chapter) and for others. The telling of the story not only involves activity that stimulates our system, but also introduces a new parallel version of what we conventionally regard as 'the same' story (using, at least, slightly different words and/or expression each time, but possibly also variations in character and plot). The creativity involved in retelling deepens the embodied meaning we experience, and this creativity can also communicate itself to a live audience through mutual attunement. This process also applies to a lesser extent in different readings of a text, and in different performances of a play.

We could also see the active sharing of meaning as occurring in the scientific communication of hypotheses, evidence, methods, and modified theories. Although the focus in scientific method is on the justification or rejection of general beliefs, in order to share the testing of those beliefs against evidence we first have to share meaning. This meaning does not usually take the form of isolated words or symbols, but mainly of propositions that can be assembled into hypothesis and theory (as we become more confident in them) as well as justificatory statements about methods and evidence. None of these, by themselves, indicate that we necessarily *accept* the new beliefs being offered or use them as a basis of further practice. However, they are the basis on which a scientific discourse can take place.

Habermas distinguished between aesthetic, moral, and scientific types of discourse, suggesting that each of them had slightly different criteria of 'validity' (that is, of integrated meaning) that allowed them to form the basis of a discourse, before conclusions were drawn. This kind of distinction should not be applied too rigidly, and may well be a product of the false fact-value dichotomy.[4] However, it can be accepted that the basis of meaning in every discourse varies from the others, because different models are being assumed. It is the embodiment of meaning that gives us the opportunity to integrate the different models involved at the level of meaning, so that we then create the basic conditions for potentially resolving disagreements of belief.

Communicative integration of meaning as a practice can obviously be engaged whenever we communicate, so is most often a matter of bringing attention to *how* we communicate. In this area, the Buddhist tradition of speech precepts seems to capture many of the key aspects of what communication should be like that aims to integrate meaning rather than fragment it. The traditional five lay precepts in Buddhism only include one speech precept – to avoid lying. However, the ten precepts, as developed by Sangharakshita from sources in the Pali Canon,[5] offer a more comprehensive list of four negative and three positive speech precepts: negatively, abstention from false, harsh, frivolous, and slanderous speech, and positively, truthful communication, kindly and gracious words, and helpful and harmonious utterance. False speech is wrong, broadly speaking, not because it involves 'falsehood', but because it undermines the shared social basis for justified belief, whilst communication motivated by truthfulness motivates mutual understanding through mutual attunement and trust.[6] Harsh speech makes mutual understanding more difficult because it alienates, whilst kindly communication obviously makes it easier. Frivolous speech disperses the attention needed for understanding of new meaning through communication, whilst slanderous speech degrades the meaning of others unnecessarily: a helpful motive is thus needed both in terms of how we speak and in terms of the content of what we communicate.

Such simple guidelines for communication as practice do not require any authority from the Buddhist tradition to be applied,

4 I.8.b.
5 The earliest of these is in the *Kutadanta Sutta*, Digha Nikaya 5.16 (Walshe 1995 p. 137). See Sangharakshita (1989) 2.2.
6 VIII.4.

but merely a recognition of their role in the integration of meaning. They can obviously be applied not only in immediate oral discussion with others, but also in body language and in written communication and interpretation. They are, of course, inseparable from other aspects of practice that may be focused more on our other actions or our mental states.[7]

---

7   II.6.

5.e. Expressive Methods of Meaning Integration

> We can integrate meaning effectively by outwardly expressing inner states, linking them to new combinations of symbols. This involves the creative recombination of art, which copies with variation rather than precisely. Art therapy and (flexibly administered) ritual provide particularly strong ways of integrating conflicting emotions. Integrating meaning expressively through the arts does not necessarily integrate belief, so can leave moral conflict, but provides a contingent basis for doing so.

Expression involves the *externalizing* of mental states, thoughts, and feelings into some symbolic form (a form that we often call art). We can distinguish expression from communication because expression is not necessarily intended to communicate – its communicative impact on others is an additional feature to its expressive value. Expression can create integration of meaning when new links within our own understanding are forged by this externalization. In effect, we learn by creating something new. We did not so fully or clearly understand what we experienced until we expressed it. For instance, we create an abstract picture to explore our emotions, we produce a figurative landscape painting to recreate our experience of that landscape, we tell a story about our recent difficulties to a friend, or we play a piece of music that becomes a channel for our grief.

The 'newness' of the thing we create or externalize is, of course, not absolute. We have had to relate experiences to symbols, and apply a combination of those symbols, so that they 'mean' the experience to us, but the symbols will often have been used in similar or even identical ways before. Perhaps we will manage to recombine symbols in new ways, but the originality consists not in their novelty, but in the way that the symbols reconnect our experience. Symbols that were previously separated become connected to each other *through* their association with our experience. For instance, the taste of mint tea develops a new piquancy if we associate it with an experience of losing a person. If we then create a poem to contextualize that sense of loss, the mint tea as a symbol then also becomes associated with the healing of that sense of loss.

Expression thus becomes inseparable from creativity. By expressing we have to bring together new meaning in response to our experience, and that bringing together of new meaning from previous resources is also creative. The meaning that is brought together is right-hemisphere or embodied meaning, of the kind that constantly combines and recombines in unpredictable new ways, rather than the left-hemisphere representations that are believed to allow precise copying through reproduction of exactly the same symbolic content.[1] As long as we recognize that meaning is embodied, however, and thus dependent on the recombination of individual experience, there can never be such a thing as precise copying of meaning. Expression is thus always new expression.

There is also a close relationship between the integration of meaning occurring in creative expression and that we experience it as beauty – as already discussed in 3.d. As I suggested there, both aesthetic and symbolic forms of beauty arise from an integrative experience of meaning created in response to an object. In aesthetic forms of meaning, it is the immediate sensory experience of the object (for instance, its colour contrasts) that makes it especially meaningful to us when focused on, and unifies our attention. In symbolic beauty, though, it is the associations of the symbols used that can integrate our attention. When we express creatively, too, we are unifying our attention and thus creating beauty within the terms of that attention, whether or not what we have produced strikes others as beautiful.

One common way into expressive meaning integration is the use of the arts in a broadly therapeutic framework. This includes formal art therapy, but also the more informal therapeutic use of the arts by individuals to engage with the conditions of conflict in their experience. 'Art therapy' may make use of the visual arts, music, drama, or creative writing, but the distinctive element is obviously that it is framed by a therapist to ensure that it stays focused on the value of the integrative value of the process rather than the results (or indeed any abstracted interpretation of the 'meaning' of the work). When people lack the confidence or initiative to engage in the arts for themselves unaided, this can be especially valuable. However, the same focus on the process is characteristic of all serious practice of the arts, with artists, writers, and musicians generally well aware that a finished 'work of art' is a side effect of an ongoing process of noting experience, sketching, drafting, or other practice.

---

1   McGilchrist (2009) ch. 7. This becomes the basis of an interpretation of creation in Ellis (2018) 4.a.

A systematic review article in 2018 found that formal art therapy had clear beneficial effects with a range of groups of patients, including patients with cancer and other medical conditions, prison inmates, the elderly, and those with 'ongoing daily challenges' – although the evidence was less clear, perhaps surprisingly, with mental health conditions.[2] Given the complexity of assessing such an area, and the assumptions that have to be made when doing so, it is hardly surprising if the evidence is patchy, even though it is positive overall. What the reviews seem less clear about is exactly how art therapy works, prior to its goal to 'improve cognitive and sensorimotor functions, foster self-esteem and self-awareness, cultivate emotional resilience, promote insight, enhance social skills, reduce and resolve conflicts and distress, and advance societal and ecological change'.[3] An integration of meaning framework has the potential to show how the barriers to overcoming reduced cognitive functions, lack of self-awareness, lack of emotional resilience or insight, and consequent lack of social skills are explicable within a framework of conflict and its integration. This can be the case even with a gap necessarily remaining between the development of meaning through these methods (which only indirectly enables conflict resolution), and the more direct use of art therapy to successfully resolve conflicts of desire or belief.

That gap between the integrative value of the arts as a creative process and their moral effectiveness is one that can be easily identified at an individual level – where it stands out in those cases of artistic refinement accompanied by acute psychological and/or moral conflict. The tortured artist is an established figure of the Western Romantic tradition, seemingly defying the whole idea that the arts can be integrally beneficial to anyone – let alone some of those unfortunate people who are sometimes abused or manipulated in the name of the higher creative process of someone else. This is a complex area that will need further unpicking in volume VII of this series,[4] but for now it can only be noted that the gap between artistic and moral value is a function of the gap between integration of meaning and integration of belief. There is no inevitable moral progress from expressive integration of meaning, but

2 Regev & Cohen-Yatziv (2018).
3 American Art Therapy Association, quoted in Regev & Cohen-Yatziv (2018).
4 VII.6.

it does create an important condition that can be used as a basis of moral progress, because integrated belief can only be founded on integrated meaning. Without integration of meaning broadly construed, however, there can be no moral progress based on more integrated judgements. That integration does not have to necessarily be generated by expressive means, but expressive integration of meaning is one of the most potent practical approaches to it.

Another area where meaning can be readily integrated expressively is through ritual. Ritual attempts to offer us archetypal inspiration through actions performed in relation to externalized symbols – often habitual and/or socially shared actions. Ritual used effectively can powerfully express our emotional states whilst bringing them into a new creative contact with symbols of a wider context that can help us avoid absolutization of those states. For instance, a funeral ceremony can provide an expression of grief, bringing our frustrated desires in relation to a deceased person into contact with a wider reflective, social, and archetypal context that enables us to adjust those desires and better channel our frustration. This will only work, of course, if we do actually experience our grief in the context of the funeral, and if the wider context we are being offered is meaningful to us, rather than the mere abstraction that may be erected by seeing the ritual just as the fulfilment of a social or religious duty.

There is thus a massive difference between 'dead' or 'meaningless' ritual mediated only through the left hemisphere, and meaningful ritual that is an expression of emotions or beliefs that we bring to it. The identification of archetypal functions only with specific symbols (such as believing that Jesus is the only way to salvation), and the lack of shared meaning across group boundaries for those symbols, has created a major challenge for the function of ritual in the modern world. This is typified by the idea that ritual is 'meaningless' (at the alienated end of the spectrum) or defined only in terms of the requirements of a particular tradition (at the group-biased end of the spectrum). Ritual can only offer an effective practice for expressive meaning integration if enough attention is paid both to the actual psychological effects of a given ritual on an individual (as opposed to its abstracted formal requirements) and to the flexible modification of a ritual so that it has beneficial psychological effects. That means, for instance, that one shouldn't ever just press ahead with ritual in a particular form because that is the traditional thing to do in a given religious context. The ritual leader needs to anticipate the feelings of the participants and take them into account.

Creative ritual, however, can rapidly assume many of the qualities of creative drama. Its central value lies in the ways in which it connects our neural systems and meaning experience into wider networks, in which our absolutized emotional surges can be helpfully contextualized. Just as a flooded river does far less harm if there is a water meadow available to absorb it, stresses to our valued desires and beliefs can be absorbed far more readily if we have created a littoral zone of wider meaning to absorb those stresses. We do this primarily by actively creating our water meadow, in a deliberate awareness that this 'useless' ground is likely to be of supreme value to us in the longer term.

5.f. Meditative Methods of Meaning Integration

> Meaning integration can be directly cultivated by associating patterns of meaning in inner experience. This can be done indirectly by relaxing intrusive patterns of disconnected meaning in mindfulness meditation, but also more directly by gradually widening our associations with people through loving-kindness meditations. Visualization (or other sensual recollection) of archetypal symbols may also integrate meaning through association with a source of inspiration.

The final method of meaning integration is one that involves working directly with the associative patterns in our inner experience. Meditation involves working directly with our mental states, but working with meaning specifically in meditation involves creating new associations or strengthening existing ones. Mindfulness meditation can be said to integrate meaning in the most basic fashion. Some meditative approaches work with emotional experience, such as the Buddhist *metta-bhavana* or loving-kindness meditation. There are also a number of meditation practices in different religious traditions that strengthen our associations with archetypal symbols.

Mindfulness meditation involves the integration of immediate associations that are caught up in loops of proliferation (reinforcing feedback loops).[1] When caught up in disconnected meaning, we reconnect it by returning to the wider object of meditation (such as the breath), constantly reinforced by relaxed body awareness that prevents our attention being dissipated. These fragmented meanings are also, of course, often associated with conflicting desires and beliefs that prevent their mutual engagement, but their re-association needs to happen initially at the level of meaning: first of all we need to recognize simply that we *experience* associations that are disconnected from others. It is the relationship between these different associations, recognized as connected within (what we assume to be) the same wider experience over time that enables us to associate them more strongly with each other, at least at that point. The repetition of that process can also gradually reinforce these new wider associations.

States of meditative absorption or *jhana* that can be achieved in mindfulness meditation connect us temporarily to more

---

1 I.1.a.

undifferentiated meaning states, of the kind discussed in 1.c. Of course, this does not remove all the differentiation of meaning that has occurred throughout our lives, but it allows us to briefly feel once again the wider relationship between all the meaning that has been differentiated, and thus make integration more meaningful by giving us a glimpse of it. As a result, conflict, which depends on lack of understanding, may at least be temporarily suspended – something we are likely to experience as a release of energy that was bound up in that conflict.

Mindfulness meditation can be a method of meaning meditation even though it does not work directly with meaning, but rather with aesthetic sensations: indeed the whole way it works is by *avoiding* meaningful symbols so as to go back to an undifferentiated state. Thus aesthetic sensations like the breath, the sight of a flickering candle flame, or the movements of walking are appropriate objects for mindfulness meditation. We do not focus on the *idea* of these things, but rather their sensual complexity as we directly encounter it. Engagement with the arts at an aesthetic level where we engage with the texture (rather than the symbolic meaning) can have similar effects, which is why listening to music, particularly, can have meditative effects. As soon as symbols and their meaning intrude into this sort of practice, though, differentiation and its long-term impact on us start to reassert themselves.

Some other sorts of meditation work directly with meaning rather than with aesthetic sensations. These can be roughly divided between those that focus on cultivating a particular emotional state, and those that focus on specific symbols. Meditation that focuses on cultivating an emotional state allows free range in terms of which symbols are used, but we need to select the symbols according to their emotional impact on us, so as to gradually lead us towards more consistently open and creative emotional states.

In Buddhist meditative tradition, the group of four meditations known as the *brahmaviharas* (abodes of God) work in this way, with each of the four focusing on the cultivation of a distinct positive emotion: *metta* (loving-kindness), *karuna* (compassion), *mudita* (sympathetic joy), and *upekkha* (equanimity).[2] These emotional states are only distinct from each other in their relationships to goals, with

---

2   *Tevijja Sutta*, Digha Nikaya 13.76-8 (Walshe 1995 p. 194). See Kamalashila (1992) ch. 2 and Salzberg (1997). Also discussed in Ellis (2020) 7.g.

karuna being a compassionate response to suffering (conditions interfering with our goals), *mudita* a positive response to success, and *upekkha* an emotional stability beyond attachment to the success or failure of goals. *Metta* is the more basic state to be cultivated that runs through the others regardless of the conditions: a state based in our embodied experience where we are open to new understanding from the other (empathy), and share those feelings (sympathy) – though in a contextualized way. When we encounter suffering, we can thus sympathize without being overwhelmed by that suffering, and when we encounter success, can share that success with enough contextualization to avoid the reinforcing feedback loops of envy. In the further state of equanimity, we are equipped to deal with conditions of either success or failure without descending into proliferating feedback loops.

This is achieved through the gradual development of meaning in response to symbols in our imagination that evoke these positive responses, whether in relation to repressed aspects of our own experience or to others. Each practice traditionally consists of five stages, focused respectively on oneself, a good friend, a neutral person, an enemy, and finally all other beings in the universe. It is assumed in this ordering that we will find it easier to develop positive emotion in relation to ourselves than to others, though of course this could be modified. Either way, we need to start by imagining people in ways that that will evoke open emotional responses of goodwill, then incrementally expand the range and difficulty of the people we imagine whilst maintaining that emotional response. For instance, we might start by remembering ourselves in a highly integrated past state, perhaps where we recognized and accommodated an aspect of ourselves that was previously repressed, and experience positive emotions in response to these other aspects of ourselves. We might imagine ourselves in a moment of happiness on a beach. We may then expand that response to one of positive feelings about a good friend, and then even towards someone we regard as an enemy. In the process we are not, of course, changing the nature of that other person externally, but we are modifying their role as a symbol for us – we are helping to make them *mean* something bigger and less prone to reinforcing feedback emotions. We are doing this by connecting together narrower, more conflicted meanings for that person as a symbol with wider ones that we have perhaps previously neglected, so that we *understand* that person better through a fuller and more generous response to them.

A third type of meditation that can enable integration of meaning is one that involves the visualization of archetypal symbols. Such symbols are usually associated with the world's religious traditions, but there is no necessary relationship with 'religion'. Rather the key importance of the symbols is that they should be inspiring over time, providing an associative link back to embodied experience of more integrated states. As I discussed in *Archetypes in Religion and Beyond*, such inspirational symbols can be seen as fulfilling broadly four archetypal functions:[3] persevering in goals (the heroic function), developing relationships with the other (the anima/animus function), avoiding long-term threats (the shadow function), and accessing unrecognized potentiality overall (the God archetype). Any of these could be visualized, but the God archetype is the most widespread.

Such visualization is well established in Buddhist tradition, where the Buddha, or other symbolic figures (such as Tara or the Bodhisattva Avalokiteshvara) are associated with 'enlightenment' as a touchpoint for our aspirations over time.[4] Christians may instead recollect or visualize Jesus, or the entire Holy Trinity, or a saint. A more temporally limited 'secular' heroic version of this is to keep visualizing the fulfilment of your goals to motivate yourself in reaching them. However, to avoid projection (that is, believing that the visualized figure does or does not 'exist' supernaturally or transcendently), reminders of the conditions of our practice and of our responsibility for them are also useful – in Mahayana Buddhism this is often done by beginning a visualization practice with a blue sky, and having the visualized figure emerge from and dissolve back into that blue sky.

Given the dominance of the visual sense in humans, visualizing in the sense of 'seeing' a potent symbol internally can be a powerful way of developing integration of meaning in a particular deliberate direction. What we see is often associated particularly with goal-orientation and predation, with the eye thus used as a symbol of the narrow focus of evil in Jung's *Red Book*.[5] However, the obsessiveness of the eye can be turned to more helpful ends too, when we use it

---

3   Ellis (2022) 1.a.
4   Ibid. 5.c.
5   Ellis (2020) 6.a; Jung (2009) pp. 288–9.

to recreate an imaginative image that will place our motives in a wider context. If we try to 'see' in too direct or wilful a way, indeed, this can be counter-productive, because the process becomes too much dominated by the left hemisphere. Rather, we need to allow an image to emerge in accordance with an overall intention. This is sometimes described as 'getting a sense of' the symbolic figure. Allowing that figure to emerge as a person is another crucial aspect of the imaginative process, because if it is too much dominated by the left hemisphere it will become an object lacking independent life.

However, the imaginative stimulus of the integration of meaning does not necessarily have to occur through the visual sense. Touch has a powerful role in developing and hence recollecting close relationships, so the memory of mutual touch may be an important aspect of anima/animus inspiration. Recollections of taste and smell may also help to shape an ambience that we associate with an archetypal symbol (for instance, the smell of incense in a temple). Imagined sound, however, is probably the second most important sense. Buddhist tradition uses mantras that are associated with particular visualized figures and may be inwardly recited during the visualization. The role of song in inspiring heroic effort is also well-known in many contexts, such as armies on the march or work-gangs engaged in physical labour. A piece of music can immediately and powerfully conjure up both an ambience and the mental state we associate with that ambience.

Integration of meaning through the deliberate inner focus of a meditation practice thus also has an immediate relationship with various communicative and expressive practices. Meditative visualizations have motivated artistic representation of Buddhas and Bodhisattvas in Buddhist tradition, with that artistic tradition both offering expressive practice to the artist and communicative integration to the viewer. In turn, such artistic representations can help to motivate and shape meditative visualization. The internal meditative recollection of music is also of course interdependent with the expressive production of music, and the use of music to communicate a strong motive to others. By encountering these symbols influenced by meditative practice, we may also absorb some of the inspiration that they can offer. In this way, four methods for the integration of meaning may come to be seen as merely aspects of one wider, inclusive method.

5.g. Ambiguity

> The integration of meaning depends on an acceptance of ambiguity and vagueness in basic meaning (beyond the context of a particular model). Ambiguity precedes differentiation, so we can reach back to a wider sense by the two-way ambiguous connection of metaphor. Loving-kindness meditation also accepts ambiguities in our view of people. Equivocation within a model, on the other hand, can maintain unnecessary conflict through contradictory belief.

The next three chapters of this section are concerned in one way or another with the breaking down of differentiated meaning boundaries, as an aspect of the process of integrating meaning. As I noted in 5.b, clarification in relation to goals is a necessary part of the development of meaning, providing a feedback mechanism whereby beliefs influence the meaning from which they are drawn. Clearly, where such clarification is needed, ambiguity is problematic, and we aim to dispel that ambiguity by clarifying. However, ambiguity is also the basis on which we can come to recognize the limitations of the models we are using in the first place. Without ambiguity, we potentially remain locked into absolutization, because we cannot conceive any alternatives to our clear-edged and representational conceptual beliefs. So how can we understand the positive role of ambiguity in the integration of meaning? How can we also understand its role in synthesis (which combines previously separated models) and in sublimity (temporary experience of integrated meaning)? The next two chapters extend the discussion of ambiguity in this chapter into those further areas. Here, however, I will be looking at the ways that ambiguity is a practically necessary part of embodied meaning, and thus of any process of meaning integration. I will also be noting the ways that ambiguity may also interfere with our integration at the belief level.

In philosophical thought, ambiguity is distinguishable from vagueness – ambiguity being a multiplicity of senses for a word, term, or proposition, whilst vagueness is a lack of determinacy in any quantity, including the boundaries of an object, the application of numbers, and the measurement of time or distance. However, vagueness is also covered in a wider sense of the term 'ambiguity' such as I am using here, because the lack of clear boundaries also implies that clear-cut senses do not apply to the objects that are supposed to lie within those boundaries. It is an aspect of representationalism to assume that a relationship between language and objects is the basis of meaning, and thus that there is some kind of defect in meaning when that relationship is *not* clear-cut.[1] Given embodied meaning, however, the relationship between objects and language is *not* the basis of meaning (except within the terms of particular schemas). Embodiment is a state of both ambiguity and vagueness.

The process of meaning integration is one of returning to the embodied basis of meaning as the common source of meanings that have become separated – not to remove the differentiation, but to make it provisional and to re-connect links that have been lost in the process of differentiation. To do this we need to venture back into a more ambiguous (and/or vague) world of experience, at least as far as is necessary to re-establish that connection. For example, a mother failing to understand her teenage son's obsession with video games needs to blur the edges of her understanding of what video games *mean* in order to empathize with why anyone would want to play them. She does not have to actually play them or enjoy them, but at least be able to imagine herself doing so. An English speaker's failure to understand a Japanese person speaking Japanese also requires a descent into ambiguity to be integrated, as she needs to recognize the non-absolute boundaries of the vocabulary terms and the grammar she is habitually using in English in order to engage with the very different boundaries habitually applied in Japanese. In the process of engaging with such ambiguity, the mother does not lose her understanding of why obsession with video games might be a bad idea, nor does the English speaker lose her grasp of the habitual boundaries in English, so the differentiation remains. However, the awareness of ambiguity extends.

The integrative effect of the arts likewise depends on this kind of re-establishment of embodied meaning connections by questioning the limitation of a model, metaphor, or schema. Perhaps the art that most directly does this is poetry, which achieves its most profound effects by making us aware of multiple meanings simultaneously. Here is an example from a poem by Yehuda Amichai:

---

1   The bias of ambiguity aversion: see V.2.g.

From the place where we are right
Flowers will never grow
In the spring.[2]

'The place where we are right' is here simultaneously an occasion of experiencing certainty that we are right, and a place – presumably a place of a kind that might have soil that flowers could grow in. 'Bodily experience as a place' is an established metaphor. The flowers are also simultaneously plants that might grow in this place (by metonymy), and an experience of growth from openness or integration, using a metaphor of 'creativity as organic growth'. By putting the experience of feeling we are right in a new context, this forces us to extend its meaning, and to reconsider any limitations we had applied to that meaning. To extend the meaning, though, we need to fully accept and inhabit the ambiguity of metaphorical extension, with neither the metaphor nor its 'basis' providing a final meaning.

Here the habitual response within the dominant representationalist tradition is to analyse the working of poetry in terms of 'denotation' and 'connotation' – 'literal' and 'metaphorical' elements, so that the 'real' meaning (the one that can be lined up with reality) becomes distinguishable from the poetic frills. In representational terms, then, this is a poem conveying a message about how feeling that we are right all the time interferes with creativity. It is not a poem 'about' flowers: the flowers are 'just metaphor'. However, there can be no such ranking in the metaphorical system. One element may be more basic to our embodied experience than another, but a metaphorical structure relates two elements of our embodied experience to each other, mixing their meaning together. From now on, we have to accept that (in this context at least) flowers carry some sense of creativity, and creativity carries some sense of flowers. Now that we have read this poem, their associations are connected, if they were not before. The representationalist prioritizing of one meaning over another is a practical one that has been mistaken for a necessary or metaphysical one,[3] in the sense that if we are to act in response to this poem it must be to limit our certainty about being right, not to cultivate flowers. But this practical prioritization in no sense needs to dictate our understanding of the *meaning* of the poetry.

2   Amichai (2000).
3   Also see V.2.j.

A similar integrative effect can be found through ambiguity in our relations with others. I described in the previous chapter how the Buddhist loving-kindness meditation (*metta-bhavana*) can open our sense of the *meaning* of others and thus create new conditions for resolving conflict. This shift in understanding of what another person *means* is one that depends on ambiguity. Whatever description we may adopt is one dependent on our own limited experience, and we normally form beliefs and act in relation to that assumed description – for instance, thinking of a manager as cruel because of his role in cutting your job. To appreciate the ambiguities in that description is not to cease to appreciate that he may be cruel, but it is to recognize the ambiguity of the label 'cruel': the manager may be cruel in some circumstances and with some people, but not others, or he may work within a system that is cruel, and be partially but not wholly shaped by that system. By recognizing such ambiguities, we can avoid the kinds of unnecessary conflict that might come from only blaming him personally for institutional actions, even if we are very clear about our opposition at an institutional level.

On the other hand, ambiguity can have the reverse effect – that of impeding integration of meaning – when taking the form of equivocation within an argument. An argument operates within the terms of potential beliefs formed within a given model, so if the model is understood in an inconsistent way, our beliefs and ensuing actions may also be inconsistent, creating rather than resolving conflict. In cases of equivocation, we use a given word or term with two different meanings, whilst assuming that it has the same meaning throughout, and drawing conclusions that apply only to one of the senses. For example, 'Nothing is more important to me than our friendship, but just staying in touch on social media is better than nothing, so I think it's more important to just stay in touch on social media than to be proper friends.' Here, 'nothing' in the first case means 'no possible thing', whilst in the second it means 'no contact at all': the equivocation then creates a contradictory conclusion.[4] More seriously, equivocation is very common in arguments about metaphysics, in which people combine both absolute and non-absolute understandings of what 'metaphysics' means whilst

---

4   See V.2.i for more on equivocation as a meaning fallacy.

determining their attitude to it, and thus allowing absolute assumptions to be adopted even whilst ostensibly arguing against them.[5]

The helpful use of ambiguity is thus one that applies it, not within the practical terms of a given model, but beyond them so as to integrate models. This is the process of synthesis, which I will discuss in the next chapter. Ambiguity is a basic feature of embodiment, and we deny it at our peril. We can only suppress it (rather than repressing it) for practical purposes within a given situation, in a context of wider awareness.

---

5   E.g. See my review of McGilchrist (2021) at https://www.middlewaysociety.org/the-matter-with-the-matter-with-things/

5.h. Synthesis

> Synthesis works both at the level of belief, where a dialectical process combines opposing beliefs, and at the prior level of meaning, where we consider possibilities that may then form new options for belief. Meaning synthesis needs to be held open to enable provisionality. Syntheses occur at different levels of development, in turn dependent on biological and cultural conditions. Integration of meaning is a complex application of synthesis, but one vital for addressing a range of conditions.

To integrate meaning is to *synthesize*. However, we need to distinguish between a variety of senses of the term *synthesis*. I have already discussed different aspects of these senses both in *Absolutization* and in *The Five Principles*. Synthesis can occur either at the meaning level or at the belief level, with the bringing together of fragmented meanings creating the possibility of provisionality of belief, as discussed in *The Five Principles*.[1] Synthesis can also occur at any level of complexity in which we combine different meanings – at the most basic 'cross-modal' level including the combination of information from different senses (visual and auditory, for instance), but also at a more complex level involving the integration of different metaphors and models.[2] It is at the more complex level where we may also start to describe synthesis as 'integration', which is a subcategory of synthesis. As synthesis is such an important and ongoing idea running throughout Middle Way Philosophy, this chapter needs to be seen as just connecting it to the integration of meaning in particular ways, not as offering the more comprehensive account that can emerge from all the volumes together.

In *Absolutization* I argued that synthesis can confer a form of justification on our beliefs, because the wider the range of conditions and interpretations we draw our beliefs from, the more likely we are to contextualize rather than absolutize any one of those perspectives. Synthesis of increasingly justified belief, however, depends on that of meaning, which I am more closely concerned with here. It is the integration of meaning that allows us to *understand* and *consider* options for belief within a provisional space. We can thus see the process of synthesis as occurring at two levels. The initial level combines with weak neural links meanings that have not been

1 II.2.d.
2 I.6.c.

Integration of Meaning 233

previously connected at all, but the belief level makes use of those weak links, strengthening their connection to the point where they can potentially be used to make practical judgements. Both types of synthesis involve an advance in our engagement with a breadth of conditions, which is the key requirement for justification.

In both cases, the process of synthesis has a generally dialectical type of structure, though much more clearly in the case of belief: a thesis is opposed by an antithesis, and the opposition is resolved by a synthesis. When beliefs are synthesized, the synthesis is a new set of beliefs that are distinct from either the thesis or the antithesis. For such new resolving beliefs to be developed, then, we need meaning resources to draw on that make them available to us. The availability of this third option requires a prior activity of meaning synthesis, in which we have come to understand, by a process of association, that alternatives are available. As described in chapters 5.c–f, the association process may be a matter of absorption, communication, expression, or meditation. It involves right-hemisphere activity by which new stimuli are accepted into the existing system of neural and associational links, and are allowed to modify that system.

The distinction between these two levels of synthesis (and our normal difficulty in distinguishing between them) helps to explain our frequent disappointment at how far we are able to change in response to what we recognize as good ideas or wise beliefs. For instance, we may recognize that it is a good idea in our personal situation to give up alcohol, which fogs our mind whenever we drink it, but this 'good idea' is only a meaning, not a belief, unless we can potentially act on it. A 'good idea' may indeed be highly impractical. We may not even have begun to address all the many conditions surrounding it – in the case of alcohol, say, all the social pressures and psychologically-entrenched habits that keep us using it. Even when the 'good idea' becomes more strongly meaningful, with more of these conditions coming into focus, it still does not imply that we *believe* that we should give up alcohol. The point at which we start to believe it is not, of course, necessarily the one where we actually act on it (the belief is not necessarily integrated), but it is the one where we start to represent it to ourselves as an intention or as a view of the 'facts'. Saying to ourselves 'I will avoid drinking alcohol tomorrow' is probably a mark of belief, even if we completely fail to act on it, whilst the mere understanding that it might be beneficial to give up alcohol is merely a synthesis of meaning – where the idea of giving up alcohol and the idea of benefit, previously separated, are united.

A similar process of synthesis can be distinguished in our supposed representation of a 'fact'. For a synthesis of meaning to take place as regards Paris being the capital of France, we only need to start to associate the ideas of 'capital', 'France', and 'Paris', even if we have no beliefs on the subject. To believe it, we need to be able to implicitly or explicitly say to ourselves 'Paris is the capital of France', or to act as though it is. Alternatives are possible at any stage, even if, in this kind of case, we have no practical motive for questioning our belief.

Maintaining the provisionality of our beliefs, once formed, also requires a kind of synthesis – in this case a synthesis of meaning that we continue to maintain, even when we have formed a belief. If our belief is not to be an absolutized belief, we need a continuing synthesis with other possible meanings that could potentially produce alternative beliefs, even when our belief is relatively clear and firm. In this case, then, the synthesis of belief and the synthesis of meaning are not entirely distinct, but rather a continuing synthesis of meaning accompanies and enables that of belief. To say that alternative beliefs continue to be available to us is also to talk about states of habitual awareness – not ones of obsessively thinking over alternatives, but rather ones where those alternatives stay in the background and can be summoned when relevant, because they are still *understood* and accepted as a wider part of the picture.

Synthesis as an aspect of the integration of meaning involves a process of development. The earliest stages of development of meaning in our lives involve cross-modal synthesis, as we associate newly experienced symbols (such as the initial words of our vocabulary) with experiences of assumed objects that we have learnt to link together across the senses. By the age of two or three we then begin to form rudimentary 'telegraphic' sentences that express potential beliefs. This initial acquisition of the apparatus of belief corresponds to the development of the 'impulsive' stage, in Robert Kegan's scheme of developmental psychology, out of the previous 'incorporative' stage.[3] Once we have met the most basic meaning expectations of our immediate environment through differentiation, then, the following stages gradually engage with the models

3   III.2.b & c.

Integration of Meaning 235

used in other environments that may interact with the initial one, and begin to synthesize the meaning in those wider models with the initial models. As Kegan notes, the movement from 'impulsive' to 'imperial' stages begins that process by engaging the child with the wider meaning found in school or in the wider community, rather than only that found in the family.[4] The wider models developed in this environment enable children to develop a more consistent set of meaning equipment with which to form beliefs about a concrete world. This initial process of synthesis between models is then succeeded by increasingly abstract and universal models that enable ever wider potential conditions to be understood.[5]

Synthesis at individual level thus depends on our progression through the stages of development, which provide the basic conditions for any given synthesis to occur. These individual conditions also depend in turn on both biological and cultural conditions for synthesis. Without the biological conditions of human evolution (and of normal individual development), we would not have the capacity to make these new neural links, in particular because of the need for development in density of neural connection both within each hemisphere and between the hemispheres.[6] The cultural development of human societies also provides a source of stimulus and expectation that may make it relatively harder or easier to reach the levels of synthesis developed in the later and more abstract stages.[7]

Not surprisingly, then, our view of synthesis needs to be synthesized. To understand it effectively, we need to hold in mind many aspects of its functioning simultaneously: perceptual, ideational, logical, biological, psychological, cultural, and developmental. This will clearly be a challenge to those of analytic habits of mind, who find a reassurance of 'meaning' by narrowing and specializing their focus, and fear that a constantly broadened focus will create a 'meaningless' picture. There is, however, no alternative to synthesis for humans to address the range of conditions around them. We cannot effectively engage with those conditions without constantly bringing our current understanding into contact with a wider understanding that is linked to experience of wider conditions. However relatively easy or difficult we may find synthesis as a process, it is

 4   III.2.b & c.
 5   II.2.e, f, & g.
 6   III.1.j.
 7   III.3 & 4.

vital. Nor can we limit our practice of synthesis only to the combination of beliefs that we already understand: to engage with new conditions we must constantly be at the edge of that understanding, searching actively for new meaning. This is perhaps the most challenging, but also the most exciting, aspect of human experience.

5.i. Sublimity

> States of sublimity, as identified in Romantic approaches to the arts, are short-term integrations of meaning, dependent both on us and on an object and its meaning (combining with other meanings). They often interact with states of temporary integration of desire that make us more receptive, boosting our attention with a sense of beauty. Sublimity is a source of inspiration (especially when associated with archetypal symbols), but it needs to be invested for longer-term practical effect.

States of sublimity have a long-standing place in the Western arts, particularly in the Romantic movement that erupted from the late eighteenth century. The raptures described by Wordsworth in response to his environment in the Lake District or at Tintern Abbey, the extraordinary intense subtlety of Beethoven's late piano sonatas and string quartets, or the transmutation of a cornfield, a sunflower, or a chair as painted by Van Gogh – these are just some of the most salient examples of works of art that seem to have come out of states of sublimity. In their turn, they may induce such states in us as we read, play, listen to, or view them. I write here partly on the basis of a longstanding personal relationship with Beethoven's last two piano sonatas, which continue to evoke sublimity for me almost every time I play them.

Sublimity is clearly an intense state of embodied meaning: not just 'emotive meaning', but also a sense of the contextualized interdependence of the symbols we are experiencing. Like all meaning, it is a state of connection. However, whilst most meaning is a long-lasting phenomenon (continuing either lifelong or until pruned, as discussed in 5.b), sublimity is a short-term effect, occurring in response to a stimulus or to a temporary bodily state. It is thus not so much the product of the creating of new associations as of the temporary strengthening of those associations.

As a state it can hardly be separated from temporary integration in general, as discussed in *The Five Principles*.[1] There, I suggested that the greater integration of desire experienced in absorbed meditative states like *jhana* was due to the relaxation of conditions that normally create conflict, allowing a greater unification of energies to be experienced. Where those energies are associated with symbols (as

---

1   II.5.f.

they most commonly are), a state of temporary integration of desire is likely to also bring with it a temporary integration of meaning, with synthesis between meanings becoming temporarily possible in a new mental state. The temporary removal of conflict, with its opposing desires and their accompanying beliefs, is interdependent with new understanding of the language or other symbols that were used to express opposing beliefs. There is also a deepening of our appreciation of symbols that we already find meaningful, as, freed up from conflict, more energy is directed towards that experience.

We cannot claim that integration of desire, meaning, and belief are entirely separate, nor that they always accompany each other to exactly the same degree.[2] However, some temporary integration of desire (for instance in an absorbed meditative state) is very likely to be accompanied by temporary integration of meaning either in that state or immediately after it. For instance, you finish a meditation based on mindfulness in an absorbed state, and are thus also in a state of greater emotional openness to others. Soon after the meditation, when you think about a problem of communication with your colleague, you start to more fully understand the meaning of some things the colleague said the previous day, and thus appreciate his or her perspective. For a short while you are able to feel a more intense sympathy with your colleague, even if this sympathy later evaporates in the face of new stressful or distracting experiences. Of course, such sympathy may lead to changes in belief about them, which may be longer-lasting.

In the other direction, a temporary boost to integration of meaning may also help to prompt temporary integration of desire. For instance, we may read a poem that leaves us with a feeling of lucidity and joy in response to the synthesis prompted by its metaphors. This is a temporary integration of meaning (that is, sublimity) dependent on our response to a particular piece of art, but may also then make us feel more generally mindful, focused, and emotionally positive. This effect is perhaps especially pronounced with the effects of music, which can alter mood in ways that are often noted. Whilst some of these effects on mood are fairly obviously due to the form of the music (for example, fast rhythms may make us feel excited, so that someone listening to *The Ride of the Valkyries*

---

2   II.5.d.

drives faster[3]), the associative effect of music in creating integrative effects is less often discussed with any precision: we may instead talk about being profoundly moved by a piece of music. Obviously, some music lends itself to this more than other music, but it is not simply a matter of any intrinsic quality of the form taken by the music either. Our sublime experience is affected by the form, because of the associations we have with that form, which are also in turn built up from embodied experience; but the potential to have a sublime experience is also dependent on our psychological state and the receptivity that it allows.

Temporary integration of meaning above all stimulates our *attention* to meaningful symbols, a property that is also the basis of the experience of beauty (as already discussed in 3.d above). We are aesthetically attracted to particular objects, often with a good deal of help both from our own biology and the conditions of the object itself. For instance we may see a marigold flower, and this arrests our attention, making us develop a strong meaning association with that object. We can talk about *aesthetic* beauty when that attraction to our attention does not depend much on prior symbolic meaning, but much more on our sensual experience (having properties like strong contrasts and bright colours, or associations with fertility that are deeply woven into our genes). We can talk more about *symbolic* or *archetypal* beauty when our response is primarily to the associations given to a symbol through culture and experience (for instance, though the archetypal functions of hero, anima/animus, shadow, and God[4]). Of course, the two can often be combined: so that we respond, for instance, both to the lapis lazuli blue of Mary's robe in a Renaissance painting, and to the image of Mary herself as the anima. Each time we respond to that image with attention, though, we reinforce the experience of symbolic beauty through that association, and create an attractor for further meaning to be integrated.

This is also the basis on which we can talk about *inspiration*. In *Archetypes in Religion and Beyond*, I discussed inspiration as the symbolic reminder of integrative functions for us, motivating us by reminding us of past experiences of more integrated states, and thus connecting our experiences together over time.[5] Inspiration

3 Brodsky (2001).
4 Ellis (2022) section 4.
5 Ellis (2022) pp. 1 ff.

is clearly a particular case of integration of meaning, but one that links together archetypal meaning with our deepest motives. In the broadest sense, learning a new word in Japanese is integration of meaning, but just learning new vocabulary is not likely to be deeply inspiring, unless the word concerned has associations that make it so. In the context of religion and the arts, however, the process of integration of meaning reaches more profound and transformative areas of our experience. Inspiration is likely to be a temporary state, as it comes and goes according to the symbols we encounter and our capacity to be inspired by them, but the regular use of such symbols as a *source* of inspiration can enable our long-term integration of meaning. For instance, if you are reminded by the sight of a Buddha figure of your deepest aspirations, perhaps linked to past experiences of meaningfulness, the power of that visual image will obviously vary depending on your circumstances and how receptive they allow you to be (as well as the aesthetic qualities of the different Buddha images you may encounter). However, the long-term impact of regularly encountering Buddha images is to help you maintain a vein of inspiration, frequently returning to that source whenever it is needed. You might then decide to incorporate the Buddha image into a regular ritual to help the regular re-kindling of that inspiration.

As discussed in *The Five Principles*, temporary integration states need to be *invested* to have long-term integrative benefit.[6] In the case of meaning integration, that means that a burst of deeper understanding is likely to need consolidating. We are more likely to be able to manage this by moving from absorptive to communicative, expressive, or meditative approaches (as discussed in 5.d–f), maintaining the strength of the neural links in the longer term by using them more actively. Thus, for instance, if we are briefly inspired by reading a poem, we can consolidate that inspiration by discussing it with someone else, writing about it in a diary, producing a new poem of our own, or reflecting on the images it leaves us with. If we are able to recall and come back to the poem itself in future, we can integrate its effects over time – which would suggest the value of learning it by heart, sticking a copy on the wall, or copying it into a commonplace book.

6 II.5.f.

The experience of sublimity, then, is probably far more important to us on a regular basis than the origins of the concept in Romantic discourse might suggest. Not everyone is inspired by Romanticism in the arts – and of course Romanticism can be made ideological and absolutized like any other movement. What the Romantics pointed to in sublime experience, however, is just a dimension of all human experience which comes from relatively brief and intense experiences of integrated meaning. Even if that dimension is an underappreciated aspect of our practice, it needs to play a role. It can do so through the integration of whatever symbols we respond to – wherever we find beauty. If we find beauty in objects that are not traditional targets of Romantic meaning, such as old postage stamps, or the design of machines, this may still be the starting point from which we discover and develop a capacity for sublimity of whatever degree. The integration of meaning always needs to start with what we find meaningful, and synthesize other objects with that.

5.j. The Meaning of Absolutes

> The integration of meaning can help us to understand the helpful role of symbols associated with absolutes, which provide an inspirational reminder of a pre-differentiated experience of meaning. Secure attachment anchored to our pre-differentiated memories, which enables us to differentiate meaning in infancy, also provides a context for the integration of fragmented meaning. But this archetypal meaning is constantly projected, confused with beliefs about absolutes.

Before leaving the topic of the integration of meaning, it is perhaps important to also discuss the supposed end-point of that process of integration. It should be clear by this point in the *Middle Way Philosophy* series that the entire Middle Way is *not* dependent on reference to end-points (such as enlightenment) to justify the process of integrative development and improving judgement.[1] In this respect it diverges from traditional Buddhism, which typically relies on some justificatory reference to that end-point (however much our view of it may be qualified and nuanced). The Middle Way is not the Middle Way *because* it leads to enlightenment, but is rather a path made up of a series of judgements that renew our sense of the value of the path as a whole at each point, our judgements synthesizing our understanding over time and putting any one given judgement in that wider context. However, the *concept* of an end-point, along with all other apparently absolute concepts (such as infinity, eternity, or objectivity), continue to rear their heads. We do not entirely dispose of these merely by dismissing them as inappropriate objects of belief, because they still have *meaning* for us. The concept of integration of meaning (built in turn on an embodied understanding of meaning) can perhaps help to cast further light on this relationship between the *meaning* of symbols associated with absolutes, which we can hardly avoid, and the *belief* in absolute (typically metaphysical) propositions, which experience justifies us in thinking we can make progress in avoiding.

The key to this issue probably lies in the distinction between differentiation and integration of meaning, already discussed in 1.c above. Specific symbols become meaningful to us because of their differentiation from a whole bodily experience in early infancy, but

1   Ellis (2019) 1.h.

this process of differentiation then also carries the danger of fragmentation, as separated experiences of meaning associated with different symbols and contexts lose touch with each other. In response to fragmentation we can integrate meaning, which does not undo initial differentiation, but rather reconnects the meanings of symbols in relation to each other, to form a web. Nevertheless, having experienced that state prior to differentiation, and having some vague and deeply embodied memory of it, we also retain a sense of non-differentiated meaning. It is this sense, I suggest, that makes absolutes meaningful to us, despite our inability to justify absolute beliefs.

In *A Systemic History*, I also suggested how maintaining this sense of a prior undifferentiated experience is emotionally important to us for the development of secure attachments.[2] In secure attachment, as understood in Bowlby's work,[3] a child is able to differentiate and make new connections with and between objects and people, without losing the underlying sense of confidence that was offered by the undifferentiated state. However, if a mother's affection is withdrawn prematurely or is unreliable in the infant's experience, confident differentiation of meaning is also likely to be lacking, and thus the confident development and testing of beliefs about the world as well. The child is thus held back in the whole process of learning without a *sense* of the absolute – that is, of a meaning unifying her experience and flowing into each new discovery.

The problem is that this *sense* of the absolute has been constantly confused with *beliefs* about the absolute[4] – such as about the 'existence' of God, about the ultimate goodness of Nature, or about the ultimate truth of a particular human account of things from a particular source (whether it is scripture, a guru, or 'science' as a set of results rather than a method). Hence a whole set of influential rationalist arguments in philosophy built on this confusion, such as the ontological and cosmological arguments for God's existence,[5] the Principle of Sufficient Reason,[6] and the common argument for the inevitability of metaphysics. In each of these cases, it's reasoned that we couldn't experience what we experience without certain

---

2   III.2.b.
3   Bowlby (1977).
4   The projection of archetypes: Ellis (2022) 2.a.
5   VI.5.c.
6   VI.2.c.

prior conditions being 'true', or at least being assumed to be true in an *a priori* universe. We couldn't have an idea of God, for instance, without a reality of God to produce that idea (Descartes' 'trademark' argument[7]); or we couldn't link ideas coherently at all without a pre-existent coherent universe framing those ideas, meaning that there is a 'reason' for everything (the 'Principle of Sufficient Reason'[8]); or we couldn't form any beliefs about the world without prior absolute assumptions (the argument for the inevitability of metaphysics[9]). All of these arguments (often used implicitly outside formal philosophy, as well as formally within it) are, I suggest, merely confused recognitions of our prior experience of absolute *meaning*, in which concepts of infinite scope have been grounded in remembered experiences of undifferentiated meaning, and connected together in the terms of models that are taken to represent 'reality'.

Without these unnecessary assumptions, however, absolute meaning is free to fulfil its archetypal function, particularly in relation to the God archetype. All that is required for us to integrate our judgements over time is sufficient awareness of a linking perspective, in which those different judgements based on differing meanings do not remain isolated, but rather take their place within a wider web of meaningful alternatives. To prompt us to maintain that linking perspective at each point, then, the linking perspective itself needs to be meaningful. It is not, however, the linking perspective of a supernatural God or all-resolving Nature beyond our own experience that is required, but rather enough continuity with our own prior, underlying experience of such a perspective. The power of an archetypal symbol such as God, then, lies in reminding us of that underlying and prior unity of experience, and bringing that awareness into contact with the shifting, highly differentiated meaning we encounter from day to day, maintaining a sense of the underlying unity of that meaning.

As we develop integration of meaning, our cultural habit is to instantly skip ahead to the beliefs that this integration of meaning does or does not betoken. But the integration of meaning is always incremental, consisting in separated meaning that has been brought together, rather than in either the presence or absence of

7   Descartes (1968) Third Meditation, pp. 118–21.
8   Leibniz (1898) §32.
9   I.4.e.

any completely justified belief. By integrating meaning, we come to appreciate another's perspective more strongly, for instance, or we recognize the existence of a perspective we had neglected – but this tells us nothing about whether we should believe or disbelieve what these perspectives offer us. The archetypal symbols we may use to help us integrate meaning also do not require any particular status to do so – it is the awareness that they prompt in us that helps us, and that is built entirely on the associations we have formed with them.

Conclusion

This book began with an exposition of what embodied meaning involves and implies. It moved on to explore the negative effects of the more traditional view of meaning that it challenges, representationalism, and the ways in which it has even hijacked our understanding of the nascent embodied meaning theory. Building on this understanding of embodied meaning, it then offered an account of the fragmentation and integration of meaning. These concepts take us directly to the *practical* role of embodied meaning in the context of Middle Way Philosophy, but they will make no sense without a prior understanding of the embodied approach to meaning. Although, in *The Five Principles*, I have previously discussed the integration of meaning as an aspect of practice interlocking with the other levels of integration,[1] there was no space there to offer all this background that will make the concept of integration of meaning more comprehensible. I hope that readers who want to put Middle Way Philosophy into practice will now be able to turn from this book back to *The Five Principles* with a deeper understanding of how the parts fit together.

I hope that this sense of synthesis between aspects of the philosophy will also extend to a connection with whatever practical experience each reader has of the arts and of other practices focusing on integration of meaning (such as loving-kindness meditation, skilful communication, or education). I do not aim to offer anything like a complete guide to such practices, but rather to show how our experience of their value fits into a wider picture. That wider picture implicitly has embodiment at its heart. Any practically-led engagement with these practices is, indeed, likely to work with embodiment, and to offer an implicit challenge to the abstracted view of meaning traditionally promoted by philosophers and linguists.

Integration of meaning practices have both an immediate value of their own, and an indirect value in their contribution to the

1   II.6.e–f.

integration of belief. Their immediate value can be felt directly – for instance in the refined enjoyment that all the arts offer, and that all their creators and appreciators will already recognize. That refined enjoyment simultaneously develops and strengthens our networks of meaning, which take the embodied form of neural links, often between the hemispheres and between different parts of the brain. These links deepen both our experience itself, and our capacity to respond to that experience throughout our lives.

Less directly and perhaps most importantly, however, the integration of meaning provides the key conditions for provisionality in judgement, and thus for a justification of our beliefs that is dependent on integration with our experience and other beliefs over the long term, rather than on an external 'proof', showing the 'reality' of the belief. As I discussed in *The Five Principles*, provisionality requires optionality – the availability of alternative possibilities to judgement.[2] These alternative possibilities are ones that are meaningful to us without being objects of belief – so that it is the integration of meaning that makes provisionality possible. The justification of all our beliefs depends on the provisionality of the judgements that support them.

The flip side of this positive contribution made by integration of meaning to all our judgements is the way in which provisionality also depends on the avoidance of absolutization. Absolutization shuts off alternative possibilities, repressing imaginative exploration, to focus our attention solely on an absolute belief and its unacceptable opposite as the only possibilities.[3] To avoid absolutization, new meaning needs to be constantly available to us – integrated into our meaning network rather than separated out inaccessibly. To avoid absolutization, which I identified in the book of that name as the central underlying problem for humankind, the integration of meaning is thus vital.

The next book in this series[4] will look in greater depth at the integration of belief in its psychological context, particularly the ways that absolutization compounds the effects of bias. In the practice of working with bias, so as neither to be deceived by it nor to react absolutely against it, it will once again be our ability to imagine a third alternative that offers us better justified judgement. The book after

2   II.2.a.
3   I.1.d.
4   V.

that[5] will then focus on the philosophical context of the integration of belief, namely the practice of agnosticism in relation to opposing absolutized pairs of beliefs. Once again, there, to find beliefs that address the complexity of conditions in relation to opposing ideologies, or to challenge simplistic assumptions about responsibility in ways that support us in actually taking it, we will need integration of meaning as a starting point. To think creatively, we have first to imagine.

This centrality of integration of meaning even to the central issues of our beliefs is what makes integration of meaning practices far more important than they are usually recognized as being. Although there are many potential integration of meaning practices, as discussed above, I will focus here on education and the arts as the most central – the integration of meaning practices that are already recognized as important by at least a sizeable section of the population. By 'education' here, though, I do not mean either technical instruction in narrowly defined skills, or the absorption of 'knowledge' that is then tested by regurgitative examination. I mean a process by which students are stimulated by new symbols to develop their own complexity of meaning networks. By 'the arts', too, I do not mean any kind of marginal recreation. We are constantly assailed by new conditions – a process that is likely to accelerate with climate change and with the human response to climate change – and to respond to new conditions we need provisionality, which means that we need integration of meaning. Education and the arts are vital to our *survival*.

Nor does the integration of meaning become any less important when we turn to areas where belief and its examination is foregrounded – for instance, science, philosophy, or political debate. I have highlighted, both in this volume (5.h), and in the previous volumes of this series, the role of synthesis in making these activities capable of adaptation. If we are to be adaptive enough to synthesize, too, we need to recognize the dangers both of over-specialization and of over-dependence on mere analysis that does not question the wider set of assumptions that accompany a given model. Not only is the integration of meaning central here for anyone practising these disciplines, but an intellectual recognition of embodied meaning – and thus that meaning is *not* a product of 'intrinsic' models – is

Conclusion 249

essential for an adequately critical understanding of the limitations of a given theoretical approach. The education of scientists, philosophers, and policy-makers needs to begin with a focus on this recognition and its implications, rather than with the entrenchment of long-dead Platonic debates about supposed 'truths' as the supposed foundation of intellectual training.

If they are to stop constantly confusing meaning with belief in the way that they currently do, scientists, philosophers, and policy-makers have a great deal to learn from the arts. It is in the arts alone that meaning is widely recognized as play, along with the importance of that play for human formation. None of us, but particularly not those in positions of influence, can afford a narrowly utilitarian education, or indeed narrowly utilitarian habits of living, in which this cultivation of meaning is neglected. It is taking this element of play seriously in a wider context, and being prepared to defend it in the wider public arena, on which our future depends. Without play, science rapidly turns into dogma, opposed in turn by opportunistic epistemological relativists who appropriate all doubts about scientific claims in the service of opposing dogma. Without play, religion continues its age-old pattern of repression and conflict, opposed only by equally absolutizing forms of secularism. Without play, authoritarian government or corporatocracy hold unquestioned sway, able to dominate all discussion with their own framing and to subvert democracy. Without play, every new progressive movement or practice – from socialism to veganism to mindfulness to rewilding – can be readily hijacked by absolutists who reduce its insights into binaries of group-identification. To credit play sufficiently, we need to constantly remind ourselves that meaning is not belief, and thus that there are other imaginable options for the interpretation of any of these positions than the one that has been explicitly prescribed in a group or by an authority. We need to remind ourselves that none of the language we are using to discuss these issues is 'essential' or unchangeable, and that the models we adopt for belief are the ones we have selected from a wider pool of meaning.

Perhaps there is no more potent symbol both of the value of the integration of meaning through the arts, and of the intense challenges facing it, than the Rushdie Affair, already discussed in 3.e. Playing with the stories around the prophet Muhammad to produce new meanings, as Rushdie did in *The Satanic Verses*, was seen at the time as a 'Western' thing to do, though the imagination is a common faculty for all humanity. To credibly threaten someone with death for doing so, with the whole apparatus of a state and the authority of a religious tradition behind the threat, is perhaps the ultimate imposition of belief on meaning, and the furthest application of disembodiment against the embodied process of the imagination. It appropriates the archetypal symbols of Islam, themselves meaningful, for purposes of socio-political power and instrumentality. Of course, Rushdie's cause in its turn can also be appropriated by the ideological absolutization of freedom out of balance with other priorities. However, the whole story suggests one general point: that there are occasions when we need to be clear enough about an embodied understanding of meaning to stand up for it and to protect it. To judge such cases carefully using the Middle Way, we will also need a much fuller discussion of the basis of political judgement before the end of this series.[6] Meaning at individual level is constantly interdependent with the socio-political conditions that allow us to explore and communicate it.

Our political protection of the integration of meaning through play, though, depends in turn on our personal practice of it. Without any practice of the arts, the defence of them can become merely an aspect of tradition or of some other ideological concept, readily open to absolutization in turn. Rather than Rushdie, then, I would like to close with a more positive image that comes to my mind: that of Edward Heath, prime minister of the UK during the 1970s, playing Chopin Nocturnes in 10 Downing Street.[7] Though his practice of music should of course not be taken to have made him immune to mistakes in political judgement, it is easy to recognize how this must have given a *context* to many of Heath's decisions that was not always present for other politicians. It is possible, as he demonstrated, to practise the integration of meaning even amongst the press of the affairs of state.

---

6   IX.
7   See Heath (1997).

The Middle Way Philosophy Series

This book is the fourth of a planned series of at least nine books on Middle Way Philosophy, to be published by Equinox over the next few years. These books will together form a highly interconnected argument for the Middle Way as a practical philosophy. In the process they will synthesize various different sources of insight, and challenge various entrenched assumptions about human judgement, its justification and motivation. This series is a substantial development, rewriting, and updating of an earlier series of four volumes.

By this point in the series, it has now ceased to be necessary to make any direct reference to the old series (as was done in the earlier volumes of this new series). Internal references to other volumes of this series are given in this book in the form of upper case Roman numerals (representing the volume number) followed by section and chapter numbers in the other volume. Obviously, references to books that have not yet been written (at the time of writing this book) must be approximate.

The full list of books in the series, including those published, in preparation, and planned, is as follows. Titles of later volumes are subject to possible amendment.

 I. *Absolutization: The Source of Dogma, Repression, and Conflict*

 II. *The Five Principles of Middle Way Philosophy: Living Experientially in a World of Uncertainty*

 III. *A Systemic History of the Middle Way: Its Biological, Psychodevelopmental, and Cultural Conditions*

 IV. *Embodied Meaning and Integration: Overcoming the Abstracted Grip on Meaning in Theory and Practice*

 V. *Bias and the Middle Way: How to Stop Absolutizing our Conditioned Assumptions*

VI. *The Practice of Agnosticism: Overcoming False Dualities across Human Thought*

VII. *Mindful Beauty: Aesthetics as Gathering Attention*

VIII. *Middle Way Ethics: Stretching across the Gap between Relative and Absolute Values*

IX. *The Middle Way Manifesto: Combining Radical Change with Political Effectiveness*

Bibliography

Amichai, Yehuda (2000) 'The place where we are right' from *A Touch of Grace*. Museum on the Seam, Jerusalem.

Bandler, Richard, & Grinder, John (1979) *Frogs into Princes: Neuro-Linguistic Programming*. Real People Press, Moab, Utah.

Berlin, Brent, & Kay, Paul (1969) *Basic Color Terms: Their Universality and Evolution*. University of California Press, Berkeley.

Bettelheim, Bruno (1975) *The Uses of Enchantment: The Meaning and Importance of Fairy Tales*. Penguin, London.

Bialystok, Ellen (2009) 'Bilingualism: The good, the bad, and the indifferent', *Bilingualism: Language and Cognition* 12:1, pp. 3–11. https://doi.org/10.1017/S1366728908003477

Bodhi, Bhikkhu (2000) *The Connected Discourses of the Buddha: A New Translation of the Samyutta Nikaya* (2 vols). Wisdom Publications, Boston.

Bowlby, John (1977) 'The making and breaking of affectional bonds: I: Aetiology and psychopathology in the light of attachment theory', *British Journal of Psychiatry* 130, pp. 201–10. https://doi.org/10.1192/bjp.130.3.201

Brodsky, Warren (2001) 'The effects of music tempo on simulated driving performance and vehicular control', *Transportation Research Part 4 F*, pp. 219–41.

Buzan, Tony (1986) *Use your Memory*. BBC Worldwide, London.

Chechik, Gal, Meilijson, Isaac, & Ruppin, Eytan (1999) 'Neuronal regulation: A mechanism for synaptic pruning during brain maturation', *Neural Computation* 11:8, pp. 2061–80. https://doi.org/10.1162/089976699300016089

Christensen, Alexander, Cardillo, Eileen, & Chatterjee Anjan (2023) 'Can art promote understanding? A review of the psychology and neuroscience of aesthetic cognitivism', *Psychology of Aesthetics, Creativity, and the Arts* 19:1, pp. 1–13. https://doi.org/10.1037/aca0000541

Costa, Albert and four others (2014a) '"Piensa" twice: On the foreign language effect in decision making', *Cognition* 130:2, pp. 236–54. https://doi.org/10.1016/j.cognition.2013.11.010

Costa, Albert and six others (2014b) 'Your morals depend on language', *PLoS ONE* 9:4, e94842. https://doi.org/10.1371/journal.pone.0094842

Darley, Emily, Kent, Christopher, & Kazanina, Nina (2020) 'A "no" with a trace of "yes": A mouse-tracking study of negative sentence processing', *Cognition* 198: 104084. https://doi.org/10.1016/j.cognition.2019.104084

Davis, Charles, & Yee, Eiling (2021) 'Building semantic memory from emotional and distributional language experience', *Wiley Interdisciplinary Reviews: Cognitive Science* 12:5, e1555. https://doi.org/10.1002/wcs.1555

Dawkins, Richard (2006) *The God Delusion*. Black Swan, London.

Descartes, René, trans. Sutcliffe (1968) *Discourse on Method and the Meditations*. Penguin, London.

Di Paolo, Ezequiel, Cuffari, Elena, & De Jaegher, Hanne (2018) *Linguistic Bodies: The Continuity between Life and Language*. MIT Press, Cambridge Mass.

Dobelli, Rolf, trans. Griffin (2013) *The Art of Thinking Clearly*. Sceptre Books, London.

Doi, Abdur Rahman I. (1984) *Shari'ah: The Islamic Law*. Ta Ha Publishers, London.

Ehrlich, Paul, Dobkin, David, & Wheye, Darryl (1988) 'Parasitized ducks', https://web.stanford.edu/group/stanfordbirds/text/essays/Parasitized_Ducks.html (accessed 2023).

Ellis, Robert M. (2018) *The Christian Middle Way: The Case against Christian Belief but for Christian Faith*. Christian Alternative, Winchester.

Ellis, Robert M. (2019) *The Buddha's Middle Way: Experiential Judgement in his Life and Teaching*. Equinox, Sheffield.

Ellis, Robert M. (2020) *Red Book, Middle Way: How Jung Parallels the Buddha's Method for Human Integration*. Equinox, Sheffield.

Ellis, Robert M. (2022) *Archetypes in Religion and Beyond: A Practical Theory of Human Inspiration and Integration*. Equinox, Sheffield.

Ellis, Robert M. (2023) 'The matter with "The Matter with Things"' (review): https://www.middlewaysociety.org/the-matter-with-the-matter-with-things/

Esack, Farid (2002) *The Qur'an: A Short Introduction*. Oneworld, Oxford.

Fideler, David (2014) *Restoring the Soul of the World: Our Living Bond with Nature's Intelligence*. Inner Traditions, Rochester, Vermont.

Friederici, Angela (2002) 'Towards a neural basis of auditory sense processing', *Trends in Cognitive Sciences* 6:2, pp. 78–84. https://doi.org/10.1016/S1364-6613(00)01839-8

Friston, Karl, Brown, Harriet, Siemerkus, Jakob, & Klaas, Stephan (2016) 'The dysconnection hypothesis', *Schizophrenia Research* 176:2–3, pp. 83–94. https://doi.org/10.1016/j.schres.2016.07.014

Gendlin, Eugene (2003) *Focusing*. Rider, London.

Godfrey-Smith, Peter (2020) *Metazoa: Animals, Mind and the Birth of Consciousness*. William Collins, London.

Habermas, Jürgen, trans. McCarthy (1984) *The Theory of Communicative Action*. Polity Press, Cambridge.

Haidt, Jonathan (2012) *The Righteous Mind: Why Good People are Divided by Politics and Religion*. Penguin, London.

Hampe, Beata (2005) 'Image schemas in cognitive linguistics: Introduction' from ed. Hampe & Grady, *From Perception to Meaning: Image Schemas in Cognitive Linguistics*. De Gruyter, Berlin.

Hampton, James (2006) 'Concepts as prototypes', *Psychology of Learning and Motivation* 46, pp. 79–113.

Haselager, Pim, De Groot, André, & Van Rappard, Hans (2003) 'Representationalism vs. anti-representationalism: A debate for the sake of appearance', *Philosophical Psychology* 16:1, pp. 5–23. https://doi.org/10.1080/0951508032000067761

Heath, Edward (1997) *Music: A Joy for Life*. Pavilion, London.

Bibliography 255

Hume, David (1975 – orig. 1777) *Enquiry Concerning Human Understanding*. Oxford University Press, Oxford.

Hume, David (1978 – orig. 1740) *A Treatise of Human Nature*. Oxford University Press, Oxford.

James, William (1902) *The Varieties of Religious Experience*. Longmans, Green & Co, London.

Johnson, Mark (2007) *The Meaning of the Body*. University of Chicago Press, Chicago.

Josselyn, Sheena, & Tonegawa, Susumu (2020) 'Memory engrams: Recalling the past and imagining the future', *Science* 367: 6473. https://doi.org/10.1126/science.aaw4325

Jung, Carl, trans. Shamdasani (2009: large format edition) *The Red Book: Liber Novus*. Norton, New York.

Just, Marcel (2008) 'What brain imaging can tell us about embodied meaning' from ed. De Vega, Glenberg, & Graesser, *Symbols and Embodiment: Debates on Meaning and Cognition*. Oxford University Press, Oxford.

Kamalashila (1992) *Meditation: The Buddhist Way of Tranquillity and Insight*. Windhorse, Cambridge.

Kant, Immanuel, trans. Kemp Smith (1929 – orig. 1787) *Critique of Pure Reason*. Macmillan, Basingstoke.

Kolk, Herman, & Heeschen, Claus (2007) 'Adaptation symptoms and impairment symptoms in Broca's aphasia', *Journal of Aphasiology* 4:3, pp. 221–31. https://doi.org/10.1080/02687039008249075

Körner, Stephan (1967) 'The impossibility of transcendental deductions', *Monist* 51:3, pp. 317–31. https://doi.org/10.5840/monist196751325

Korzybski, Alfred (1933) *Science and Sanity: An Introduction to Non-Aristotelian Systems and General Semantics*. International Non-Aristotelian Library, Lancaster, Penn. & New York.

Kövesces, Zoltan (2002) *Metaphor: A Practical Introduction*. Oxford University Press, Oxford.

Lakoff, George (1987) *Women, Fire and Dangerous Things: What Categories Reveal about the Mind*. University of Chicago Press, Chicago.

Lakoff, George (2002) *Moral Politics: How Liberals and Conservatives Think*. University of Chicago Press, Chicago.

Lakoff, George, & Johnson, Mark (1980) *Metaphors We Live By*. University of Chicago Press, Chicago.

Lakoff, George, & Nuñez, Rafael (2000) *Where Mathematics Comes From: How the Embodied Mind Brings Mathematics into Being*. Basic Books, New York.

Lamotte, Etienne (1983) 'The assessment of textual authenticity in Buddhism', *Buddhist Studies Review* 1:1, pp. 4–15. https://doi.org/10.1558/bsrv.v1i1.16227

Leibniz, Gottfried, trans. Latta (1898) *Monadology*. https://plato-philosophy.org/wp-content/uploads/2016/07/The-Monadology-1714-by-Gottfried-Wilhelm-LEIBNIZ-1646-1716.pdf (accessed 2023).

Lewis, Bernard (1963) *Istanbul and the Civilization of the Ottoman Empire*. University of Oklahoma Press, Norman.

Lytle, Sarah, & Kuhl, Patricia (2017) 'Social interaction and language acquisition: Towards a neurobiological view' from ed. Fernandez & Cairns, *The Handbook of Psycholinguistics*. Wiley, New York.

Marx, Karl, ed. McLellan (1977) 'On James Mill' from *Selected Writings*. Oxford University Press, Oxford.

Maturana, Umberto, & Varela, Francisco (1980) *Autopoiesis and Cognition*. D. Reidel, Dordrecht.

Maturana, Umberto, & Varela, Francisco, trans. Paolucci (1987) *The Tree of Knowledge: The Biological Roots of Human Understanding*. Shambhala, Boston.

McGilchrist, Iain (2009) *The Master and his Emissary: The Divided Brain and the Making of the Western World*. Yale University Press, New Haven.

McGilchrist, Iain (2021) *The Matter with Things: Our Brains, our Delusions, and the Unmaking of the World*. Perspectiva Press, London.

McNeil, Mary, Polloway, Edward, & Smith, J. David (1984) 'Feral and isolated children: Historical review and analysis', *Education and Training of the Mentally Retarded* 19:1, pp. 70–9.

Momen, Moojan (1985) *An Introduction to Shi'a Islam*. Yale University Press, New Haven.

Nagel, Thomas (1986) *The View from Nowhere*. Oxford University Press, New York.

Oakeshott, Michael (1989) *The Voice of Liberal Learning*. Yale University Press, New Haven.

Paul VI, Pope (1965) *Dei Verbum: Dogmatic Constitution on Divine Revelation*. https://web.archive.org/web/20140531175312/https://www.vatican.va/archive/hist_councils/ii_vatican_council/documents/vat-ii_const_19651118_dei-verbum_en.html (accessed 2023).

Plato, trans. Cornford (1941) *The Republic of Plato*. Oxford University Press, Oxford.

Regev, Daphna, & Cohen-Yatziv, Liat (2018) 'Effectiveness of art therapy with adult clients in 2018 – What progress has been made?', *Frontiers in Psychology* 9:1531. https://doi.org/10.3389/fpsyg.2018.01531

Riaz, Ali (2008) *Faithful Education: Madrassahs in South Asia*. Rutgers University Press, New Brunswick NJ.

Riesenberg, John (2000) 'Catastrophic Forgetting in Neural Networks'. MA Thesis, University of Cincinnati.

Salzberg, Sharon (1997) *Loving-kindness: The Revolutionary Art of Happiness*. Shambhala, Boston.

Sangharakshita (1989) *The Ten Pillars of Buddhism*. Windhorse, Glasgow.

Scott, Sophie, Blank, Catrin, Rosen, Stuart, & Wise, Richard (2000) 'Identification of a pathway for intelligible speech in the left temporal lobe', *Brain* 132:12, pp. 2400–6. https://doi.org/10.1093/brain/123.12.2400

Searle, John (1989) *Minds, Brains, and Science*. Penguin, London.

Sessions, Roger (1941) 'The composer and his message' from ed. Centeno, *The Intent of the Artist*. Princeton University Press, Princeton.

Sheldrake, Rupert (2012) *The Science Delusion: Freeing the Spirit of Enquiry*. Coronet, London.

Shigetsu Roku, trans. Luk (1961) 'The finger pointing at the moon' from *Ch'an and Zen Teaching: Second Series*. Rider, London.

Stamenkovic (2011) 'Verbs and prototype theory: State of the art and possibilities'. Proceedings of English Language and Literature Today Conference, Novi Sad.

Suarez, Mauricio (2015) 'Deflationary representation, inference, and practice', *Studies in History and Philosophy of Science* 49, pp. 36-47. https://doi.org/10.1016/j.shpsa.2014.11.001

Taleb, Nassim Nicholas (2012) *Antifragile: Things that Gain from Disorder*. Penguin, London.

Tang, Jeremy, LeBel, Amanda, Jain, Shalee, & Huth, Alexander (2023) 'Semantic reconstruction of continuous language from non-invasive brain recordings', *Nature Neuroscience* 26, pp. 858-66. https://doi.org/10.1038/s41593-023-01304-9

Tononi, Giulio, Boly, Melanie, Massimini, Marcello, & Koch, Christof (2016) 'Integrated Information Theory: From consciousness to its physical substrate', *Nature Reviews Neuroscience* 17:7, pp. 450-61. https://doi.org/10.1038/nrn.2016.44

Trudgill, Peter (1995) *Sociolinguistics*. Penguin, London.

Turner, John Robert, Allen, Jeff, & Hawamdeh, Suliman (2023) 'The multifaceted Sensemaking Theory: A systematic literature review and content analysis on sensemaking', *Systems* 11:3, p. 145. https://doi.org/10.3390/systems11030145

Van der Kolk, Bessel (2014) *The Body Keeps the Score: Brain, Mind and Body in the Trauma of Healing*. Penguin, London.

Vervaeke, John, Lillicrap, Timothy, & Richards, Blake (2012) 'Relevance realization and the emerging framework in cognitive science', *Journal of Logic and Computation* 22:1, pp. 79-99. https://doi.org/10.1093/logcom/exp067

Walshe, Maurice (1995) *The Long Discourses of the Buddha: A Translation of the Digha Nikaya*. Wisdom Publications, Boston.

Wernicke, Carl, trans. Eggert (1977) *Wernicke's Work on Aphasia: A Sourcebook and Review*. Mouton, The Hague.

Wilber, Ken (1982) 'The pre/trans fallacy', *Journal of Humanistic Psychology* 22:2, pp. 5-43. https://doi.org/10.1177/0022167882222002

Wittgenstein, Ludwig, trans. Anscombe (1967) *Philosophical Investigations*. Blackwell, Oxford.

Index

4E cognition, 5

a priori, 92, 94, 135, 244
absoluteness, 3–4, 7, 9–10, 36, 43, 53, 73, 75, 84, 86, 89, 92–4, 100, 108–9, 125, 135, 138–40, 148–9, 158, 177, 181, 188, 199, 217, 228, 230–1, 242–4, 247. See also absolutization
absolutization, 17, 39, 50, 56–7, **59**, 62, 68, 70, 83, 85–6, 92, 94–5, 99, 101, 107–8, 131, 149, 155, 166, 168, 171, 179, 180, 184, 190, 220, 227, 247, 250
Absolutization (book), 3, 59, 64, 70, 92–4, 99, 149, 162, 171, 232, 247, 251
absorptive meaning integration, 188, 190, **202–9**, 233, 240
abstraction, 1–2, 10, 31, 36–7, 39–40, 42, 45, 51–2, 55, 60–2, **66–8**, 93, 95, 98, 103, 114–15, 132, 134, 137, 142, 167–8, 184, 186, 193, 195, 199, 217, 220, 235
abundance mentality, 190
accent, 162
action, 3, 7, 12, 14, 20, 22, 44, 71, **73–4**, 76–7, 81, 84, 86–7, 93, 104, 108, 110–11, 119, 174–5, 196, 198, 216, 220, 230. See also activity
activity, 18, 20, 25, 38, 39, 44, 46, **47–8**, 52, 60, 69, 105, 174, 176, 188, 192, 214, 233. See also action
ad hoc argument 92–3. See also circularity
ad hominem argument, 105
adaptability, 14. See also adaptation, adaptivity

adaptation, 28, 85–6, 119, 179–80, 190, 211, 248. See also adaptability, adaptivity
adaptivity, 74, **85–6**, 195. See also adaptability, adaptation
adequacy, 81, 85
adjectives, 38
adulthood, 22, 95, 188, 209
adverbs, 38
aesthetic attention 165–6
aesthetic beauty **122–3**, 239
aesthetics, 22, **32–3**, 118–19, **122–3**, **165–6**, 192, 214, 218, 223, 239–40, 253
aetiological myth, 160
age difference, 176
aggression, 38
agnosticism, 66, 107, 111, 114, 156, 248
agriculture, 176
AI, 12, 15–16, 18
alienation, 21, 132, 162, 166, **192–3**, 220
Allah, 126. See also God
allegory, 110
ambiguity, 5, 33, 128, 130, 146, 153–4, 156, 201, **227–31**
ambition, 20, 177
American usage, 171
Amichai, Yehuda, 228–9, 253
amodality, 66–7
analysis, 42, 104, 146, 186, 190, 196, **200**, 201, 235, 248
analytic philosophy, 66, 137–9, 200
anatta, 131
anima/animus, 9, 108, 207, 225–6, 239
animals, 14, 40, 43, 46, 51, 60, 70, 176. See also organisms

Annunciation, 122-3
antinomianism, 131
antithesis, 233
apperception, 136
appetitive soul (Plato), 136
appropriation, 53, 62, 64, 144, 157, 249-50
Arabic, 126
arbitrariness of linguistic forms, 66-7, **170-3**
archetypal fragmentation, 169, **179-82**, 186
archetypal function, **107-9**, 113, 115, 244
archetypes, 5, 9, 21-3, 36, **39**, 94, 103, 105, **107-11**, 113, 115, 124, 125 (n3), 131 (n16), 151, 153, 168-9, **179-82**, 183, 186, 200, 207, 214, 220, 222, 225-6, 237, 239-40, 242, 243 (n4), 244-5, 250
Archetypes in Religion and Beyond, 5, 9, 107, 124, 179, 225, 239, 254
architecture, 176
argument, 56, 90, 92, 97-8, 230. See also logic, scepticism
Arnheim, Rudolf 120
art: see visual art, arts, art therapy
art therapy, 217, **218-19**
artefacts, 89, 174
arts, 4, 6-7, 75, 84, 90, 105, **117-23**, 138, 153, 174, 176, 191, 202, 207, 209, 217-19, 223, 228, 237, 240-1, 246-50
association, 3, 5-10, **12-19**, 20-87 *passim*, 95, 99-100, 102-23 *passim*, 136, 139, 150, 152-3, 156, 165-6, 170-87, 188, 193-4, 201-4, 207, 211, 217-18, 222, 225-6, 233-4, 237, 239-40, 242-3, 245
assonance, 123
atheism, 8, 100, 181
atonement, 178
attention, 3, 5, 18, **21-4**, 25, 31-3, 53, 55, 70, 75, 80, 100, 117, **120-4**, 156, 162, 165-7, 192-3, 196, 202-4, 207, 212, 215, 218, 220, 222, 237, 239, 247
attenuation of meaning, 114

attunement, 211, 212, 214-15
Austen, Jane 208
Australia, 204
authoritarianism, 249
authority, 82, 125, 127, 129-31, 142, **144**, 199, 215, 249-50
autocatalysis, 37
Avalokiteshvara, 225
awareness, 1, **3-5**, 10, 25, 26, 27, 30, 55, 79, 84, 90, 98, 111, 113-15, 119, 149, 152-3, 156, 158, 167, 182, 184, 187, 192, 199, 206, 219, 221, 222, 228, 231, 234, 244-5
awe, 109, 113
Ayer, Alfred 139

Babel, 160, 162
balance, 47, 104, 121-2, 250
balance schema, 47, 121-2
balancing feedback loops, 29, 190
Bangladesh, 167
bar mitzvah, 174
basic level categories, 4, 25, 38, **40-3**, 44, 45, 47, 48-50, 53, 54, 57, 70, 81, 85, 104, 107, 155, 168, 193
beauty, 16, 20, 23, 32, 109, 117, **119-23**, 134, 180, 218, 237, 239, 241
Beethoven, Ludwig 55, 118, 237
behaviour, 12, 17, 64-5, 75, 144, 191
behaviourism, 17, 138
belief, *passim*
  ~ and absolutization **59-60**, 92-6, 107-11
  ~ and archetypal inspiration 107-11
  ~ and desire 20-1
  ~ and judgement 73-6
  ~ and knowledge 84-7
  ~ and meaning **5-9**, 14, 104-6
  ~ and metaphysics 92-6
  ~ and sense-making 104-6
  conflicting ~ 155-9
  revelatory ~ in religion 124-33
Bettelheim, Bruno 208-9, 253
bias, 10, 30, 59, 71, 77, 97, 153, 171-3, **184-5**, 198, 220, 228, 247
  confirmation ~ 59
  domain dependence 185

group/social ~ 10, 30, 77, 153, 220
survivorship ~ 198
Bible, 22-3, 110, 128-32, 160
bilateral asymmetry, 70
bilingualism, 205
biodiversity crisis, 167
biographies, 90
biology, 24, 45, 80, 191, 232, 235
birth, 25, 58, 188
blind men and the elephant (parable), 162
blind spot, 97, 105
bodhisattvas, 226
body, 1, 3, 4, 5, 8, 45, 48, 51, 67, 72, 100, 106, 129, 134, 136, 137, 165, 169, 183, 185, 186, 191, 211, 222
Body Keeps the Score, The, 185, 257
body language, 212, 216
body orientation schemas, 47
bodywork, 4
botany, 28
boundaries, 13, 37, 39, **42-3**, 45, 76, 77, **78-9**, 95, 103, 206, 220, **227-8**
Bowlby, John 243, 253
brahmaviharas, 223
brain, 15, 69, 70-1, 77, 80, 152, 191. See also Broca's Region, left hemisphere, neural links, neuroscience, pre-frontal cortex, right hemisphere
brain lateralization, 70. See also left hemisphere, right hemisphere
brain scanning, 69
breasts, 24, 194
breath, 165, 222-3
Britain, 36, 145
Broca's Region, 69-72
Buddha, 108, 130-1, 162, 172-3, 225, 240, 253-4, 257
  authority of historical ~ 130-1
  ~ as archetypal inspiration 108, 225-6, 240
Buddhas, 226
Buddhavacana, 124, 130
Buddhism, 2, 99-101, 112-14, 124, 130-1, 181, 210, 215, 222-3, 225-6, 230, 242. See also Buddha, Mahayana, Theravada

bureaucratic language, 162
bureaucratization, 163
Buzan, Tony 194, 253

capitalism, 157
care, 142, 144, 178
catastrophic forgetting, 197
categories, 2, 4, 18, 24-5, 29, 31, **36-43**, 45, 47-50, 53-4, 57, 70, 81-2, 88, 93, 104, 107, 134-6, 168, 193. See also basic level categories, prototypes
Catholicism, 124, **128-31**
causality, 12, 17, 46, 55, 64-5, 89, 136. See also determinism, linear causality
centre-periphery schema, 47-8, 121
ChatGPT, 15
childcare, 176
childhood, 22, 43, 45, 89, 153, 163, 193, 195, 198, 203, 208. See also infancy
children, 34, 58, 77, 126, 152, 166, 177, 198, 202, 208, 235, 256
China, 150
Chinese, 15-16, 66-7, 77, 150, 161, 176
Chinese Room Analogy, 15, 66
chords, 117
Christ, 94, 129, 175, 178. See also Jesus
Christianity, 22-3, 38, 55, 59, 76, 82, 94-5, 113-14, **128-33**, 172, 175, 178, 181, 193, 225. See also Bible, Catholicism, Church, evangelical church, Protestantism
Church, 23, 128-30
circularity, 59. See also *ad hoc* argument, reinforcing feedback loops
clarification, 8, 153, **196-201**, 227
class, 82, 117, 157, 177
class conflict, 157
classification: see categories
cleanliness, 176
cliches, 55
climate change: see global warming
clothes, 174, 176
cognition, **5-6**, 16, 58, 64-5, 81, **84-7**, 89, 102, 168

Index

cognitive linguistics, 5, **59**
cognitive meaning, 5–6, **21–2**, 26–7, 43–4, 48–9, 58–9, **84–7**, 88–9, 135, 138, 153, **160–4**, 165–6, 168, 170, 173, 175, 181
cognitive models: see models
cognitive science, 62, 64–5, 105
cognitiveness, 160–1
collection schema, 60
collective unconscious (Jung), 107
colours, 38, 239
commodities, 167
communication, 34, 38, 51, 64, 66, 74, 76, **77–83**, 89, 102, 104, 112–13, 153, 158, 161, 176, 178, 198, 204–5, 209, **210–16**, 217, 226, 233, 238, 246
communicative action, theory of (Habermas) 212
communicative integration, 190, **210–16**, 240
commutative justice, 61
compassion, 150, **166**, 182, 185, 223–4
compatibilism, 100
compulsion schema, 54
computationalism, 62, **66–7**
computers, 12, 15, 16, 66–7, 117, 211
concentration, 113. See also attention, mindfulness
concepts, 8, 17, 22–3, 29, 32, 37, **44–61**, 84, 86, 91, 95, 100, 106, 108, 119, 120, 142–3, 147–8, 153, 192–3, 200, 213, 227, 242, 244, 246. See also categories, models
concreteness, 43, 45, **51**, 55, 60–1, 93, 115–16, 195, 235
conditionality, 99. See also conditions, contingency, interdependence, systems, truth-conditional theory
conditioning, 98, 186
conditions (general), 4, 8, 9, 26, 30, 42, 43, 55–9, 71, 74, 83, 92, 112, 139, 143, 161, 166–7, 169, 183, 195–6, 199, 213, 215, 218–19, 224–5, 230, 239, 244, 248, 250
~ for absolutization 68
~ for conflict 149, 153–4, 237

~ for embodied meaning **12–13**, 31–2, 57, 71, 104, 136–7, 141, 150, 191
~ for language 77
~ for provisionality 112, 247
~ for synthesis 232–6
environmental ~ 109, 178
truth ~ : see truth-conditional theory
confabulation, 97
confidence, 28, 214, 243
confirmation bias, 59. See also bias
conflict, 3, **7**, **9**, 26, 30, 59, 75, 96, 107, 129, 131, 149–54, **155–9**, 163, 167, 172–3, 176–80, 185, 212–13, 217–19, 222–4, 227, 230, 237–8, 249
conformity, 119. See also group biases, group binding
connotation, 6, 33, 35, 229
consciousness, 52, 257. See also awareness
conservatism, 143
consonance, 123
contact schema, 47
container schema, 18, **46**, 48, 50–1, 54, 89, 106, 121
contiguity, 12
contingency, 24, 41, 49, 58, **75–6**, 84, 86, 181, 210, 217. See also conditions
conventions, 37, 59, 76–8, 81, 83, 129, 170
copying, 108, **192–3**, 218, 240
corporatocracy, 249
cosmic justice, 181
cosmological argument (for God's existence), 243
counterforce schema, 185
creation, 28, 152, 181, 188, 193. See also creativity
creative writing, 218
creativity, 22, 51, 64, 82, 95, 166, 193, 200–2, 207, 214, **217–21**, 223, 229
critical thinking, 196
cross (Christian), 38, 55, 172–3, 175
cross-modality, 67, 232, 234
crucifixion, 38, 172

cultural fragmentation, 169, **174-8**
culture, 2, 6, 24, 26, 29, 34, 36, 38, 41, 44-5, 49, 52, 55-8, 62, 80, 81, 89, 95, 102, 109, 124, 127-8, 132, 149, 152-3, 165, 167, 169, **174-8**, 186, 191, 193, 203, 207, 211, 232, 235, 239, 244
curia, 130
Curie, Marie, 108
curiosity, 29, 207
curriculum, 205
custom, 143, 174, 176. See also culture, tradition
cycle schema, 46, 122

data, 18, 67, 200, 204
Dawkins, Richard 156, 253
death, 51, 128, 172, 250
deep generic skills, 205
defeasibility, 78
definite article, 204
definition, 33, 34, 36, 38, **57-9**, 68, 74, 77, **81-2**, 84, 95, 101, 145, 157, 188, 196, **199-200**. See also categories, essentialism, stipulation
dementia, 186
democracy, 108, 143, 148, 213, 249
demonization, 181
denotation, 6, 33-5, 229
depression, 8, 52
Descartes, René, 111, 136, 244, 254
describability, 112
desert, 146
design, 16, 104, 117, 174, 176, 211, 241
desire, 3, 13, **20-4**, 26, 30, 51, 70, 71, 149, 154-5, 177, 219-22, 237-8
determinism, 8, 10, 12, **17**, 100, 186
developmental psychology, 234. See also stage theory
dhamma, 131
diachronicity, 179, 208
dialect, 162, 170
dialectics, 210, 212-13, **232-3**
dialogue, 5. See also discourse
diary, 35, 77-8, 240
dichotomy, 10, 116
dictionary, 33-4, 77, 81-2, 84, 199

differentiation, 12, 17, 18, 24, **25-30**, 41, 54, 75, 106, 152, 175, 201-3, 223, 227-8, 242-4
differentiation learning, 28, 188, 195
disagreement, 155
disassociation, 53
discontinuity, 59-60, 120
discourse, 34, 83, 143, **213-15**, 241
distributive justice, 146
dogma, 10, 56, 129, 166, 168, 249. See also metaphysics
Dogmatic Constitution on Divine Revelation, 128
domain dependence, 183-5
doubt, 139
drama, 33, 214, 218, 221
dual aspect monism, 100
Dublin, 177
dysconnection, 183-4, 254

early life: see infancy
economic relationships, 166
economy, 51
ecosystems, 14, 42
education, 6-7, 27, 34, 126, 148, 176, 188, **195**, 202, **205**, 209, 246, 248-9
effort, 22, 28, 45, 52, 58, 114-15, 179, 226
ego, 114, 164. See also identification
electrical signals, 12, 14
embeddedness, 5, 44-5
embodied meaning, *passim*, especially 12-61
  archetypal symbols in ~ 107-11
  basic conditions for ~ 12-30
  distinction from 'cognitive linguistics' 6-7, 84-7
  distinction from representationalism 62-148
  formation of language in ~ 40-61
  non-linguistic symbols in ~ 117-23
  prototypes in ~ 36-9
  symbols in ~ 31-5
embodied practice, 1-2, 5. See also bodywork
embodied schemas: see schemas
embodiment, **1-2**, 4-5, **8**, 30, 44-5, 59, 95, 215, 228, 231, 246

Emma (novel), 208
emotion, 25-6, 28, 38, 47, 51-2, 64, 69, 72, 81, **84-7**, 89-91, 93, 105, 113, 121-2, 127, 138, 150, 161, **165-9**, 172, 175, 181, 185, 199, 208, 212, **217-25**, 238. See also emotive meaning, feeling
emotive meaning, 6, **20-4**, 27, 43-4, 48-9, 58, **84-7**, 88-9, 153, 160-70, 173, 175, 237
empathy, 153, 155, 224. See also sympathy
empiricism, 12, 76, 134-7
emptiness, 97, 99, 131
enaction, 5, 45. See also action, activity
energy, 3, 20, 52, 122, 136, 191, 223, 238. See also desire
England, 49, 53-5
English, 144, 160, 170, 174, 176, 204, 206, 228, 257
enlightenment (nirvana), 51, 100, 113-14, 130, 154, 181, 225, 242
environment, 13-14, 28, 38, 41, 44-5, 48, 52, 59, 85-6, 150, 166-7, 176, 177, 186, 190, 197, 202, 206-7, 234-5, 237
episodic memory, 186, 188, 193-4
epistemology, 138-9
equality, 146
equanimity, 223-4
equivocation, 53, 171-2, 227, **230-1**
essentialism, 34, 67, 73, 82, **92-6**, 135
essentiality, 39, 76
eternity, 242
ethics, 30, 51-2, 74, 110, 134, 138, **140-1**, 142, 144, 148, 162, 177, 191, 199, 205, 206, 213-14, 217, **219-20**
etymological fallacy, 67
etymology, 55, 67, 82, 106
eucharist, 103, 108, 129, 176, 178
Europe, 126, 145
evangelical church, 178
even-handedness, 6
evil, 109-10, 180-1, 225
evolution, 70, 152, 235
exclusion of options, 59

experience, *passim*
aesthetic ~ 117-23, 165-6
archetypal inspiration in ~ **107-11**, 112-16, 180-2, 239-40, 244
associative ~ and meaning 12-19, 36-7, 50, 104
denial of ~ in representationalism 66-8
expression of ~ 88-91, 217-21
individuality of ~ 34-5, 78-82
ineffability in ~ 112-16
infantile ~ **25-7**, 38-9, 242-3
meditative ~ 222-6
metaphors in ~ 52, 228-9
related to neural processes 17-18
religious ~ 107, 109-10, 112-16, 118, 125, 132-3, 168, 244
schematic linking of ~ 44-5, 136-7
sensory ~ 95, 117, 120
starting point for embodied meaning 1-11
sublime ~ 118, 237-41
symbols and ~ 31-2
experiment, 196
expression, 47, 53, 64, 72, **88-91**, 121, 161, 214, **217-21**, 233
expressive integration, 190, **217-21**, 240
expressivism, 65-6, **88-91**
extension (feature of body) 4, 45, 47
extension (of meaning) 39, 41, 48, **49-56**, 60, 67, 81, 85, 104, 108, 194, 229. See also metaphorical extension, metonymic extension
eye, 2, 30, 225

fact-value dichotomy, 140, 215. See also cognitive meaning, emotive meaning
fairy tales, 202, 208-9
falling in love, 180
false dichotomy, 10, 21, 84, 117. See also restriction of options
false speech, 215
falsehood, 3, 215
falsity, 137, 141
family, 50-1, 161, 174, 177, 198-9, 235
fantasy, 3, 78, 203

fatwa, 128, 130
fear, 20
feeling, 3, 21, 24, 71, 85, 88–90, 108, 153, 166, 176, 181, 208, 217, 221, 224, 229, 238. See also emotion
film, 33, 208
fissiparousness, 132, 157
Five Principles of Middle Way Philosophy, The, 7–8, 26, 40, 97, 105, 140, 154, 156, 188, 200, 232, 237, 240, 246–7, 251
flipping, 118
flow, 3, 22
focusing (practice), 4–5
food, 13–14, 51, 80, 174, 176, 199, 211
force schemas, **47–8**, 54–5
foreign languages, learning, 202, 205–6
Forms (Platonic), 107, 134–6, 138
foundationalism, 59
fragility, 50, 59, 109
fragmentation of meaning, 5, 7, 9, 25–30, 102, 105, 124, 127, 132, 143, 145–8, **149–87**, 188, 200, 202, 222, 242–3, 246
France, 77, 172, 234
freedom, 32, 58, 142–4, **147–8**, 167, 250
freewill, 8, 10, **17**, 43, 100
freezing (of judgement), 73–4, 77
French, 77, 172, 206
Friston, Karl, 183–4, 254
frivolous speech, 215
full-empty schema, 46
fundamentalism, 132
funerals, 220

Gaelic football, 176
Ganesha, 75
garden, 28, 75, 93, 122
gender roles, 176
Gendlin, Eugene, 5, 254
generalizations, 92, 99
Genesis, 160
genocide, 110
German, 27, 206
gestalt, 12, 15, 17, 44, 120
Gettier, Edmund, 84

global warming, 165, 167, 199, 204, 248
globalization, 178
goals, 4, **20–4**, 29, 34, 35, 45–6, 70, 73, 85, 104, 108, 126, 160, 167, 192, 195–8, 202, 207–8, 212, 219, 223–5, 227
God, 9, 23, 39, 43, 94, 107–15, 125–30, 161, 168, 181, 223, 225, 243–4. See also God archetype
God archetype, 108–9, 113, 168, 181, 225, 244
God's eye view, 30. See also absolutization, metaphysics
goodness, 134, 243. See also ethics
government, 172, 176, 249
grammar, 4, 71, 77, 126, **202–5**, 211, 228. See also propositions
group biases, 10, 30, 153
group binding, 59, 109
groups, 2, 7, **10**, 26, 29–30, 34, 60, 103, **108–9**, 110, 119, 125, 127–8, 130, 132, **152–3**, 157, 160–2, 168–71, **174–8**, 181, 198, 219–20, 223, 233, 249
guru, 243

Habermas, Jürgen, 212–14, 254
habit, 1, 6, 24, 42, 52, 86, 143, 152, 166, 176, 244. See also custom, tradition
Haidt, Jonathan, 142, 144, 254
harmony, 121, 123
Harry Potter, 108
harsh speech, 215
hatred, 3, 147, 152
health, 51–2, 219
heartbeat, 25, 47, 121, 207
Hebrew Bible: see Old Testament
hemispheres (of brain), 29, 70, 72, 134, 235, 247. See also left hemisphere, right hemisphere
Hercules, 108
heroic schema, 107
heroism, 9, 107–8, 179, 186, 207–8, 225–6, 239
hijacking (of integrative practice), 179–80

Hinduism, 75-6, 114
Hitler, Adolf, 110
Holy Trinity, 225
hormones, 185
human relationships: see personal relationships
humanities, 138
Hume, David, 12, 135-8, 255
humour, 7, 154, 194
hypernyms, 41-2
hyponyms, 41-2, 82
hypothesis, 137, 183, 196, 214, 254

icons, 32, 33, 38, 40, 46, 55, 117, 211. See also images, visual art
idealism, 8, 10, 62, 65-6, 100
idealized models: see models
identification, **26**, 48, 79, 113, 128, 145, 178, 208, 220, 249
ideological stage (Kegan), 195
ideology, 7, 34, **142-3**, 145, 147, 157, 166, 241, 248, 250
idiolect, 162, 170
ijma, 127
images, 5, 19, 31, 44, 55, 104,117, **120-1**, 132, 162, 226, 239-40, 250. See also visual art
image schemas: see schemas
imagination, 3-4, 7, 22, 24, 52-3, 70, 83, 92, 105, 126, 173, 183, 191, 208, 224, 226, 247, 249-50. See also integration of meaning
imam, 127
imperial stage (Kegan), 152, 195, 203, 235
impressions, 79, **135-8**, 207
impulsive stage (Kegan), 195, 203, 209, 234-5
incorporative stage (Kegan), 234
incrementalism, 140-1
incrementality, 21, **36-7**, 59, 86, 88, 90, 100, 112, 116, 119, 134-5, **139-41**, 143, 144, 148, 154, 176, 224, 244
indeterminacy, 78
India, 72, 162, 176, 206
indifference, 160, 167
indirect realism, 64

individual, 5, 10, 26, **34-5**, 43, 51, 54, 75, 77, 86, 89, 106, 118, 131, 135-6, 138, 149, 152, 160-1, 164, 174, 177, 193, 195, 203, 210-12, 218-20, 235, 250
individualism, 10-11
individuality, 88. See also individual
individuation: see integration
ineffability, 103, **112-16**
inequality, 146-7
inevitability, 59, 243-4. See also determinism
infallibility, 130
infancy, 2, **24-8**, 30, 38, 48, 54, 95, 106, 122, 152, 177, 191, 197, 242-3
infinite rationalization, 59, 149
infinite scope, 110, 244
infinity, 59, 93-4, 116, 149, 242
inflation of metaphysics, 53 (n6), 59, 64
innateness, 203
inner-outer dichotomy, 10, 88-9. See also private language argument
innovation, 143
inspiration, 6, **9**, 21, 23, 39, 105, **107-11**, 114, 126, 154, 169, 179-81, **207-9**, 220, 222, 225-6, 237, **239-40**, 242
instrumentality, 163, 250
integrated information theory, 18
integration (in general) **5**, **26-30**, 75, 80, 100, 105-6, 124, 127, 149, 154, 185, 212-13, 222, 232, 237-8, 240, 246-8
~ of belief 27, 30, 75, 106, 186, 212, 219, 238. See also belief
~ of desire 30, 154, 237-8. See also desire
~ of meaning 5, **7-9**, **26-30**, 73, 75, 106, 149, **153-4**, **188-250**
integration learning, 188
intellectual understanding, 1-2, 4, 120, 166-7, 248-9. See also cognitive meaning
interdependence, 12, 20-2, 30, 42, 45, 60, 81, 85, 89-90, 94, 158, 160-1, 168, 170, 183, 186, 193, 203, 226,

238, 250. See also conditionality, systems
interindividual stage (Kegan), 195
interoception, 1
interpersonal stage (Kegan), 195
interpretation, **32–4**, 72, 90, **92–6**, 104, 107, 112, 115, 125–6, 128, 131–2, 143, 156–7, 160 (n2), 216, 218, 232, 249
intolerance, 127
intoxicants, 176
intuition, 1, 60, 134
intuitionism, 181
Inuit, 24
investment, 21, 237, 240
Ireland, 130, 176
Islam, 124–31, 250
isomorphism, 62, **67–8**, 80–1, 98, 140
Israel, 152
iteration schema, 46, 122

James, William, 115, 255
Japanese, 150, 228, 240
jargon, 160, 162
Jesus, 55, 94, 172, 220, 225. See also Christ
jhana, 113, **222–3**, 237
Jibreel, 125
Johnson, Mark, 2, 4–5, 25, 31, 36, 44, 46, 49, 51–3, 62, 102, 120–1, 255
joy, 238
judgement, **3**, 6, 9, 30, 64–5, 72, **73–6**, 79, 101, 105–6, 110–11, 119, 139, 143, 145–6, 154, 171, 194, 220, 233, 242, 244, 247, 250
Jung, Carl, **5**, 33, 108, 124, 225, 254–5
Jungianism, 107
justice, 142–4, 146–7
justification, 6, 74, 85, 97, 134, **139–41**, 142, 170, 172, 214, 233, 247
justified true belief (knowledge), 84–5

Kant, Immanuel, 136–7, 255
Kantianism, 44, 134
karuna, 223–4. See also compassion
Kegan, Robert, 152, 195, 234–5
Khomeini, Ayatollah, 130

knowledge, **5–7**, 17, 27, 29, 40, **57–61**, 65, **84–7**, **97–8**, 115, 134–5, 163, 188, 194, 195, 205–6, 248
Körner, Stephan, 137, 255
Korzybski, Alfred, 67, 255
Kövesces, Zoltan, 51, 255
Küng, Hans, 130

Lake District, 237
Lakoff, George, 2, 4–5, 31, 36, 40, 44, 46, 49, 51–3, 58–62, 102, 144, 255
language, 2, 4, 7, 19, 21, 24, 26–7, 29, **31–61**, 62, 64–8, 72, 74, **77–83**, 84, 88, **95–6**, 104, 108, 112, 116, 120, 123, 131, 137, 150, 155, 157–8, **160–4**, 166, 168–9, **170–3**, 174, 176, 178, 186, 198, **203–6**, 210–16, 228, 238, 249. See also symbols, words
 communicative use of ~ 77–83, 198, 210–16. See also communication
 ~ change 95–6
 ~ differences 160–4, 170–4, 176
 ~ forms 47, 110, 170–3
 ~ learning 26–7, 77, 95, 205–7, 211, 214
 ~ teaching 211, 214
 propositional ~ 69–72. See also propositions
law, 21, 95, 126, 162, 176
learning, 7, 23, **25–30**, 39, 57–8, 77, 80, 152, **188–90**, 195–7, 202, 205–6, 240, 243. See also education
left hemisphere (of brain), 4, 12, 16, 23, 29, 52–3, 56, 58, **69–72**, 87, 91, 97, 120, 126, 132, 134–5, 139, 143, 148, 183, 152, 160, 167, **183**, 186, 192–3, 197, 199, 201–2, 218, 220, 226. See also brain lateralization, right hemisphere
leisure, 176
letters, 171
libertarianism, 147
lying, 78, 215
linear causality, 17, 89. See also causality
linear processing, 16

linear relationships, 17
Linguistic Bodies, 6, 10, 254
linguistic fragmentation, 168, **170-3**, 174
linguistic idealism, 65
linguistics, 5-6, 10, 59, 64-6, 170-1, 203. See also language
link schema, 46
listening, 24, 27, 155, 165, 207-8, 223, 237-8
literalism, 110, 128
Locke, John, 135
logic, 64, 92, **94**, 200
London, 177, 204
Lord of the Rings, 6, 208
love, 3, 38, 71-2, 110-11, 178
loving-kindness, 222-3, 230, 246
loving-kindness meditation, 222, 227
loyalty, 142, 144
lumping, 157

madrassahs, 126
Mahayana Buddhism, 99-100, 131, 225
maladaptation, 197-8
mantras, 226
map, 67
Marseillaise, 172
Marx, Karl, 157-8, 256
Marxism, 34
Mary (mother of Jesus), 122-3, 239, 256
mass (Catholic): see eucharist
Master and his Emissary, The, 4, 256
materialism, 8, 10
maternal attachment, 28
mathematical model, 23
mathematics, 57, **60-1**, 118, 137, 200
Maturana, Umberto, 13, 72, 85-6, 256
maturation, 191, 194-5. See also stage theory
McGilchrist, Iain, viii, 4, 53, 69-70, 118, 132, 134, 143-4, 192, 218, 231, 256
meaning, *passim*: see embodied meaning, meaningfulness, meaning resources, representationalism, undifferentiated meaning
meaning crisis, 8, 9
meaning of life, the, 8
meaning resources, 7, 105, **188-95**, 210, 214
meaningfulness, 11, 14, 28, **34**, 70, 178-9, 240
meaninglessness, 11, 76, 150
mediation, 154
medicine, 56, 176
meditation, **2-3**, 4-5, 112, 166, 192, **222-6**, 227, 230, 233, 238, 246. See also mindfulness
meditative integration, 190, **222-6**, 240
melody, 117, 121-3, 172, 207
melody schema, 47
memory, 14, 27, 79, 126, 183, 186, 188, **193-4**, 198, 226, 243
memory engrams, 188, 193
memory palace, 194
mental states, 147, 216-17, 222. See also belief, desire, meaning, mindfulness
merging schema, 47, 54
metaphor, 4, 18, 39-40, 43-4, 46, 48, **49-56**, 57, 60-1, 67, 70, 81-2, 85, 90, 95, 104, 107-8, 113-14, 117, 120, 122, 125, 128, 132, 139, 143-4, 155, 168, 175, 181, 227, **228-9**, 232
metaphorical extension, 31, 39, 48, **49-56**, 60, 67, 81, 85, 104, 108, 229
Metaphors We Live By, 49, 255
metaphysics, 8-9, 17, 40 (n2), 43, 53 (n6), 59, **62-8**, **92-96**, 97, **99-100**, 102-3, **107-11**, 118 (n1), 124-5, 129, 134, **138-9**, 171, 178, 186, 229-30, 242-5
  claimed inevitability of ~ 59, 243-4
  inflation of ~ 53 (n6), 59, 64
  ~ appropriating archetypal meaning 107-11
  ~ appropriating embodied meaning 102-3
  process ~ 99-100
  religious ~ 124-5, 129

representationalism and ~ 17,
    62–8, 92–6, 138–9, 225
metonymy, 39, 48–9, **53**, 172, 229
metonymic extension, 39, **53**, 172
metta, 222–4, 230
metta-bhavana, 222, 230
Middle Way, **3**, 8, 11, 30, 62, 91,
    99–101, 104, 106–7, 149–50,
    155–6, **190–1**, 200, 232, **242**, 246,
    250
Middle Way Philosophy, 2, 3, 8, 100,
    149–50, 200, 232, 242, 246
mind, 4, 7, 45–6, 65, 81, 85, 100, 130,
    135, 138, 158, 186, 233, 235. See
    also mental states, privacy
mindfulness, 1, 3, 5, 51, 113, 165–6,
    192, **222–3**, **238**, 249. See also
    meditation
mishearings, 162
misprints, 162
mnemonics, 194
mobility, 178
models, 6, 10–12, 18–19, 23, 33–4,
    37, 41, 44, 49, **57–61**, 62, 65–73,
    75, 77, 79–84, 87, 92–5, 100–1,
    109–10, 112–15, 120, 124, 134,
    136–7, 139–40, 143–4, 147–8,
    155–6, 158, 178, 181, 184–6, 195,
    197, 199–206, 209, 212–15, 227–8,
    230–2, 234–5, 244, 248–9
  clarification within ~ 198–201
  formation of ~ 57–61
  integration of ~ 232–6
  ~ as basis of action 73–6
  ~ in communication **77–83**, 113–14,
    214–15
  ~ in fragmentation 155–9, 184–5
  ~ and propositions 69–72
  ~ in psychological development
    195, 203–4, 209
monasteries, 131
monastic rules, 131
money, 51–2
morality: see ethics
motive, 12–13, **20–24**, 31, 73, 74,
    108–9, 162–3, 180, 202–3, 215,
    226, 234, 239. See also desire
motor skills, 25, 69

movement (bodily), 1, 20, 45, 51, 55,
    161, 212, 223
mudita, 223–4
Muhammad, 125–6, 128, 175, 249
mujtahids, 127
multivalence, 33
muscles, 52, 185
music, 19, 55–6, 85, 90, 103, 117–18,
    121–2, 123, 172, 202, 207, 211,
    217–18, 223, 226, **238–9**, 250
musicology, 90
Muslims, 126–8, 175, 181. See also
    Islam
mutual causality, 89. See also inter-
    dependence, systems
mystical experience, **113–15**, 124, 130,
    132–3, 168. See also religious
    experience
mysticism, 112–15, 125

Nagarjuna, 99, 101
Nagel, Thomas, 65, 256
narrative: see story
nation, 51, 236
naturalism, 5, 103, **139–40**
Nature, 181, 243–4
near-far schema, 47–8
necessity, 77, 93. See also determin-
    ism, inevitability
needs, 29, 80, 146, 152, 166, 169, 179,
    212
Neoplatonism, 118
nervous system, 89, 211, 221. See also
    neural links
neural links, 12, **17–18**, **25–6**, 32, **43**,
    77, 104, 149, 153, 167, **183**, 185,
    188, 191, **193–4**, 195–7, 202, 204,
    211, 221, 232–3, 235, 240, 247. See
    also synaptic pruning
neuro-linguistic programming, 212
neuroscience, 4, 17, 62, 69, 118, 183,
    193. See also brain, nervous
    system
nirvana: see enlightenment
noesis, 115
non-linguistic symbols, 38, **117–23**,
    175, 211. See also images, music,
    symbols

nostalgia, 145
nouns, 36-7, 40, 54, 93
novels, 21, 128, **208**
novelty, 217
numbers, 57, 60-1, 67, 227, 251. See also mathematics
Nuñez, Rafael, 60-1, 255

object schema, 47, 60, 106, 185
objectification: see projection
objectivity, 89, **117-20**, 148, 242
objects, 17, 20, 24-6, 28, 38, **40-8**, 50, 54, 60-1, 65, 67, 70-1, 73, 93, 99, 117, 120, 126, 131, 134, 158, 161, 168, 180, 183, 185, 202, 204, 206, 223, **228**, 234, 239, 241-3, 247
observation, 8, 17-18, 29, 48, 93, 135-6, 156, 202
Ockham's Razor, 196, 201
Old Testament, 22-3. See also Bible
omnipotence, 181
onomatopoeia, 26, 67, 123, 171-2
ontological argument (for God's existence), 111, 243
ontological metaphors (Lakoff and Johnson), 52
ontological obsession, 59, 101
ontology, 53, 59, 101. See also metaphysics
opportunities, 24, 45
optionality, 3, 157, 232-3, 247, 249. See also restriction of options
organisms, 12-17, 20, 25, 29, 37, 42, 44, 50, 65, 86, 108. See also animals
orientational metaphor, 51
originality, 217
Ottoman Empire, 130, 255
over-specialization, 162, 248

paganism, 181
painting, 117, 120-3, 192, 217, 239
Palestinians, 152
Pali, 130-1, 215
Pali Canon, 130-1, 215
Papua New Guinea, 174
paradox, 100
paralinguistic features, 161

part-whole schema, 47-8, 60
path, 25, 44-6, 48, 60-1, 121, 242. See also Middle Way, source-path-goal schema
peace, 38, 127
perception, 64, 97, 120-1, 135-6
perfection, 94, 160. See also absoluteness, metaphysics
personal relationships, 50-1, 110, 166, 174, 185, 195, 198, 208, **225-6**
perspective schema, **47**, 121
Philosophical Investigations, 137, 257
philosophy, 2, 15 (n5), 21, 57, 61, 64-8, 98-100, 103, 111 (n11), 124, **134-41**, 142-3, 145-6, 157-8, 162, 200, 243-4, 246, 248. See also analytic philosophy, epistemology, metaphysics, Middle Way Philosophy, philosophy of language, philosophy of mind, philosophy of perception, philosophy of religion, political philosophy
philosophy of language, 2, 65-6. See also embodied meaning, representationalism
philosophy of mind, 15 (n5), 100
philosophy of perception, 64
philosophy of religion 107-16
phrases, 52, 104, 117, 122, 145, 204
physical properties, 3, 47, 51, 132, 136, 157, 176
physical substrate, 17. See also materialism
physicalism, 8
physics, 35, 42, 205
physiology, 12
pictures, 22, 26, 36, 38, 40, 88, 118, **120-1**, 131, 135, 138, 192, 203, 212, 217, 246. See also images, visual art
Plato, 118, 134-8, 256
Platonism, 8, 39, 61, 107, 118, 134-8, 249
play, **22**, 24, 128, 130, **249-50**. See also creativity
poetry, 85, 89-90, 114, **123**, 217, **228-9**, 238, 240

political action, 7
political correctness, 95
political organization, 176
political philosophy, 142–8
politics, 7, 51, 54, 64, 95, 103, 124, 130, **142–8**, 152, 163, 167, 174, 176–8, 248, 250
Pope, 128–30, 256
Popper, Karl, 139
positive emotion, 113. See also emotion, *metta*, temporary integration
potentiality, 225
power structures, 132
pragmatics, 6, 66, 138
Prajñaparamita, 100
Prakrit, 162–3
precepts, 215
predation, 70–1, 225
pre-frontal cortex, 4, 26, 70. See also Broca's Region
pre-trans fallacy, 27
Pride and Prejudice, 14
priesthood, 126, 128
Principle of Sufficient Reason, 243–4
principles, 12, 40, 74, 136, 148
privacy (of meaning), 31, **35**, **77–81**, 83, **89**, 138
private language argument, 78
probability, 18
probabilizing, 140
process philosophies, 99
process schema, 46
professionalism, 177–8
projection, 59, 107, **109–11**, 114, 125 (n3), 168, 179, **180**, 225, 243 (n4)
proliferation (mental), 4, 59, 65, 166, 190, 222, 224. See also reinforcing feedback loops
pronunciation, 170
prophets, 110
propositional revelation 125, 128
propositions, 4, 27, 49, 52–3, 59–60, **69–72**, 94, 104, 117–18, 120, 125, 128, 131, 138–9, 142, 158, 166, 192–3, 196–7, 200, 203–4, 214, 226, 242
Protestantism, 131–2

prototype theory, 36–9. See also prototypes
prototypes, 18, **36–9**, 41, 42, 46, 50, 70, 81–2, 120, 144–7, 173, 210
provisionality, 8, 22, **73–6**, 78, 83, 92–3, 96, **99–100**, 105, 111, 112, 114, 116, 119, 140, 158, 168, 196, 205, 228, **232–4**, 247–8
pruning: see synaptic pruning
psychology, 12, 30, 62, 77, 98, 105, **111**, 149, 158, 162, 168–9, 184, 193–4, 208, 213, 219–20, 233, 235, 239, 247
  association in ~ 12, 77. See also association
  cognitive ~ 62, 184. See also belief, bias, meaning
  developmental ~ 162, 208, 234. See also stage theory
  psychological conflict: see conflict
  ~ of archetypes 111. See also archetypes
  ~ of memory 193–4. See also memory
public policy, 142
publicity, 79
pulse, 47, 90, 121, 207
punishment, 192
puritanism, 132
purity, 134, 142, 144
Putin, Vladimir, 110

qualities, 29, 55, 61, 66, 88, 119–21, 180, 240
Qur'an, 124–9

rational soul (Plato), 136
rationalism, 61, 76, 94, **134–7**, 181, 243
rationality, 57–61, 108, 124, 134–8, 148, 181, 186, **199**, 201, 208–9, 213
rationalization, 110, 168
reading, 14, 21, 175, 208, 237, 240
realism, 62, 64, 66, 100
reality, 2, 4, 57, 60, **62–8**, 72, **73–6**, **92–6**, 98–9, 107, 110, 117–18, 140, 142, 145, 192, 203, 229, 244, 247. See also metaphysics

Index

reason, 93, 135, 243-4. See also logic, models, rationality
Received Pronunciation, 170
receptivity, 114, 202, 239
recollection, 108, 163, 222, 226
Red Book (Jung), 5, 225, 255
Red Book, Middle Way, 5
redemption, 55
reductive appropriation, 53
reductiveness, 8, 23, 53, 69, 79, 110
reflection, 5, 166, 195, 198, 207, 220
reframing, 155, 210, 212
reification, 52, 54, 88, 110. See also projection
reinforcing feedback loops, 29, 59, 92, 180, **190**, **224**. See also proliferation
relationships between objects schemas, 47
relationships (human): see personal relationships
relativism, 100, 249
relevance realization, 102, 104-5
religion, 6, 9, 51, 64, 75, 94-5, 103, 105, **107-15**, 118, 122, **124-33**, 166, 168, 172-8, **181**, 220-2, 225, 240, 249-250
religious experience, 9, 107-15, 118, 132. See also mystical experience
Renaissance, 122, 239
representation, **12-13**, 16, 18-20, 26, 33, 37, 41, 45-6, 49-50, 52, **57-8**, **64-5**, 67-76, 80, 84-94, 97-9, 101, 109-10, 112-14, 117, 123, 125-9, 132, 134-5, 137, 139, 140, 142-6, 152, 157-8, 160-1, 171, 183, 188, 190, 192, 195, 197, 204, 211, 218, 226, 229, 233-4, 244. See also representationalism
   belief and ~ 20, 84-7, 103-4, 124-5, 181-2, 233-4
   freezing of ~ 73-4, 77-8
   goals and ~ 20, 24, 45-6
   judgement and ~ 73-6
   models and ~ 18-19, 41, **57-8**, 71-2, 203-4
   propositions and ~ 71-2
representation blindness, 97-8, 101

representationalism, 2, 9-10, 16-17, 31, 37, 49, 57-8, **62-101**, 102-4, 106, 109-10, 112-20, 123-49, 156-8, 160-1, 171, 181, 183, 188, 190, 192-3, 228-9, 244, 246. See also representation, truth-conditional theory, Wittgensteinianism
   absoluteness of ~ 75-6
   abstraction of meaning in ~ 66-7, 98-101
   cognitive-emotive dichotomy in ~ 84-6, 117-20, 140-1, 229
   conceptual definition in ~ 37, 81-2, 228
   conflict and ~ 156-9
   copying and ~ 192-3, 218
   definition of ~ 64-5
   essentialism and ~ 75, 82, **93-6**, 109-10, 134-5, 228
   expression and ~ 88-91
   fragmentation and ~ 149-59
   ineffability and ~ 112-16
   language privileged in ~ 37, 117-19
   left-hemisphere over-dominance 16, **69-71**, 134, 183, 218
   metaphysics and ~ 17, **92-6**, 97-103, 124-41
   representation of reality 67-8, 75-6, 97-9, 109-10, 117, 125-6, 244
   transparency 97-8
   signs in ~ 33-5
   values and ~ 140-8
repression, 59, 70, 91-2, 110, 127, 129-30, 144, **157-8**, 224, 231, 249. See also conflict
resemblance, 12, 26, 135. See also metaphor
responsibility, 109-10, 112, **115-16**, 141-2, 156, 160, 179-80, 225, 248
restlessness, 3
restriction of options, 92, 94-5
revelation, 107-8, 110, 124, **125**, 126-31, 181
rewilding, 249
rhythm, 25, **47**, 55, 117, **121-3**, 238

rhythm schema, 47
Ride of the Valkyries, The, 238
right hemisphere, 4–5, 8, 16, 23, 29, 52–3, 58, **69–72**, 87, 91–2, 114, 120, 130, 134, 144, 160, 166, 187–8, **191–3**, 197, 202, 218, 233. See also brain lateralization, left hemisphere
Rimbaud, Arthur, 177
rites of passage, 176
ritual, 7, 21, 123, 129, 174, 177–8, 217, **220–1**, 240
role-playing, 22
Romanticism, 219, 237, 241
Rosch, Eleanor, 36
rules, **57**, 131, 138, 187, 199
Rushdie, Salman, 128, 130, 249–50

sacraments, 129
saints, 71, 225
samsara, 100
Sangharakshita, 215, 256
Sanskrit, 162
Satanic Verses, The, 128, 249
scale schema, 47
scent, 117
scepticism, 6, 40, 97–8, 139, 186
schemas (embodied), 4, 18, 25, 31, 38–40, 42, **44–8**, 49–50, 52–5, 57, 60–1, 70, 81–2, 89, 104, 106–7, 117, 120–2, 136–7, 139, 155, 168, 179, 181, 185, 193, 228. See also names of specific schemas
schizophrenia, 53, 79, 184
school, 143, 150, **177**, 192, 235
science, 8, 13, 62, 134, **137–41**, 142, 196, 200, 205, 214, 243, 248–9. See also biology, cognitive science, neuroscience, physics, psychology, scientific method, social science
scientific method, 214
scripture, 128–9, 243. See also Bible, Pali Canon, Qur'an
Searle, John, 15–16, 66–7, 256
secularism, 10, 249
self, 136
self-organization, 13–14

semantic memory, 186, 188, 193–4
semantic understanding, 70
semantics, 6, 138
sense-experiences: see experience (sensory)
sense-making, 8, 73, **102–6**
senses, 22, 25, 44, 53, 70, 80, 89, 92, 134, 146, 199, 202, 227–8, 230, 234
sex (activity), 71, 176, 194
sex (distinction), 24, 29, 198
sexual practices, 176
sexuality, 24, 176, 194
shadow (archetype), **108–10**, 181, 207, 225, 239
Sheldrake, Rupert, 140, 256
Shi'a Islam, 127
sign language, 161
signs, 5, 31, **33–5**, 65
Sikhism, 190
simplicity, 196, 211
sin, 178
skills, 8, 77, 205, 219, 248
slanderous speech, 215
sleep, 25
smells, 24, 38, 207
social conformity: see groups
social fragmentation: see socio-political fragmentation
social integration: see socio-political integration
social meaning 9–11, 34–5, 37, 66, 77–80, 83, 134, 138, 148, 184, 199
social organization, 176, 195
social science, 105, 138. See also linguistics, psychology, sociolinguistics
socialism, 249
sociality, 11
social status, 52, 54–5, 170–1
society, 34, 51, 140, 143, 152, 163, 164, 177
sociolinguistics, 170
socio-political fragmentation, 152, 163, 168–9, 174, 250
socio-political integration, 210–11, 213, 250
solipsism, 79

solitude, 80
somatic fragmentation, 169, 183, 186
somatics, 1, 4
song, 175, 211, 226
soul, 134, 136
sounds, 32, 38, 77, 104, 121, 171, 226. See also music
source domain (metaphor), 50–2, 55–6, 60
source-path-goal schema, **44–6**, 60–1, 121
space, 45, 47, 136
speech precepts, 210, 215
spelling, 82, 170–1
spirited soul (Plato), 136
spiritual lineage, 51
splitting schema, 47, 54
sports, 176
stage theory 152, 195, 234–5
Standard English, 170–1
state, 144
status: see social status
stipulation, 33, 62, 64, 82, 196, 199, **200**
stories, 16, 22, 128, 160, 172, 179, 194, 202, **207–9**, 210, **214**, 217, 249
strict father morality, 144
structural metaphor, 51
subjectivity, 89, 117–20
sublimity, 23, 112, 118, 154, 201, 227, **237–41**
substance, 136
substitution, 59, 83
subtilization slope, 97–101, 112
sub-vocalizing, 77
suffering, 55, 224
sufficiency, 77
Sufism, 130
Sunnah, 127
Sunni Islam, 130
superficiality, 207
supernatural, 9, 94, 109, 139, 244
surface schema, 47
survivorship bias, 198
suspension of disbelief, 7
Sword verse, 127
symbolic fragmentation, 173

symbolism, 9, 22–3, 25, 27, **31–5**, 39, 48, **107–9**, 111, 117, 122–3, 129, 131, 160, 165–6, 170, 172, 174, 177, 179–80, 186, 204, 206, 217–18, 223, 225–6, 239
symbols, *passim*, especially **31–5**
 archetypal ~ 9, 94, **107–8**, 180–1, 222, 225, 245, 250
 linguistic ~: see language
 non-linguistic ~ 38, 103, 117–23, 175, 204, 211
 ~ distinguished from signs 33–4
sympathetic joy, 223
sympathy, 7, 114, 224, 238
synaptic gain, 184
synaptic pruning, 26, 77, 153, 190, **196–8**, 201, 204
syntactic processing, 70
synthesis, 2, 5, 154, 158, 183–4, 196, 200–2, 207, 227, 231, **232–6**, 238, 246, 248. See also integration
system independence (assumed), 59–60
Systemic History of the Middle Way, A, 70, 124, 179, 190, 194, 243, 251
systems (general), **6**, 12, **14–17**, 42, 45, 92, 103, 185, 190

tai chi, 4
Taleb, Nassim Nicholas, 184–5, 257
talking to ourselves, 77
Tantra, 131
tanzil, 126
Tara, 225
target domain (metaphor), 49–2, 55, 56, 60–1
taste, 24, 117, 175, 217, 226
Tchaikovsky, Pyotr, 55
teleology, 46
temporary integration, 154, 237–9
terrorism, 128
testing, 196, 198, 214, 243
theism, 8, 100, 110, 156, 181
theology, 38, 95, 115, 168
theorization, 8, 62
theory of ideas, 135–6
therapy, 5, 217–19

Theravada Buddhism, 130
thesis (in dialectic), 233
thought, 4, 15, 21, 40, 51, 66, 75, 78, 88, 118, 134–5, 144, 158, 227
thought experiment, 66, 196
threats, 23–4, 108–9, 167, 179, 181, 207, 210, 225, 250
Tibetan Buddhism, 131
time, 45, 51, 54, 57, 107, 136, **143–4**
Tintern Abbey, 237
Tipitaka, 130
tipping point, 15
toilet practices, 176
tolerance, 127
Tolkien, John, 6, 208
Tononi, Guilio, 17, 18, 257
touch, 4, 9, 27, 47, 108, 117, 226, 230
trade, 146, 167, 176, 178
trademark argument (for God's existence), 244
tradition, 94–5, 113–14, 124, 132–3, 137, 142, **143–6**, 148, 158, 200, 203, 225
transitiveness, 61, 71
transmission, 34
transparency, 97–8, 158
transport, 176
trauma, 28, 38, 183, 185–6
travel, 7, 202, 206, 209
truth, 3, 59, 61, 76, 84, **107–9**, 118 (n1), 125–6, 134, **137–41**, 142, 205, 243
truth-conditional pragmatics, 66
truth-conditional theory (of meaning), 66, 72, 76, **137–41**
tune: see melody
Turner, John, 103–4, 257
two mules, 212–13
two truths (Buddhism), 100

ugliness, 121
ulema, 126, 128
uncertainty, 65, 115–16, 184
understanding, *passim*: see meaning
undifferentiated meaning, 57, 243–4
undifferentiated state, 25, 27, 223, 243
unholy alliance, 156
univalence, 31, 33

university, ideal of, 163
upekkha, 223–4
utilitarianism, 249

vagueness, 33, 227–8
Vajrayana, 131
validity, 94, 213, 215
values, 128, **140–48**, 170, 174, 178, 209
Van der Kolk, Bessel, 185, 257
Van Gogh, Vincent, 237
Varela, Francisco, 13, 72, 85–6, 256
Vatican, 130
veganism, 249
verbs, 37, 71, 93
Vervaeke, John, 102, 104, 257
via negativa, 114
violence, 176
visual art, 22, 33, 60, 88, 90, 95, 103, **117–23**, 132, 174, 192, 207, 217–19, 226, 228, **237–40**. See also images, pictures
visual images: see images, pictures, visual art
visualization, 222, 225–6
vocabulary, 7, 105, 162–3, 190, 202, 205, 211, 228, 240
voice, 47, 55, 121–2, 207
voters, 142–3, 148, 163

wahi, 126
war, 38, 55, 110, 128
weak analogy, 56
weighing up, 105, 140
Wernicke, Carl, 12, 257
Western culture, 100, 134, 135, 141, 143, 176, 212, 219, 237, 249
Where Mathematics Comes From, 60, 255
Whitehead, Alfred, 99
Wilber, Ken, 27, 257
William of Ockham, 196
Wittgenstein, Ludwig, 34–5, 78, 79, 80, 134, 137–8, 257
Wittgensteinianism, 66, 76, 79, 102, 213
Women, Fire and Dangerous Things, 2, 255
wonder, 113, 157

words, 15, 18, **25–8**, 33, **36–9**, 41–2, 45, 49–50, 55, 58–60, 67, 74, 92, 104, 110, 112–13, 118, 121, **123**, 125–6, 129–34, 160–3, 165, 172, 175, 184, 186, 193, 198, 203–4, 210–12, 214–15, 234. See also language

Wordsworth, William, 90, 237
work, 176

Yeats, William, 177
yoga, 1, 4–5

Zen, 112, 122

www.ingramcontent.com/pod-product-compliance
Lightning Source LLC
Chambersburg PA
CBHW051631230426
43669CB00013B/2256